301
WAYS TO USE
SOCIAL
MEDIA TO
BOOST YOUR
MARKETING

301

WAYS TO USE
SOCIAL
MEDIA TO
BOOST YOUR
MARKETING

CATHERINE PARKER

New York Chicago San Francisco Lisbon London Madrid Mexico City
Milan New Delhi San Juan Seoul Singapore Sydney Toronto

    2 3 4 5 6 7 8 9 10 11 12 13 14 15 16   QFR/QFR   1 9 8 7 6 5 4 3 2 1

ISBN   978-0-07-173904-7
MHID   0-07-173904-1

This publication is designed to provide accurate and authoritative information in regard to the subject matter covered. It is sold with the understanding that the publisher is not engaged in rendering legal, accounting, securities trading, or other professional services. If legal advice or other expert assistance is required, the services of a competent professional person should be sought.

—*From a Declaration of Principles Jointly Adopted by a Committee of the American Bar Association and a Committee of Publishers and Associations*

Library of Congress Cataloging-in-Publication Data

Parker, Catherine, 1978-
        301 ways to use social media to boost your marketing / by Catherine Parker.
        p.   cm.
        ISBN 978-0-07-173904-7 (alk. paper)
        1. Internet marketing.   2. Marketing—Blogs.   3. Social media—
Economic aspects.   4. Online social networks—Economic aspects.   I. Title.
II. Title: Three hundred one ways to use social media to boost your marketing.
III. Title: Three hundred and one ways to use social media to boost your marketing.

HF5415.1265.P367   2010
658.8'72—dc22   2010014713

Interior design by Monica Baziuk

Contents

MICROBLOGGING

Getting Started on Twitter

Leveraging Twitter

FriendFeed

Tumblr

 # 4 SOCIAL NETWORKING

Facebook Pages

Facebook Advertising

LinkedIn

Orkut

Plaxo

Ning

MySpace

Meetup

6 ## MULTIMEDIA

Video-Sharing Sites

YouTube

SlideShare

Podcasting

7 REVIEWS AND OPINIONS

Reviews and Opinions Overview

Yelp

Epinions

RateItAll

Yahoo! Answers

8   WIKIS

Acknowledgments

Many thanks to McGraw-Hill, without whom this book would not be possible, and thanks in particular to Donya Dickerson for her support throughout the project. I am also grateful to Sallie Randolph and Ceridwen Dovey for their sound advice and guidance at this book's inception; to Claire Currie for her friendship and encouragement; and to MJ Otto, Velma Botha, and my family strewn across the globe for their support and humor as I made my crossing from marketer to writer.

Introduction

Toward the end of 2008, Tourism Queensland, Australia's tourism body for the country's second-largest state, was faced with a problem. As a result of the global financial crisis, people were spending less on international leisure travel, which for the Australian government meant a threat to the country's $88-billion-a-year[1] tourist industry. In the tough economic climate, Tourism Queensland wanted to increase tourism revenue to the Great Barrier Reef islands off the Queensland coast, which would require a completely new marketing approach, due not least to a shrunken budget. Opportunity came in the form of Hamilton Island, one of the seventy-four Whitsunday Islands on the edge of the Great Barrier Reef, which boasts pristine beaches, immaculate weather, and unspoiled coral reefs. And so, in January 2009, Tourism Queensland began publicizing its search for someone to be Hamilton Island's "caretaker"—a career opportunity it dubbed the "Best Job in the World." In return for a salary of AUS$150,000 (about $133,000), the successful applicant would work on the island for six months, performing duties such as feeding the island's fish, collecting the mail, and "generally enjoying and exploring the islands of the Great Barrier reef," all while reporting back via a blog and video and photo diaries. To apply, interested candidates had to submit a sixty-second video of themselves making a case for why they should get the job. Almost immediately the campaign captured the world's imagination: within six weeks the campaign website had received around 3.4 million unique visitors and more than thirty-four thousand video applications from 201 countries. The media latched on, too, and the unusual job advertisement was featured in more than six thousand news stories worldwide, which translated into media coverage valued at over $80 million.

So What Does This Mean for Me?

By anyone's standards, Tourism Queensland achieved monumental marketing success on a relative shoestring budget. How? Integral to its success was the fact that it came up with a truly original idea that piqued people's interest at the right time—in the middle of the Northern Hemisphere winter. Then, to spread its idea, it used social media channels like video sharing and blogging, which allowed it to start a conversation online with people who in turn spread the message to their own circles of influence. Supplementing this communication with social media sites like Facebook and Twitter, Tourism Queensland was able to grow its target audience exponentially and generate enormous buzz about the campaign in a very short span of time and at relatively little cost.

But how does this apply to you? The Tourism Queensland example is relevant because no matter what the size of your business or industry, you can use the same social media strategies to grow your own brand and increase your customer base. Social media's accessibility stems largely from the scalable nature of the Web, as well as the fact that most social media tools are easy and free to use, so you don't need special technical skills or extraordinarily deep pockets to run a successful social media campaign. With all this in mind, the only real things you need to be successful on the social media scene are a good strategy and a healthy dollop of time.

So are social media just a collection of websites and tools? On one level, yes, but they're also much more than that. At their core, **_social media_ can be defined as uses of Web technology to spread messages through social interaction that happens online.** Put another way, social media in a business context are ways to spread the word about your brand or product on the Web using tools and websites that allow a conversation to take place between you and your target market. Related statistics speak volumes about the potential of social media to market your brand. For example, as of early 2010, Facebook has more than four hundred million users,[2] while Twitter was receiving around fifty million updates a day from its users, which is an average of six hundred tweets per second.[3] In other words, getting involved in the social media space means you're accessing a large, active group of people who in turn use these channels to spread your brand message further. If done correctly, a social media campaign can result in broad-reaching brand exposure and influence that you'd struggle to achieve on your own without leveraging an online community.

Luckily, you don't have to engage in every social media tactic there is. In fact, you shouldn't: no business will be suited to every available tool, and using all of them would be an unproductive use of your time. For example, if you're a film and photography school wanting to market yourself using social media, sites like Flickr and YouTube will hold a lot more potential for you than if you sell office supplies. Like all other marketing tactics, the key to success with social media is to get into the head of your target market to pinpoint where its members are interacting and then spread your brand's message there. The effort you spend on a social media campaign is only as good as its success in converting potential customers into real ones, after all—so it's worth thinking carefully about who is included in your target market and where these people are likely to be.

This book aims to reveal the best-kept secret about social media campaigns: they're surprisingly simple to do. With this major myth debunked, you can start to pick and choose from various tactics outlined in these pages to tailor a campaign that's suited specifically to your business and industry. With a little effort, your campaign can bring rewards that far outweigh the time you took to create it. And when this happens, you'll wonder what took you so long to start one.

How to Use This Book

To help you create a social media campaign that is best suited to your business, this book organizes the most popular and widely used social media tools into seven categories: **blogging**, **microblogging**, **social networking**, **social bookmarking**, **multimedia**, **reviews and opinions**, and **wikis**. Within each category you'll find examples of sites and tools—for example, Twitter and FriendFeed within microblogging tools and Facebook and LinkedIn within social networking tools.

In each subsection, you'll find one-page tips that cover one main strategy for that particular tool. Although the tips are structured so that each one can be read in isolation, you'll get the most value if you read all the tips in one section in context with each other. For example, if you read all the tips on blogging, you'll be well equipped to create, market, and monetize your business blog. The tip structure also helps you manage the time commitment that's part of starting a social media campaign. For example, you could try reading and implementing one tip every week, which structures things so you can make steady progress. As you build up your skills, you'll be able to implement each of the tips in less time, especially within the same section. Above all, even if your progress is slow, keep it steady. The best social media campaigns are built up consistently over time, which allows your brand's message to be spread fluidly among others your audience is connected with.

Finally, it's important to note that while the contents of this book are current as of printing, this is unlikely to stay the case for long given the social media industry's lightning-fast evolution on almost a daily basis. So while this book will give you a good basic understanding of social media principles, it's impossible to guarantee the ongoing accuracy of all specific information contained within it.

	Blogging	Microblogging	Social Networking
What is it?	An informal conversational medium for writing and publishing content about your business and industry online on a regular basis	Short-form blogging where posts are usually limited in length and format	A way to engage and interact with a specific online community by way of a fan or profile page
Examples	Blogger, TypePad, WordPress	Twitter, FriendFeed	Facebook, MySpace
Best suited to your business if	You want to establish yourself as an industry expert and encourage a conversation with your target audience	You want an immediate way to interact with your consumer base	You want to build a fan base where current and potential customers can interact in one central location
Key advantage	Comprehensive	Immediate and mobile	Large associated community
Strengths	Simple to start Convenient way of providing useful resources to your target audience Potential to share detailed information Potential to earn money based on the amount of traffic you receive	Quick and easy to post updates Can grow exposure to a large group of influential online users in a short span of time Good way of finding out news on a particular topic as it happens Effective way to dissipate negative brand sentiment from customers Easy to update from mobile devices	Lets users interact with each other in a central location Effective medium for conversation with your customers or target audience Increases your brand's exposure through the public broadcast "feed" system Can tap into specific community types
Weaknesses	Requires a time commitment to set up and maintain Requires regular production of unique, useful, interesting content	Requires a time commitment to post regular updates Not built for sharing in-depth information	Target audience is there to socialize, not conduct business Can be ineffective if the network contains the wrong demographic for your product or service Needs to be active regularly —so a need to produce regular content that is engaging to your audience
Opportunities	Build up loyal readership Generate income	Build up loyal followers Drive traffic to specific blog posts or website content Cover live events	Build a community around your brand Spread your brand to your community's network of influence

Social Bookmarking	Multimedia	Reviews and Opinions	Wikis
A central location for posting links to useful resources which can be seen and shared by other users	Sharing rich media such as video, images, and presentations online	A way for customers to share opinions and reviews of your products and services online	A central repository designed to be edited by a group rather than one person
Digg, StumbleUpon, Delicious	YouTube, SlideShare, Flickr	Yahoo! Answers, Epinions, eHow	Wikipedia, Wikia
You want to share useful resources relating to your industry with your target audience	Your business lends itself to how-to or viral videos or rich content such as images and presentations	You have high-value products or services and have traditionally relied on referrals for new business	You want consumer input on product development, you want group collaboration and internal exposure for company projects, or you want to share your industry knowledge
Traffic driver	Cuts through the noise of text marketing	Objective recommendations of your product or service	Allows group collaboration
Allows quick spread of your content Useful place to read news, insights, and updates about your industry, partners, and competitors Drives external traffic to your Web properties Bookmarks are stored remotely so they can be accessed from anywhere	More engaging and interesting than text-based media More likely to be shared than other forms of media Allows you to create a stronger call to action to your target audience Compact way to communicate a large amount of information	Reaches users in the impressionable "research" phase of the buying cycle Objective word-of-mouth recommendations that are more likely to be trusted by your target audience Can establish yourself as an expert knowledge provider in your industry Allows you to quickly dissipate negative brand sentiment in a public forum	Effective platform for group collaboration, idea generation, and problem solving Useful central repository of information to be shared internally, externally, or both Easy way for consumers to make themselves heard by a business Allows you to establish yourself as an industry expert through contributions to public wikis
Seen as self-promotion if you submit your own links Strong competition with other content being submitted Resulting traffic is a short burst rather than a steady increase over time	Labor-intensive to produce rich media content on a regular basis Requires a certain level of technical expertise to produce Can appear amateurish if not done properly, which can be damaging to your brand	Negative reviews need to be handled in a specific way to contain damage What's said about your brand is out of your control	Requires knowledge of wiki syntax to edit Hard to contain negative feedback from consumers if used as an external channel Multiple editing capabilities means it potentially lacks ownership and attention within a business
Spread interesting and useful content Monitor your competitors Generate brand buzz	Reach consumers who prefer visual media over text Engage more effectively as a result of richer media Educate over geographical distances	Establish credibility for your brand via objective sources Extend your brand reach to your customers' own circle of influence	Effective bridging tool between your business and your customer Save time in internal processes Promote team building and pride within your business Drive traffic to your website through information about your brand on public wikis

1

Social Media in Action

ALTHOUGH THIS book provides hundreds of specific ways to enhance your marketing using social media, none of them will be effective if you don't have a good strategy underscoring your overall campaign. Although social media are the new favorite kid on the block, you should think of them as just another marketing channel (albeit with a fancier tool kit). When you think like this, you'll recognize the need to have a goal and motivation for your entire campaign, as well as the value in aligning it with your other marketing efforts, both online and offline. By making sure they all work in unison, you increase the overall effectiveness from each channel.

Part of making sure all your ongoing marketing strategies work together is keeping a consistent voice across all of the marketing channels you use, social media and otherwise. Using a consistent voice will help you define your brand and messaging more clearly to your target audience, which will ultimately increase the chances that they'll be influenced by your brand or convert into customers.

When structuring your social media strategy, first decide on a central arm around which your campaign should focus, such as your blog or your website. This central arm will be the place where someone will fulfill a specified call to action that is marketed across all your social media channels. Once you've decided on this central arm, you can start piecing together which social media tools you'll use. Remember that less is more: while literally hundreds of social media tools and channels exist, not all of them will suit your business and your target market. For example, a company targeting a younger demographic may find more success on Facebook than

1

companies targeting high-net-worth individuals. Also, social media take time, so the more channels you engage in, the more resources you'll use.

Many people think of social media as a "magic bullet" that produces automatic success after they create an account on a social networking site, say, or post one or two updates online. The truth is far less magical; social media campaigns involve time and effort just like any other form of marketing. Of course, if you're streamlined and using only tools that work for your business, you'll have less to manage. No matter what tools you're using, though, you'll be able to manage this effort more effectively by designating an internal "social media champion" who will assume ownership of the social media function within your business and act as the day-to-day point person for all communication and administration relating to the campaign. Also, no matter how big or small your social media campaign is, you should be tracking its return on investment. Defining what this return is and what you want to track will depend on the goal of your campaign, whether it's to drive traffic or generate brand awareness. Once you've allowed your statistics to gather data for a significant period of time, you can start rearranging resources to make your campaign more efficient.

No matter what your reasons for running a social media campaign, realize that with the exception of runaway successes like the Queensland Tourism campaign, most campaigns take time to produce results. Even though the "Best Job in the World" campaign saw significant results from social media, it kept this social conversation going long after the competition had ended. And in the end, this should be the ultimate goal of any marketing campaign—not just one that involves social media.

Think of the bigger picture

Social media can be a highly effective way of engaging with your current and future customers, increasing your brand's exposure, and driving traffic to your site. However, if you think of your social media plan as one aspect of your greater marketing mix, you'll get even more benefit from your efforts. Do this in the following ways:

- **Have one consistent voice:** Remember that many current and future customers are exposed to your brand on more than one place online, as well as offline, so don't confuse them with different messaging on each channel. Whether you're using only a website and a blog, or you're using Twitter, Facebook, and LinkedIn as well, keep the contents of your message and the way you deliver it consistent across all channels. Doing so creates more coherent brand messaging, which can be more effective in converting a site visitor into a customer.

- **Decide on your goal and a central aim:** Is it to drive more traffic to your blog, or is it to make more people buy products off your website? Once you have your overall goal, delegate one central focus for your strategy and then use separate channels to drive traffic there. For example, if your aim is to drive traffic to your blog, use Twitter, Digg, and Delicious to advertise your blog posts. Or your goal could be to drive traffic to your website by encouraging visitors to access articles, white papers, or tools on your site and then to buy your products and services. In this case, link to the resource section of your website from your Facebook, Twitter, and YouTube channels.

- **Don't forget your offline messaging:** More traditional forms of marketing within your business can be an excellent way of driving traffic to your social media sites and other channels. For example, include your blog and website addresses in promotional material such as brochures and business cards. Include your website address, along with your Twitter and Facebook URLs, in presentations you give.

TIP 2 | Use less rather than more

With so many social media tools available, the choice of which ones to use can be overwhelming, and many people feel pressured to use as many as they can. But, in fact, the success of your social media campaign depends less on how many different kinds of social media you use than on how effectively you use each one as part of one coherent strategy. There are two main steps toward achieving this:

1. Know your business's strengths and weaknesses. For example, if you're a business that doesn't use any kind of professional imaging in your product offering (for example, if you're tax consultant), you wouldn't choose to use Flickr and engage with its community of photography enthusiasts. On the other hand, if you publish regular research and how-to documents, you could connect much more effectively with your target market by contributing to Yahoo! Answers and a niche finance wiki or holding Meetups where you provide workshops about, for example, organizing your tax structure as a small business.

2. Know your target market. By knowing where your target market engages online, you'll better be able to choose which social media tactics will be more effective. For example, if you're targeting upper-level executives, you're likely to have more success on sites like LinkedIn and Plaxo than on sites like MySpace that have a younger user demographic.

Engaging properly with a social media channel requires a time commitment, so the more tools you use, the more time you'll spend managing those separate campaigns and engaging with each separate audience. And letting this interaction slide can be bad for your brand's perception: for example, if you don't follow up with a customer comment or question on Facebook due to lack of time, that customer could see your business as one that doesn't respond to its customers, which could result in the customer's moving to another competitor to get the desired product or service. As always, you should measure the returns of any social media tools you use so that you can see which ones give you real returns (for more on this, see Tip 4).

TIP 3 | Appoint a social media champion

Having a social media champion within your organization can heavily impact the success of your business's social media campaign. Whether this champion is you or someone you delegate, the individual should take ownership of the day-to-day running of the social media campaign, both externally in terms of engaging with customers and internally in terms of getting other employees in the business on board with the campaign. Having a champion is also a good way of ensuring constant monitoring of your brand's reputation, so that swift action can be taken where necessary (for example, in the case of a negative review on a reviews website). Overall, a social media champion's main duties should include:

- **Engaging regularly:** The champion should ensure that there is regular activity by your business on whatever social media channels it's using. For example, a champion would ensure that content is regularly added to your company's Facebook page, and that updates are posted to Twitter each day.

- **Selling internally:** A social media champion can help sell the idea of a social media campaign internally, such as by publicizing successes on an internal blog or by giving presentations that contain examples of the strategy in action and what effect it's having on the company as a whole. The champion should also be responsible for tracking the impact your social media efforts have had on the business, such as an increase in traffic to the company's website as a result of using Twitter to market it (for more on how to track social media campaigns, see Tip 4).

- **Coordinating employees' personal social media activities:** Nowadays most employees engage with social media on some level personally, for example via a Twitter, Facebook, or MySpace page, a personal blog, or a Flickr account. A social media champion can coordinate this independent activity by integrating the social activity of the business and the employee: in this way, you can spread the word about your brand throughout those employees' own circles of influence. For example, if you've uploaded new content to your Facebook page, you could ask employees to mention it on their own Facebook accounts. Or, if you post articles on Digg, you could ask your employees to vote for articles you've posted.

TIP 4   Track the effect

No matter how large or small your social media campaign is, you should be monitoring its return on investment to your business. What you should track depends on your goals for your social media campaign—driving traffic, converting visitors to customers, or encouraging your site contents to be shared by others, among others.

To track a social media campaign effectively, you should already have an analytics package (for example, Google Analytics or Omniture SiteCatalyst) interfacing with your website to give you information such as site traffic trends, referral origins, and click paths of your visitors through your site. When it comes to social media efforts on your site, most website analytics packages will let you create campaigns that isolate referral traffic to a specific domain. For example, you could create a campaign that tracks which visitors are coming from MySpace, Facebook, or your own blog. If you're already using Google Analytics, you can install the "Better Google Analytics" extension for the Firefox browser that gives you social media metrics within the Analytics interface.

Besides using your site analytics to track your campaigns, several tools specifically track social media campaigns. Some examples are:

■ For Twitter, Hootsuite (www.hootsuite.com) shows statistics associated with your Twitter account, such as the number of users who clicked on a link within a tweet. SocialToo (www.socialtoo.com) tracks who follows and unfollows you on Twitter, TweetStats (www.tweetstats.com) provides graphs of Twitter stats such as your tweets over time and reply statistics, and Twittercounter (www.twittercounter.com) shows you statistics of followers and whom you're following, plus your tweets over time.

■ If you're using social bookmarking as part of your campaign and want to track how others are sharing your article, tools like PostRank (https://analytics.postrank.com) track bookmarks of your content on Digg and StumbleUpon (as well as shares on Twitter).

■ If you're using Facebook Advertising, Facebook Insights contains built-in statistics that can tell you the performance of your ads if you're using Facebook Advertising (for more on Facebook Insights, see Tip 95).

■ Along with paid tools like Radian6 (www.radian6.com), free tools like Addictomatic (www.addictomatic.com) let you monitor your brand across blogs, forums, social networking sites, and more.

■ Finally, for quick and free monitoring, Google Alerts (www.google.com/alerts) e-mails you new content picked up by Google that relates to keywords you want to track, such as your brand name.

TIP 5 | Take action

A crucial part of your social media campaign's success is taking action and tweaking your campaign in response to knowing what's giving you a return on your investment and what isn't. To find out what's working for you, you'll need to know your campaign goal (e.g., to drive traffic to your website), and you should be using website analytics or another specialized tool to track how your campaign elements are fulfilling this goal (for more on tracking, see Tip 4). Once these are in place, you should allow a period of time for your analytics package to gather data. Then, when you have enough data to make a sound analysis, compare your social media efforts side by side to see which is performing better and make changes based on these learnings. For example, if your Facebook account is resulting in a large amount of traffic, but your MySpace account isn't, you may decide to devote more time to Facebook and less time to managing your MySpace community. Similarly, if you find that your YouTube videos aren't resulting in the traffic or customers you thought they would, you may want to try running video campaigns on other video sharing sites such as Viddler or Yahoo! Video.

Knowing your target demographic may help you initially identify which social media sites are likely to perform better than others—for example, Plaxo rather than MySpace if your demographic is older. Above all, you should invest time in social media that provide a real benefit to your business, and this means accepting that some social media tactics will work better than others, because no two businesses are alike. There are also other reasons it's better to use fewer tools than too many; for more on this, see Tip 2.

TIP 6 Keep going

Although the tools used to implement a social media campaign may be newer and shiner, using social media is just like any other form of marketing in several key ways:

- A social media campaign requires a strategy and a goal.

- A successful campaign needs to use channels that are appropriate for your business and your target market.

- A social media campaign takes time to show results.

Since implementing a social media campaign can be as simple as signing up for a Twitter account in just a couple of minutes, some businesses believe the campaign should yield results just as quickly. In reality, the basic principle of social media is to connect with your target audience on a shared platform and then give them a reason to keep engaging with you. Doing this takes time. For example, providing useful resources to the point where you become known as an expert in your industry, resulting in more people visiting your website or reading your blog, takes time. If you persevere, the rewards are worth your persistence—people are given more of an opportunity to learn more about your brand and develop a positive sentiment about it. In turn they are more likely to become your customers by visiting your website and buying your product or service.

The easiest way to make sure you persevere with your social media campaign is to build it into your daily work tasks. For example, you or your social media champion (for more on this, see Tip 3) could spend a set amount of time each day or every couple of days to tend to the campaign. This could mean responding to questions, participating in conversations, uploading content to your blog and other social media profiles, or commenting on other content provided by those in your industry. Spending regular time on your social media campaign also helps you monitor your brand's reputation online and stay up on news relating to both your industry and your business.

2

Blogging

BLOGGING HAS come a long way from the late 1990s, when it was started as a way for people to share personal commentary with other Internet users in an online diary format. More than ten years later, with hundreds of millions of blogs in existence, the industry has matured far from beyond the fad that many critics initially proclaimed it to be. Today blogging is far more than just a personal diary tool (although millions of those types of blogs still exist)—for a business, it can be an effective marketing tool as well. Besides being able to spread the word about your brand quickly and easily, maintaining a business blog gives you an informal way of connecting with, listening to, responding to, and engaging in conversation with your target audience.

The barriers to entering blogging are low: platforms like WordPress, TypePad, and Blogger are free, it's simple to set up a blog on them in a matter of minutes, and you don't need any extraordinary technical skills to maintain or publish content. Once your blog has been established, there many ways you can market it to grow your readership and, ultimately, expand your customer base. Although writing good content is critical to a blog's success, if no one can find all your well-crafted posts, your hard work is going to waste. There are several ways you can make sure people find it, including optimizing it so you're visible on search engines and joining other blogging communities.

Many bloggers are able to make money from their blog by capitalizing on the traffic their site gets. This traffic is used as a selling point to potential advertisers: if your blog has a significant number of readers, and it falls within a specific topic, advertisers are often willing to pay in some form for exposing their product or service to an audience that's specifically suited to that product or service.

Setting Up Your Blog

TIP 7   Decide between a hosted and a self-hosted blog

So you've decided you want to start a blog. The next major decision you need to make is whether you want it to be **hosted** or **self-hosted**.

A self-hosted blog means that you manage the blog's software yourself and organize your own server space to store your blog's content. For most people, this means paying a monthly fee to have their Web hosting company look after it. Besides this cost, the main issue with having a self-hosted blog is that you need to set up and manage the blogging software yourself, which requires you to have a certain level of technical skill. If you don't have these, you'll need to factor in the added cost in time and money to find someone who does. Although having a self-hosted blog costs more money and requires more technical resources, you're less restricted in terms of how much data you can upload to it, and you have maximum flexibility with its structure and look and feel. In general then, most businesses that want an optimal brand experience for their audience on a blog that is highly customizable opt for a self-hosted blog.

The hosted alternative involves signing up with a third party to host your blog on its domain. The main advantage with a hosted blog is its cost savings: in most cases, it's free to sign up for a basic option, and you don't have to pay a monthly hosting fee. The other main advantage of a hosted blog is its simplicity: you don't set up or manage the software yourself, and setting up and posting to your blog is a quick and simple process. However, unlike with a hosted blog, you're more limited with your blog's structure and look and feel and how much data you can upload to it.

These pros and cons notwithstanding, if you're new to the world of blogging, it's probably a good idea to start with a hosted one. This option is the simplest to come to grips with if you're a beginner, and you won't have to commit a lot of resources in terms of time, money, and technical expertise to set it up. For the sake of simplicity, the rest of the tips in this section on setting up your blog will assume that you have a hosted blog.

TIP 8 Choose a blogging platform

Assuming you've chosen a hosted blog (where a third party keeps your blog on its domain), the next major decision that you'll need to make is which blogging platform to use. You can choose from a wide range of platforms, all of which offer a basic level of quality, functionality, and ease of use. There are certain notable differences between them, however, and which platform is right for your business will depend on what you want to do with your blog. For example, if you want your blog to be simple and fuss-free but want to generate revenue from it through advertising, Blogger is your best option. If you want maximum flexibility but don't want to generate revenue, WordPress is a better choice. The following comparison chart shows the pros and cons of having a basic blog on three popular blogging services: Blogger, WordPress, and TypePad.

	Pros	Cons
Blogger	Free Simple to set up—targeted specifically to beginners Simple to associate your own domain name with your blog Owned by Google, so you can easily integrate other Google products such as Google Analytics and Google Reader Easy to set up Google AdSense so you can make money off advertising Offers a wide range of highly customizable templates	Limited functionality in terms of menus, pages, and categories Allows content to be organized only by labels, not by category
WordPress	Free A large number of plug-ins let you add extra functionality such as creating pages, menu items, categories, and subcategories Built-in statistics Built-in spam blocker	Doesn't allow advertising (e.g., on Google AdSense) Free templates are limited and not very customizable If your traffic grows significantly, you have to pay for an upgrade to accommodate extra traffic
TypePad	Easy integration of advertising programs such as Google AdSense Built-in image uploader for hosting your images straight from your computer Mixed media templates available Allows guest accounts	Nominal monthly subscription fee Slightly complicated to have your blog hosted on your own domain

TIP 9 Set up your blog's look and feel

Although the user interface differs among blogging platforms, with some offering more functionality than others, most blogs have common elements that allow you to customize it for your business. Four of the most important areas of your blog that you'll typically customize are:

- **Templates:** All hosted blog applications let you choose a template, which is another name for the basic design layout options for your blog. Some platforms are more flexible than others in terms of what you can customize, but most will let you change the fonts, colors, and footer and header image. Applying a template to your blog is easy to do, so experiment with different ones to see which works best in communicating your brand's image.

- **Blog profile:** This is an introductory paragraph about your blog that is displayed somewhere on your blog's home page. Since it's usually the first thing a new visitor will read when trying to find out more about you, it pays to spend some time writing a well-thought-out profile paragraph. Think of it as your blog's elevator pitch, so make it informative and memorable while still keeping it brief and as nonsalesy as possible.

- **Blogroll:** A blogroll is a list of links to other blogs that you choose to link to from your own, and this list usually appears on the right or left column of your blog's home page. In the context of a business blog, think of a blogroll as a list of blogs you're endorsing as resources for your readers, so be picky about what you include. If you're looking for ideas of blogs to include, think about blogs written by your clients, partners, or employees and blogs written by influential thinkers in your industry.

- **Comments or no comments?** Blogging platforms let you choose how stringent your comment policy is: you can choose to allow anyone to post a comment or require that readers be logged in to do so, or you can make it so you have to approve a comment before it is posted. How you handle comments has a surprising amount of influence on your readers' behavior on your blog and their perception of your brand: allowing people to comment without logging in, for example, opens up your blog to comment spam, but adding this extra log-in step means you may discourage some people from commenting at all. Usually opting for the middle ground is best, where you require people to log in to leave a comment but you don't have to approve the comment before it is published.

TIP 10 **Point your own domain name to your blog**

When you create a hosted blog, your blog's address, or Uniform Resource Locator (URL), will display as part of the particular blogging platform you're on. For example, if you're using WordPress, your blog address will be in the format http://myblog.wordpress.com, and if it's on Blogger, it will be in the format http://myblog.blogspot.com. While this is fine to leave as is, many blog owners prefer to have their own domain show as their blog address: http://www.mybusinessblog.com or www.mybusiness.com/blog.html if they want their blog to be part of their main website. For business blog owners especially, having your own domain as your blog address looks more professional, and it allows you to create a better brand association between your blog and your website. This brand reinforcement carries over if you're listing your blog on other places such as your Facebook page or even on printed marketing material such as brochures and business cards.

If you want your blog to have its own domain name, you'll first need to purchase the Web address you want. The cost will depend first on whether the domain name is available: if you buy a domain name that someone else owns, the price you'll pay depends on how much the seller is willing to sell it for, which in turn depends on how much of a demand there is for that domain. If you buy a domain that isn't owned by anyone straight from a domain registrar like EasyDNS or GoDaddy, you'll pay much less. Domain names that end in *.com* are also usually more popular than other endings, like *.net* or *.biz*, so you'll pay more for a *.com* domain than one that ends with *.net*. As a general estimate, an unused *.com* domain bought from a domain registrar will cost you in the region of $10 to $20 per year. You can also buy domain names directly through your blogging platform if you have a WordPress or Blogger blog.

Once you've bought your domain name, you'll need to link it to the standard address that your blog was created with (for example, http://myblog.blogspot.com). You do this by changing the DNS settings for your domain name so that they point to the server where your blog is hosted (the process is simple and well documented by both domain registrars and blogging tools). Once you've updated the server settings, you may have to wait several hours for the change to take effect.

TIP 11 | Set up an RSS feed

Depending on who's talking, you'll hear that RSS stands for *real simple syndication*, *rich site syndication*, or *RDF site summary*. In all cases, though, its meaning remains the same: an RSS feed is a file created using a programming language called *XML* that contains an aggregate of all your blog's content in one place. The file is then updated as more content is added to your blog, so that it remains an accurate and up-to-date record of all the content on your blog. Having an RSS feed for your blog is useful for two main reasons:

1. It's in a standardized format, which means that many different software platforms, websites, and devices can access your blog's content, no matter what platform you're on.

2. It allows subscriptions, meaning that as your content is updated, people or programs that have subscribed to your feed will be notified of the update.

These two features make an RSS feed an easy way for people and programs to access the latest content on your blog without needing to visit the blog each time you add more. Through this simple "push" syndication of your blog's content, an RSS feed is an excellent way of staying connected with your blog audience, and promoting your feed is a good way of attracting new readers.

The most common way that people interface with an RSS feed is through an RSS reader, also known as an *aggregator* or a *feed reader*. In the RSS reader interface, content is usually shown in the form of post headlines and summaries—sort of like looking at an e-mail inbox. Then, as with e-mail, you click the headline to read the entire post, which opens up in a new window.

If you're already using a major blogging platform such as Blogger or WordPress, your RSS feed is automatically created and updated as you add new content. However, the degree to which you promote your feed to gain more readers depends on you. At the very least, make sure you include an RSS link on your blog home page for people to subscribe to your feed. Most blogging software tools will allow you to do this through the inclusion of an RSS widget into your blog interface. Besides including this link on your blog, you can also add it to your website, e-mail signature, and anywhere else you have a presence online.

TIP 12   Use FeedBurner

An RSS feed gives people and programs a standardized way of automatically accessing your blog content without needing to visit your site each time it is updated. While all major blogging tools today generate a standard RSS feed for your blog, your RSS feed can be leveraged even further via feed management tools. These tools help you enrich the content your feed pulls from your blog, and they also help you monetize and advertise your feed— all of which allows you to grow your audience base even further. One of the most popular feed management tools available is FeedBurner, which works with your existing RSS feed in the following ways:

- Allows you to customize the titles and descriptions of post content in your feed, which in turn encourages higher click-through to your blog

- Lets you see who's clicking through on your feed, what other feeds they're reading, and which feed reader they're using

- Allows your readers to share articles that they find useful with others in their community, such as by bookmarking them on sites like Digg and Delicious

- Integrates Google AdSense into your feed to monetize the traffic you're getting through RSS

- Includes an e-mail subscription form on your site so that your readers have another way of subscribing to your content

- Notifies major blog aggregators such as Technorati, My Yahoo!, Newsgator, and Bloglines when you post new content so that your subscribers using these services get your freshest content as soon as possible

- Lets you display the number of subscribers to your feed on your blog or website, which serves as another avenue of blog promotion

FeedBurner is now a Google product, so if you already have a Google account, you can log in with your Google account details at www.feedburner .com to get started. Once you've logged in (or created an account), you'll be guided through the setup process, during which you'll be prompted to add the feed URL into the FeedBurner interface. After your account is set up, you can begin promoting and enhancing your feed.

TIP 13   Upload pictures to your post

Including images in a blog post is a good way of capturing your readers' attention and making the post more interesting. Some people connect better to visual formats than written ones, so by including both images and text you'll be appealing to a wider base of readers.

Uploading images to posts is easy and intuitive on most blogging tools: when you're creating a post, simply navigate to where the image is stored on your computer and upload it into the body of the post. When you upload an image, you'll be given various options for the size the image is uploaded as, such as thumbnail, medium, or large. You'll also be able to add a caption, description, and URL to the image if you want it to link to another site or post on your blog. If you want to include an image on your blog that you don't own, be aware of copyright issues: credit the image source by linking back to the site where the image originally appeared or e-mail the owner directly for permission to use it. Another option is to purchase the rights to an image through stock photography sites like www.istockphoto.com and www.gettyimages.com.

If you don't want to store your images on your own hard drive, you can store them on an external image-hosting site. Doing so saves space on your own computer and gives you a centralized image storage location—particularly useful if you have multiple contributors to the same blog. Examples of popular free image-hosting sites include:

- **Flickr:** A free account allows you to upload two videos of 150 MB each and 100 MBs' worth of photos per month. Image size is limited to 10 MB each.

- **Picasa:** A free account gives you a maximum of 1 GB of storage space for images and videos. Image sizes are limited to 20 MB each, and videos are limited to 1 GB each if uploaded from Picasa.

- **TinyPic:** Unlimited storage space and bandwidth, but images are limited to 1,600 pixels in either length or height, and videos are limited to 100 MB and five minutes or less in length.

- **ImageShack:** Unlimited storage space and bandwidth, but images are limited to 5 MB in size, and videos are limited to 15 minutes for free accounts.

- **Photobucket:** A free account gives you 500 MB of storage space and up to 10 GB of bandwidth per month. Image size is unlimited for images up to 1024 x 768 pixels, and videos can be 300 MB or less and must be 10 minutes or less in length.

TIP 14   Leverage stats for your blog

When you start a blog for your business, you're putting time and effort into another marketing channel. As for any other investment, you should monitor the return you're getting —with a blog, this return could mean growing your reader base and increasing your brand exposure, or selling your product or service as a result of your blog, or generating revenue from ads that you're displaying on it. No matter what your goal is, the best way to monitor your return is to analyze your blog's statistics. These will give you information such as:

- how many people are visiting your blog

- how many people are arriving at your blog but then leaving again

- the average amount of time people spend on your blog

- where your readers are coming from

- if your readers come from a search engine, what search phrases they used to arrive at your site

- which posts they read

Armed with this knowledge, you can get a clearer picture of the audience that is reading your blog and what content is most useful to them.

Most major blogging tools such as WordPress and Blogger provide basic blog statistics. If you're looking for more extensive analysis, such as returns on ads you're displaying on your blog, you're better off using an external tool. One of the best free tools available is Google Analytics, which you can access using your Google log-in (if you already have one) at www.google .com/analytics. Like most statistics packages, Google Analytics provides you with custom tracking code that you'll need to include on the pages of the blog that you want to track. With a blog's template structure, tracking the whole blog is easy—you simply paste the code into the part of the template that is common to all the pages of your site. Doing this also means that new content will be tracked without your needing to add the tracking code to the new page of content each time. Once the code has been included on your blog, visitor activity is tracked and translated into the statistics you see in the Google Analytics reporting interface.

Writing Useful Blog Content

TIP 15 It's about your readers, not you

When it comes to content for your business blog, it's really all about what your readers want. This may seem counterintuitive; after all, you're writing about your business, so shouldn't you be the one to decide what to write about? Yes and no. At a high level, it is true that you'll be writing about content that's related to your industry. But within your chosen subject, you should write content that is useful primarily to your readers and that answers the main question when they're on your blog: "What's in it for me?"

The type of content that works best on a blog is very different from the content you'd include on your website. Your website is best for outlining details and specifications about your products or services or as a place to give general information about your company. In comparison, while your blog can still be related to the products or services you sell, it should offer something that adds value to your readers *without asking anything from them in return.* Rather than writing a post that outlines the benefits of one of your products, write a post that mentions your product or industry in the context of something that adds value, such as unique research you've done or insights you have about your industry. If you sell accounting services, for example, don't just talk about the great value pricing you offer on your accounting services; rather, teach your readers how to file their tax returns or provide objective critiques of popular automated tax software products.

When your blog content adds value to your readers without trying to push your products or services on them, they're more likely to associate your brand with quality and usefulness. In turn they're more likely to become loyal readers who will return to your blog for the insights you provide. The best part about all of this is that if your insights lead your customers to want to know more about your product, they're more likely to convert from readers to customers, which in turn grows your business even further.

TIP 16 Carve out a niche

Starting a new blog can feel overwhelming once you realize how many established bloggers already exist in nearly every major subject area. Despite this strong competition, you can make a dent in your industry by creating a specific niche for your blog's subject matter. For example, if you sell greeting cards, a unique take within the greeting card industry could be to document the real lives of the greeting card writers on your blog. You could write about the real events that happened in their lives to inspire the messages that they write, or you could describe the process they use to come up with new greetings. When you write original content, you create a unique angle with your blog, increasing your chance of standing out from your competitors even if your blog is new.

To find out what kind of niche you should carve out, start by familiarizing yourself with what other established bloggers in your industry are writing about. Using blog search engines like Technorati and normal search engines like Google, search on keyword phrases relating to your industry to find the blogs that you'll be competing against. Once you're familiar with what's already being written, you'll be better equipped to brainstorm ideas for new content on your blog that will be original.

Carving out a niche applies not just to what you write about but to how you write your blog posts as well. Some bloggers may draw cartoons or pictures each day instead of writing text, while others may choose a specific style of writing. Whatever format you choose for your blog, if you let your unique voice show through in your blog, you're more likely to cut through the noise of other bloggers competing for the same readership. Carving a niche also means that you narrow your focus, which is a good route to establishing yourself as an expert in a particular area. Only blogs associated with the most well-established brands can post very general news and still be successful; in general, if you're a moderately to little-known brand worldwide, sticking to a specific focus will help you establish better traction in the blogosphere. This, in turn, leads to a steady and loyal reader base.

TIP 17   **Know your subject matter**

Similar to the advice given in a creative writing class, the key to having a blog that adds the most value to your readers is to write about what you know. That means you should either be an expert on the topic at hand or have the personal experience to back up what you're saying. If you're writing a business blog, you'll most likely be writing about your business in the context of your own industry, so it should be an easy task to give examples of real-life situations or pass on expert knowledge about the subject you're talking about. When you give real-life examples, don't be afraid to write about your own failure points as well as your successes. By being a company that can admit its mistakes and learn from them, you come across as being humble and honest, which improves your brand perception among your readers and makes for a more loyal blog audience. Overall, by giving insights in a real-life context, you not only provide a better explanation for the point you're trying to make but also make your blog more colorful and interesting to read.

A good way to ensure that you're always writing about what you know is to have multiple contributors to your blog from within your company. Choose people who have different roles and skills within your organization so that they can bring varied knowledge to the blog in a personal context. For example, your technical staff can write about technical problems and solutions they've come up with, while someone from your sales team can write about the marketplace in general. If you do go the route of multiple authors, make sure you don't have too many contributors so that the voice of your blog begins to seem disjointed. Another idea is to have a theme week, where different people within your company write about the same issue and how it affects them or their department.

Whatever you choose to do, the overarching strategy for your blog should be that every post be written by someone who has earned the authority to write about his or her chosen topic, either by being an expert or by having gained personal experience with that topic.

TIP 18 | Write viral content

To attract new readers to your blog, you need some way of spreading the word about it. The fastest way to do this is to have one of your blog posts reposted or referred to on other blogs. When this happens, the other blogs' readers are exposed to your content, which increases the chances of their visiting your blog and becoming your readers as well.

A blog post that lends itself to being shared easily because it is interesting or new in some way is said to be viral in nature. The word *viral* describes how it is passed on—someone who finds a post interesting might repost it on his or her own blog, and then readers of that blog may in turn repost the post or link to the post on their own blog. Like a virus, the blog post then spreads quickly in its exposure among increasing groups of people. Writing a blog post that is viral in nature means you quickly get traction beyond your own readers, which builds up your blog's audience as a result of your original post.

So what does a post that's viral look like? There is no single answer to this. Sometimes a post "sticks" simply because it taps into the zeitgeist of the moment —for example, you may be one of the first bloggers to talk about a hot topic that subsequently grows in popularity. At other times your post may simply be amusing to a large proportion of people who then share it with their own community. Overall, types of posts that tend to spread virally include:

- controversial or timely posts that talk about a current hot topic

- posts that consist of lists; these are easy to scan and often touch on real-life examples

- humorous posts

- posts that give unique insights into a particular topic

- posts that talk about useful resources or tools for your readers

- contest posts, where readers are asked to provide input in return for the chance to win something

Since it's hard to define what works and what won't, especially among different industries, you'll need to experiment with different types of posts to see what works. You won't always be successful, but it's worth the effort of writing twenty or thirty posts if only one of those becomes a viral success.

TIP 19   **Avoid the jargon**

As with any other reading matter, the best way to connect with your audience is to write content to which they can relate. Every industry and company has associated jargon that its members use, and you may not even realize you're using these technical phrases or words in everyday conversations with your clients or colleagues. Remember, though, that when you write your blog a varying proportion of your readers won't be in your industry, and most of them won't be a part of your company. So, to make sure you connect with your readers, steer clear of jargon and even from writing posts that are too theoretical. If readers don't follow what you're saying, they may end up leaving your blog and not returning. And even if every one of your readers does understand the jargon you use, you'll still have a better chance of connecting with them if you illustrate your point clearly and simply.

An easy way to keep it clear and simple is to allude to a personal experience—an actual real-life situation. Blogs are also a more informal medium than other communications such as press releases or even website copy, so blog writing lends itself to being less like a lecture and more like an informal discussion. Also remember that if you write clearly and simply, people will associate "clear" and "simple" with your brand. On the flip side, blog posts that are unclear, too complex, or too hard to follow may result in your audience associating those qualities with your brand and related products or services.

Sometimes, because you're so immersed in your industry, it's hard to recognize when you're using language that is too jargon-filled or too technical. Consider having a trusted friend or other blogger outside of your industry give you feedback about how easy your posts are to understand. If you can have someone proofread them when they're in draft format, you'll have an opportunity to revise them before they go public, but even if read after being published, the feedback you get can help you refine your writing in the future.

TIP 20　Don't be self-contained

One mistake that bloggers often make is to keep their blog self-contained—they don't link out to or refer to other blogs for fear that these blogs will take their audience away. By its very nature, though, the blogosphere is open and democratic, and therefore functions best when there is an easy flow of information in and out of blogs on the same topic. Assume that your audience is reading other blogs besides yours anyway and that linking out to or mentioning others won't jeopardize the size of your readership. Embrace this easy information flow by acknowledging other blogs that inspire you in your own posts and linking out to other blogs that you feel may be useful or interesting to your readers. By providing extra resources, your blog will show that your business is willing to learn from others. As a spin-off, trackback functionality on most blogs means that those blogs will know you're linking to them, so you're exposing your content to other bloggers who may in turn link back to you for their own readers' enrichment.

It's important also to acknowledge when you're mentioned on another blog. Whether it's in a positive or negative light, don't shy away from a response in your own post—this is another way of showing that your business is open to learning from others.

To find extra resources to include in your blog posts, join blog networks and use blog search engines and directories to see what other bloggers are saying in your subject area. Research who the influential bloggers are in your industry and read their blogs for ideas and information that you can share with your own audience. This can include anything from a plain blog post to rich resources like white papers, presentations, photos, or podcasts.

As well as linking out from within your posts, your blogroll is a place where you can refer your readers to quality resources. Since a blogroll is usually highly visible on your blog's home page, be discerning about the blogs you include on this list and keep them relevant to your industry.

TIP 21   **Experiment, track, and respond**

Until you've been blogging for a while, it's hard to predict what kind of posts will work best for your particular audience and industry. And, you may define what works best differently from to someone else: does a successful post for you mean that it's shared often, that it generates a lot of comments, or that it results in inquiries about the business services you're offering? Once you've identified what a successful post means to you, experiment by writing in varied formats to gauge which types of content work best. For example, try writing a few of the following types of posts:

- Lists

- Case studies

- Roundup posts that compare different products, services, businesses, brands, or solutions in one subject area

- Posts that experiment with associated graphics: with pictures and without, or using photographs versus illustrations

- Video posts

- Podcasts

Once you've published a few posts in different formats, use your statistics linked to your blog to analyze how they're performing. Over time, you should be able to see a trend where certain types of blog posts attract larger audiences than others, generate more comments, or attract more inquiries. Once you've identified what format is working, create more posts like these and fewer in the formats that don't work as well. Doing this will help you build momentum for growing your readership: the larger your audience becomes, the quicker your blog will grow since more people will be sharing the content you produce.

Besides changing the type of post you're writing, you can experiment with more subtle attributes on your blog such as the format of your post title, the look and feel of your blog, the length of your blog post, and how much you link to other blog posts or link out to external resources. To help you with this, you can even ask your readers for input into what they'd like to see on your blog that's not already there. By involving your readers in the testing process, you're also encouraging more audience participation, which is likely to make them a more engaged audience.

TIP 22 Encourage audience interaction

Stripped down to its bare essentials, a blog is made up of two basic elements: the poster (you) and the commenter (your reader). The ability to write content that can easily be commented on is at the core of the blogging medium and is what separates it from the "one-way conversation" marketing channels, such as brochures, advertising, press releases, and company websites. A blog facilitates a two-way conversation easily, so you should leverage this ability as much as possible to make your blog as successful as it can be.

Besides fostering the creation and sharing of new ideas for both you and your readers, encouraging audience interaction keeps your readers engaged and loyal to your blog. A loyal reader is more likely to share your blog with others, which in turn increases your readership and raises your blog's profile. Finally, when you position your blog as one that encourages a conversation, people will begin to perceive your business as being one that listens and responds to its customers and learns from what they have to say.

To encourage audience interaction, write posts that encourage a debate among your readers. This can mean writing posts that are slightly controversial or ones in which you give a strong opinion and then explicitly ask your readers within your post what they think of the issue. When a reader does leave a comment, respond openly so that the conversation is continued long after your post has been published. Besides being active in your comments section, you can create posts that by their very nature encourage readers to participate. Examples of these types of posts include things like reader polls and surveys, or competitions where you ask for reader input and award a prize for the best answer or the correct answer. You could also ask for reader feedback on a certain topic, the best of which you'll then share in a subsequent post.

Attracting a Loyal Reader Base to Your Blog

TIP 23   Let people know about you

If you're spending a lot of time writing your content, you should also be spending time publicizing your blog. After all, if you don't have readers, you're not getting a return on the time you're spending on it. By far the easiest and most obvious way of attracting new readers to your blog is to ask people you already have relationships with to visit your blog. Begin by tapping into the network you already have: think about your customers, employees, business partners, suppliers and vendors, or industry groups to which you may belong and send them your blog address as well as a brief description of what your blog is about. These are people who already know you and trust you—so they can start the process of generating subscribers, comments, and other blog activity.

Once you've told people you know about your blog, include it in other marketing materials that you may have as well. This could include writing about your blog in your e-mail newsletter or linking to it on your website, in your e-mail signature, on your business cards, and on other signage you have. If you have a presence on other sites such as forums, social media sites such as Facebook and LinkedIn, or multimedia sites like Flickr or YouTube, include a link to your blog from within your profile area. The overall goal with posting a link to your blog on these sites is to capitalize on traffic that you are already generating to your other sites and profiles. Also, marketing your blog to people who are already familiar with your brand by interacting with it via these other channels makes them more likely to visit your blog and become loyal readers.

Other useful ways to publicize your blog are to include it on major blog directories and blog search engines such as Technorati. You should also spend time making sure your blog has a presence in search results of major engines like Google—for more on this, see Tips 27–32. Finally, networking in blogging communities such as MyBlogLog (see Tips 41–46) is another way to make sure your blog is exposed to as many people as possible.

TIP 24   Write regularly

One of the main reasons many blogs fail to attract and retain readers is lack of perseverance: if you don't blog regularly, you'll start to lose readers since they know they won't be likely to find fresh content on your blog. According to a 2008 Technorati survey, only 7.4 million out of the 133 million blogs that were being tracked at the time had been updated within the last four months. This means that even if you're a new blogger, you have a good chance of being successful and building up a large readership in the blogosphere just by making sure that you post often.

Although this is a simple concept, it can be hard to put into practice. Just like any other type of business promotion, a blog takes time, which means taking resources away from other essential daily activities. Not surprisingly, then, many companies simply can't keep up this commitment. However, if you do keep at it, you'll reap the rewards in the form of a large, loyal readership, a respected brand, and a wider selection of content visible on search engines.

To keep your existing readers, the golden rule of blogging after writing interesting, unique content is to write good content *often*. To get yourself into the habit of posting regularly, see your blog as an essential part of your marketing effort, which allows you to justify the time you'll be spending posting. The more frequently you post, the better; the most successful blogs in any industry typically post several times a day. If this isn't manageable for you, try to post at least every day and not less than twice a week. One option to make this a reality is to have multiple contributors within your company who will share the load of posting every day or multiple times a day. You can also build up a stock of fresh content by writing extra blog posts when you have downtime and then storing them up to post when you're too busy to write new ones. Remember that these "spare" posts can't be time sensitive, so write about general topics that won't become dated anytime soon.

TIP 25   Use your blog to handle criticism

Many businesses shudder at the thought of their product or brand being criticized in the blogosphere. After all, if a negative story surfaces, the viral nature of blogs means that this negative message can spread to hundreds or even thousands of readers within the space of a few hours or days. Many companies react to bad publicity by burying their head in the sand and pretending the criticism isn't happening, because they believe that getting involved in the debate will only make things worse. The reality, though, is that ignoring what is happening can be a costly mistake that can cause your brand long-term damage. The Internet is a democratic medium where lively debate is highly likely to take place whether you are participating or not, and widely differing tastes and opinions mean that you can't please everyone all the time. If you accept this reality, you'll realize that it's OK to make mistakes or to face disagreement, as long as you react quickly to what is happening.

If you find your business or product being criticized on the Internet, your business blog can be a useful tool with which to react to the situation and in many cases serves as a potent tool for getting across your side of the story. A sound action plan will help you to mitigate any disasters and prevent the situation from becoming worse than it already is:

1. Acknowledge the problem. Facing the criticism early and acknowledging you've made a mistake means you'll be able to contain the negative criticism before it spirals into something much bigger.

2. Apologize. If you weren't in the wrong, state your side of the story without becoming defensive. If you were wrong, admit it. People are far more likely to forgive a company that admits its mistakes than one that comes across as arrogant and aloof.

3. Present a solution as quickly as you can. Get people's minds off the issue that caused the problem and on ways you're being proactive about solving it.

4. Encourage feedback. The very nature of the Internet encourages discussion, so don't be afraid to ask for feedback. Ask your blog readers for their honest opinions about how you can improve and then take their comments to heart.

5. Stay calm. Remember that your blog is an extension of your brand and is a showcase for your company philosophy. When you respond to criticism, be balanced and objective.

TIP 26 Become a guest blogger

Whether you're starting a personal or a business blog, one of the main initial challenges of blogging is how to build up a base of regular readers. This is not surprising: as a new blogger, you're not well known within your industry's blogging circles, and you may well be competing with other blogs that have been around for longer and are therefore better established. Even if you spend significant amounts of time writing a useful blog that contains interesting and informative content, attracting new readers to your blog can be difficult if they're already finding the information they need from another blog that's similar in subject matter. A good way to start building your blog's brand and reputation is to offer to guest-blog for other established blogs in your industry. Guest posting allows you to provide a blogger with fresh content for his or her blog in return for giving your blog exposure.

Start the guest-blogging process by doing research into respected blogs that are related to yours and that have a synergy with your particular blog style. Once you've found blogs you like, browse through their archived content to see the type of content they prefer. From here, brainstorm topics to write about that are similar in theme but that the author hasn't covered before. Now you're ready to contact the author about your proposed guest content. Compose an e-mail to the blogger, letting him or her know that you've read the blog and are new to blogging in the same industry. When you mention the post you're proposing to write, be specific about what the contents would be, and to increase your chances of acceptance, give the author a choice of two or three topics you could write about. Be sure also to include a link back to your blog in your e-mail so that the author can read your blog. Because you'll be showcasing your blog by doing this, it's probably best to offer to guest-blog only once you have a few weeks' or months' worth of writing to show.

If the author agrees, and you do write a post, make sure the blogger's site links back to you at the end of your post. Not only will this encourage people to click through to your site, but it will enhance your blog's visibility on search engines as well.

Making Your Blog Best Friends with Search Engines

| TIP 27 | **Check that you're in Google Search and Google Blog Search** |

The first step in ensuring your blog is best friends with search engines is to see how good a friend you are with it to begin with. If you've just started your blog, there may be a lag in how long it takes for your blog to be indexed in major search engines like Google, Bing, and Yahoo! This time period depends on various factors, but primarily on how easily the engines can find you, which in turn is determined mainly by how many links point to you from other sites. If you're a new blog, getting links to your blog from other blogs and communities is therefore very important in being visible to search engines.

To check whether search engines like Google have indexed your blog, do a keyword search on your blog's name; for example, "The Final Frontier blog." You can also enter "site:" followed by your blog's URL, such as "site:www.finalfrontier.com." If you see your site listed, great. If not, try to arrange for a link to your blog from another already established site, as search engines find new content by following external links on sites they already know about. After you've done this, check again in a few days or weeks to see whether you've been indexed.

In addition to Google.com, Google Blog Search (http://blogsearch .google.com) is a specialized Google search that produces results from blogs only. This can be another major source of traffic for people looking for blog content on a specific topic. Occasionally blog results are also pulled into Google's main page results, which can increase traffic to your blog even more. To see whether your blog is indexed in Google Blog Search, do the same search that you did on Google.com—either search on your blog title or by using "site:" followed by your blog's URL. You can also submit your blog manually to Google (otherwise known as "pinging" Google) by entering your blog address at http://blogsearch.google.com/ping. Usually your blogging software program will do this automatically, but if your blog isn't showing up, this can be worthwhile to do manually. Pinging Google also means that you're ensuring your most recent posts are indexed and appearing on Google's blog search results.

TIP 28 — How to do keyword research

Part of how a search engine ranks Web pages in its search results is by matching the content on that page to the query someone enters into the engine. The more closely your page's content and someone's query match, the higher the chances that your page will rank in a search engine's results. The first step in this process is to find out what your target market is searching for by performing keyword research. Luckily, finding out what people are searching for is easy thanks to several keyword research tools available. One of the most popular and easy-to-use tools is Google's free keyword tool (https://adwords.google.com/select/KeywordToolExternal). Although paid keyword research tools like Wordtracker (www.wordtracker.com) provide more extensive data, if you're doing fairly basic keyword research for your blog, Google's tool is more than sufficient.

Start with Google's tool by entering a word or phrase that's fairly general, such as *sofas*, even if your blog post is specifically about *leather* sofas. This will give you a wider range of keywords from which to choose, since the tool returns all phrases and synonyms that fall within that topic. In our example, Google might return phrases like *three-seater sofas* or *antique couches*. The list can be sorted by search volume per month, and you can restrict your research to searchers in a particular country.

From the list of these phrases, choose a primary (main) keyword phrase and one secondary keyword phrase that's similar to the first one. Continuing with our example, *leather sofas* and *leather furniture* may be your two most applicable phrases that have a high search volume. Note that most people search with phrases that are between two and three words long, so this is the optimal phrase length to select. One-word phrases, while producing large search volumes, can be difficult to rank since there is so much competition—if you're trying to rank for just *sofas*, you'll be competing with every Web page about sofas, as opposed to pages that talk only about leather sofas.

TIP 29 **Incorporate keywords into your blog post**

Now that you've selected your primary and secondary phrases, you're ready to incorporate them into your blog post.

Search engines treat different areas of the page with varying importance, which influences where in the post you should place your keyword phrases. One of the most important areas of a page to a search engine is the header, since that's the most likely place to contain a summary of that page's content. Your post's title should therefore be the first stop for keyword optimization. For example, if you're writing a blog post about your grandma's roast chicken recipe, and *roast chicken* is your main keyword phrase, your post heading can be something like "Roast Chicken: A Surprisingly Easy Dinner." When optimizing the title, or any other piece of text, don't sacrifice readability for search engine visibility. Your post should always sound natural and easy to read to a human being, so don't overdo it by repeating keyword phrases until the text becomes painful to read.

Once you've created an optimized title, include instances and variations of your keyword phrases into the main text of your post. Variations could include plurals and synonyms—for example, *computers*, *laptops*, and *laptop computers* all contribute to thematic relevance for a post on laptops. If you're hosting your own blog, put your keywords in the meta title (you can see this in the blue browser bar when the page is loaded) and within a summary sentence in the meta description. While meta descriptions don't actually count in ranking algorithms, they appear as the snippet of text in a search engine result, and so a description that's useful and compelling can influence click-through to your blog. If you're using free blogging software such as Blogger or WordPress, you won't have as much freedom to edit these fields. However, most tools will automatically populate your meta title field with your post title, so you'll still be covered for the basics.

Tag your blog content

Tags can be thought of as themes that you assign to a particular blog post. For example, if you're writing about the Apple Conference in San Francisco, applicable tags for that post that you create may be words like *Apple*, *Apple Conferences*, *San Francisco*, and *Tech Conferences*.

Because tagging helps you organize your blog posts thematically, it makes the posts much easier to find for your blog readers. Usually a blog is defaulted to organize content by date—but while you may know what you were writing about in August of 2006, your readers won't have a clue. Organizing the content by subject provides a quick way for them to find the content they're looking for.

You can add tags in a "tag" or "label" field (the name depends on the blogging software you're using) on your blogging interface either while you're composing your post or after the post is published. Once you've created the tags, you'll see them under the post as hyperlinked words, and you can also choose to have them appear on the side navigation links under the heading "Categories" or something similar. If you click on a particular tag, you'll be taken to a page that aggregates all the posts that fall under that topic.

As well as a way of organizing content, tags are an excellent way to make the pages of your blog visible to search engines. Besides on-page copy, search engines look at the quantity, quality, and contents of the inbound links pointing to a particular page to determine that page's relevance to a particular subject. For example, if you have lots of links pointing in to one of your posts that say "Apple conferences," it's reasonable to assume that your post is probably about Apple conferences. The more of these topical links you have pointing to your page, the more likely it is that page will rank well for the corresponding keyword search. From the example above, tagging your content with *Apple Conferences* means you're creating an inbound link to your post that will increase its relevance to that topic. This, in turn, improves your visibility in search results for related queries.

TIP 31 Attract inbound links to your blog

The main way that search engines decide which Web pages rank high on their results is by determining which page has the highest quantity of topically relevant, *quality* links pointing in to it from other websites. A large number of inbound links to a page suggests that other people think that page is important, and if the words in the links and the sites that link all fall under a similar topic, the page will be deemed thematically relevant for similar queries. While on-page content is important to search engines, inbound links are even more heavily weighted by them since they're harder to fake. For this reason, if you want to ensure that your blog ranks highly, you need to make sure it has a good amount of inbound links pointing to it from relevant, high-quality external sites.

The best long-term strategy for gaining thematically relevant inbound links to your blog is to write content that people find useful and interesting. Doing this makes people naturally want to link to you for their readers' benefit without your even needing to ask. This works best if you have a large number of readers, so if you're still building your readership, start by adding your blog to aggregators and directories to increase exposure. Read other blogs in your subject area and comment on posts there, since your user name alongside the comment typically lets you add a link back to your blog.

Another way to get inbound links is to be included in someone else's blogroll, the list of blogs the blogger links to from his or her own blog (usually in the left or right column; see Tip 9). You can either ask for this link or build up your exposure so that you become known as a good industry resource, and people will start linking to you without being prompted. You can also increase your blog's inbound links by offering to write a guest post on someone else's blog. As well as getting a link back to your site, you'll be exposed to a wider audience.

Your own marketing materials are easy places to place links back to your blog since you can do them yourself. If you have other websites, forums, articles, or online press releases, include a link in them back to your blog. As well as boosting the inbound links to your blog for search engines, you'll be giving your readers an extra resource.

TIP 32   Leverage other communities' search engine presence

Making sure that your blog has a presence in other sites such as blog portals and social networking sites means that you can take advantage of the high search engine rankings that those sites already have. If your blog is new and hasn't yet built up credibility through a lot of inbound links, this can be very important in supplementing your search engine traffic until your blog is better established. For example, if you do a keyword search on a topic related to one of your blog posts that's on Technorati or Digg, there's a chance that your post on those sites will appear in search engine rankings while your own blog post won't. This is because Google considers sites like Technorati to be highly credible and so will rank them higher in results pages. Even though it's not your own blog that's ranking, users who click through from search engines to your post on another site like Technorati will often end up clicking through to your blog afterward. In this way, being included on other blog networks allows you to get indirect search engine traffic to your blog.

Having a presence on social media sites can help your blog's search engine visibility in the following ways:

- Facebook allows you to choose your own user name, which appears as part of the URL for your page in the format www.facebook.com/username. Including a Facebook user name that is related to your blog's name means that your Facebook page will appear in search results for searches on your blog name, which creates another way to occupy real estate on search engine results pages for searches related to your blog.

- Similarly, choosing a Twitter name or "handle" that's consistent with your Facebook user name and your blog name means when people search on your blog name your Twitter account is likely to rank in search results.

- Although tagging content on social bookmarking sites such as Digg or StumbleUpon won't give your blog inbound link value (most major social bookmarking sites instruct Google not to follow their links to avoid people tagging solely for SEO purposes), they can still help to make your blog more visible on social bookmarking sites to a targeted audience. This in turn encourages them to link back to your posts or to your blog as a whole—and the more inbound links your blog has, the higher your blog's rankings in search engines will be for related keyword searches.

Making Money from Your Blog

TIP 33   Understand Google AdSense

One of the most popular ways for blogs to generate revenue is via AdSense, Google's free contextual advertising program. When you enroll in the AdSense program, Google uses a relevance algorithm to display text or image ads on your blog that are related to your blog's subject matter. In this way Google acts as a middleman between you and independent advertisers.

The AdSense model lets you make money in two main ways: cost per click (CPC), in which you receive a portion of money the advertiser is willing to pay for someone to click on its ad, and cost per thousand impressions (CPM), where you earn money in return for the ads appearing on your site. With the cost-per-click model, an advertiser doesn't pay (and you don't earn money) when the ad is displayed—you earn only when someone actually clicks on the ad. Advertisers choose which model they would like based on the goal of the ad: if the ad is intended mainly for general branding purposes, a cost-per-thousand-impressions (CPM) model will work better. If the main goal of the ad is to generate clicks so that the user performs some kind of action, a cost-per-click model is more suitable. The type of ad that will ultimately show on your site depends on which ad has the potential to make the advertiser more money.

Google pays its content providers (you) on a monthly basis and imposes a "payment threshold" where you're paid only once you reach a certain earnings level. This threshold varies according to the currency of your country; in the United States, it's $100. Many bloggers generate significant revenue through AdSense; generally, the amount of money you make will depend on your blog's subject matter and how much traffic it has. AdSense is free, so it's worthwhile to try it out for a period of time since it won't cost you anything. Bear in mind that although you can include AdSense on blog platforms like TypePad and Blogger (which is probably the most seamless platform on which to run AdSense since Blogger is also a Google product), WordPress does not allow advertising on its platform.

TIP 34   Set up Google AdSense

To set up an AdSense account, you first need to submit an application for approval through the AdSense website at www.google.com/adsense. During this process Google checks that your blog is in line with its publishing policies by looking at what type of content you publish, whether you are publishing content in a language that's compatible with the AdSense program, and that, as the blog owner, you are over eighteen years old.

Once your account has been approved, you'll be able to log in to the AdSense interface to set up your account. If you already have a Google account (which you will have if you have a blog on Blogger), you can use the same log-in details. During the setup process, you'll be able to choose whether to have text or image ads display on your blog. You'll also be able to customize the ads in terms of their size and format and where on the page they'll appear so that they fit in with the look and feel of your blog.

Once this setup is finalized, Google will provide you with a snippet of code for your customized ad unit that you'll need to paste into the source code of your blog. You should place this snippet in the part of your blog's code that is common across your whole blog so that the ad unit will appear on every page of your blog. Google provides you with comprehensive instructions for doing this.

When the AdSense code has been added, ads will start showing on your blog and you can track their performance and your earnings from within your account interface. The interface will show you how much money you're earning as a result of the impressions and clicks the ads are generating on your blog. You can either view your ads' performance as a high-level snapshot on your account dashboard or download reports that will give you more detailed information such as the total number of page and ad unit impressions, number of ad clicks, the ad's click-through rate, effective cost per impression, and your earnings per ad.

TIP 35 Understand Text Link Ads

Another popular blog advertising program that's quick and easy to implement is Text Link Ads (www.text-link-ads.com). Similar to Google AdSense's contextual matching model, Text Link Ads are placed on your blog where the ad content is thematically relevant to the content on your page. For example, if you have a blog post talking about travel to Greece, contextually related Text Link Ads may include ads by travel companies or travel agencies promoting Greek vacation packages. Like Google AdSense, Text Link Ads acts as the middleman between the advertiser and you, the content provider.

In return for displaying ads on your blog, Text Link Ads pays you a portion of the revenue that the advertiser is paying to have its ads appear on your blog. Although Text Link Ads is similar to traditional banner advertising in that they both pay based on the number of impressions that an ad generates, the main difference is that Text Link Ads are displayed only alongside content that is contextually relevant. This means that those who see the ad are more likely to be interested in its content, since the blog post they're reading is thematically related. As a result, there is a higher chance that the reader will take action based on the ad, such as visiting the website of the company that is advertising and ultimately becoming a customer down the line. Consequently, the higher rate of return to an advertiser that Text Link Ads generates makes it a more effective mean of advertising than traditional impression-based advertising.

More recently, Text Link Ads and other text selling services have come under the spotlight since advertisers were buying ads simply to drive up the amount of inbound links pointing to their site from an external source. This strategy is controversial because it is seen as a way of "gaming" search engines, since a website's search engine ranking depends heavily on the number of links pointing into it, and Text Link Ads were a quick and easy way of gaining these links. However, even if a site is found guilty of doing this, as the content provider you won't be penalized. This fact, and that the program is free to implement, means that it is still a worthwhile form of revenue generation to try on your blog.

TIP 36 Set up Text Link Ads

To sign up to be a content provider for Text Link Ads, visit the publisher's section of the Text Link Ads site at www.text-link-ads.com/r/publishers. To be a part of the program, you first need to be approved as a publisher. During this approval process, Text Link Ads will evaluate the popularity of your blog to see whether the potential advertisers are likely to gain a worthwhile return by displaying adverts on your site. Once you've been approved, which usually takes around twenty-four hours from when you submit your application, you'll be given code to add to your blog so that the ads start appearing alongside your posts. You can implement Text Link Ads on most blogging platforms except for WordPress, so if you are planning on generating revenue for your blog you should opt to use a platform that does allow advertising, such as Blogger or TypePad.

One of the main advantages that Text Link Ads offers is that you have control over the ads displayed in your blog. Every time an advertiser pays for an ad to appear on your blog, Text Link Ads will e-mail you and let you either approve the ad or prevent it from being published. This process means that while you're earning money from advertising on your blog, you're still in control of the kind of ad content associated with your blog.

Once your ads are displaying, you can log back into your Text Link Ads account and see the impressions and earnings that you're accruing. The potential amount of revenue your blog can earn by displaying Text Link Ads depends mostly on how popular your blog is: advertisers are charged a flat rate per month per link, which is determined by your blog's traffic, theme, ad position, and link popularity. If your blog receives a large volume of traffic, the advertiser will be charged more to display the ad on your site and you'll receive a portion of this fee.

Payment to publishers is made monthly, and you can choose to receive it either as a check or via PayPal, Payoneer, or a Text Link Ads (TLA) voucher. The payment threshold or minimum amount of earnings you have to reach to receive a check is $25, but there is no minimum for PayPal, Payoneer, or TLA voucher payments.

TIP 37 **Write paid reviews**

Besides having ads appear on your site, a popular way to make money from your blog is by being paid to write a review of someone's product or service. In the paid review marketplace, review broker companies act as the middleman by matching you with products to review that are related to your blog's overall theme. In return, the company or brand that owns the product is exposed to your blog's audience.

If you decide to write paid reviews, make sure your blog still consists predominantly of regular, unpaid posts. If the balance of your blog's content is made up of paid reviews, your readers may become disillusioned with your motives for blogging—they'll see you more as an advertising platform than as a blog that can give them genuinely useful content. Even if the product or service you're reviewing is on topic with your blog, writing too many paid posts puts you at risk of permanently losing your readers, who may go elsewhere for more authentic content.

Two of the most popular paid review brokers in the market are www .reviewme.com and www.payperpost.com:

■ **Reviewme.com:** Through the site, the advertiser chooses the publisher it would like to review its product. The money you can earn per review varies according to your blog's popularity but ranges from $20 per review to as much as $200. As the blogger, you're required to state that the review is sponsored, although you can write the review honestly and give negative or positive feedback. To be approved as a reviewer, your blog needs to be generating fairly significant amounts of traffic, which can be a problem if your blog is new.

■ **Payperpost.com:** This works similarly to Reviewme.com, except that you can proactively choose to write reviews from the PayPerPost marketplace instead of waiting for reviewers to approach you. Advertisers can also specify whether you can write a "fair" review or whether it has to be positive. In general, PayPerPost is more accessible if you're just starting out blogging, although the amount you earn per post will typically be less than the maximum you can earn on Reviewme.com.

TIP 38 — Use blog-specific advertising networks

Blog-specific ad networks serve as a marketplace where ads are matched to display on a publisher network that consists only of blogs. When you sign up as a publisher with a blog-specific network, contextual ads are displayed on your blog alongside content that is related to the ad. In return, as the publisher you then receive a percentage of the money that the advertiser is paying for the ad to appear.

There are a variety of blog ad networks that you can sign up with, and each varies in terms of the requirements for joining. Most regular blog ad networks simply require that your blog be fairly well established (more than a couple of months old), that it be updated regularly, and that it be hosted by a service that can support ads. Others, such as BlogAds (www.blogads .com), don't allow just any blog to sign up—they require blogs on their network to have a certain audience size and popularity level in order to join the network. Some blog networks may require your blog to fall within a specific niche in order to join—for example, a women's blog network that features only women's lifestyle blogs.

Payment for publishers on blog-specific ad networks is usually structured in one of three ways: **cost per impression** (where you're paid a certain amount per a certain volume of your readers who are exposed to the ad), **cost per click** (where you're paid a percentage of the money an advertiser pays for a reader to click on an ad), or **cost per action** (where you're paid every time a reader fulfils an action as a result of clicking on the ad, such as signing up for a newsletter). In general, ads on your blog will be more successful (and you'll end up making more money) if your blog content is closely aligned with the product advertised.

Most networks give you a choice of ad formats that are displayed on your blog, such as banner ads, text ads, or related product units. You'll also usually be able to choose a color scheme and dimensions for the creative so that the ads fit in with the overall look and feel of your blog.

TIP 39 **Use general affiliate networks**

Affiliate networks were one of the first ways that website owners began to make money when the Internet began to be used commercially, and being part of an affiliate program today can still be an effective way to monetize your blog. At a high level, the business model for an affiliate program is that the business running the program will pay other websites (known as *affiliates*) for referring a visitor or customer to its site. How the affiliate refers the visitor involves some kind of promotion on the affiliate's site, such as a text link, product mention, or banner ad.

Websites like Commission Junction (www.cj.com) or Amazon (www.amazon.com) are called affiliate networks, because they act as intermediaries between the websites running affiliate programs and the affiliates themselves. The payment structure in an affiliate program varies among the different networks and programs available, but you'll typically be paid using one of the following payment models:

■ **Pay per click**—you receive a certain portion of the amount that the owner of the affiliate program pays for a reader to click through to its site from yours.

■ **Pay per impression**—the traditional banner-advertising revenue model, where you're paid according to how many people view an ad for the business's product on your blog.

■ **Pay per lead**—you're paid a certain amount of money if the ad on your site generates a lead from one of your readers.

■ **Pay per action**—similar to pay per lead, this is where you're paid if someone fulfills a certain action, such as signing up for a newsletter, as a direct result of clicking an ad from your site.

Many bloggers choose to run a variety of affiliate programs on their blogs to cobble together a larger flow of income that they wouldn't be able to get from running just one program alone. Other bloggers also combine regular affiliate programs with contextual advertising such as Google AdSense or Text Link Ads. If you are considering becoming an affiliate, make sure the affiliate network you sign up with is reputable and that the sites offering affiliate programs are genuine businesses. It's important to make sure this is the case—if not, your blog's reputation will be compromised since you'll be associated with the product or service in question, which means you'll risk losing your readers for good.

Joining Blogging Communities

TIP 40 | Participate in blogging communities

Across every industry, the most successful bloggers are those who are pro-active about gaining new readers and who initiate a conversation with others writing on similar subjects. These days just setting up your blog and posting content is rarely enough to attract a significant amount of new readers initially. Especially if you're starting a new blog, you need to expose your blog as widely as possible to people who are interested in your content so that they can become familiar with your blog and become regular readers. One of the most effective places to do this is on blogging communities. These are sites that pull in content across multiple blogs that are usually organized on the network by subject. Joining blogging communities allows exposure for your blog across an entire industry and across different audiences. As a new blogger, it also helps you tap into an existing audience in your specific subject area.

Popular blogging communities include sites like MyBlogLog (www .mybloglog.com), BlogCatalog (www.blogcatalog.com), Blogged (www .blogged.com), and NetworkedBlogs (www.networkedblogs.com). When you join these networks, you can interact with other bloggers writing about topics similar to yours, which allows you to build up recognition for your blog within your industry. The other advantage of joining a blogging network is that it lets you build up your blog's readership much faster than if you're attempting to do it on your own. For example, if your blog is featured or linked to on the home page of a blog network, it will be exposed to a much larger audience of readers who are already reading other blogs on that same network. Another example is cross-posting, where a related post from one blog will appear under another post as a related link.

Most blog networks and communities contain profile pages for each blog, where you can comment and interact with the author. Many networks also have internal communication systems such as forums, e-mail lists, and wikis that give you even more ways to connect with other bloggers in the same industry.

TIP 41   **Submit your blog to directories**

Although your blog is most likely to be found via blog networks and search engines (both general ones and blog-specific engines), blog directories can also be a useful way of exposing your blog to people who are looking for your content. Like most directories, blog directories are organized by subject matter, so readers will see your blog if they browse in a specific category that is related to you. The main difference between a blog directory and a blog search engine is that directories typically provide information on the blog as a whole, rather than returning results containing specific blog posts within that blog. This is useful for you if you're researching influential blogs in your industry rather than looking for posts on a specific topic. Some examples of blog directories are:

■ **Blogged (www.blogged.com):** Blogged gives you information on each listed blog, including its topic, tags, length of time it has been in existence, and who its authors are. Blogged.com editors also review and rate the blogs that are part of its directory, and readers are able to give feedback on each blog.

■ **BlogCatalog (www.blogcatalog.com):** Besides browsing for blogs in a particular category, or searching on a keyword relating to a particular topic, you can rate and review blogs, which then appear as comments on the blog's profile page. You can also connect with other bloggers by adding them as friends to your account—after which you can keep up to date with actions they take on the site such as new blogs they're reading or comments they write. You can also connect with bloggers through Shoutboxes, private groups, or general discussions.

■ **Technorati Blog Directory (www.technorati.com):** Although it is better known as a blog search engine, Technorati also has a blog directory where you can browse by topic to find blogs in a specific area. Examples of categories include small business, music, gadgets, fashion, science, and food. To be part of the blog directory, you need to sign up for an account with Technorati and claim your blog to prove that you're the owner. For more on Technorati, see Tips 47–49.

TIP 42   Join MyBlogLog

MyBlogLog is a social blog-sharing network owned by Yahoo! that allows your blog to be exposed instantly to an existing audience of other bloggers who are already part of the network. Besides being a traffic-building tool for your blog, MyBlogLog is an excellent tool for monitoring statistics on your blog such as the amount of traffic you're getting and what links people are clicking on within your posts.

To create an account with MyBlogLog, click the "Join/Sign In" tab on the home page of www.mybloglog.com. On the account creation page, you'll need to choose a username, password, and e-mail address to associate with your account, and you'll need to provide the URL of your blog. Since the site is owned by Yahoo!, you can sign in using your Yahoo! ID if you already have one. Once your account has been created, you'll need to claim your blog to prove that you are its owner. To do this, you'll be provided with a unique snippet of code to paste into your blog's template. Doing this associates your own blog with your account. Once your blog has been claimed, you can make changes to your profile to enhance your branding such as uploading your company logo. From your profile, you can access most of MyBlogLog's functionality, such as viewing statistics related to your blog, including who's visiting it and what links they're clicking on within a post.

Although a basic MyBlogLog account is free, you can pay a monthly subscription fee for a MyBlogLog pro account. Having a pro account gives you added functionality such as being able to access real-time stats and the option to download logs that you can slice and dice independently on your own using other analytics tools. While a pro account is useful if you have a significant amount of traffic to your blog or have a large number of links in each post, the basic version will be more than adequate if you're just starting out. A good idea is to start with a basic account and upgrade later if you want to by going to the "Edit" settings in your account.

TIP 43 Network with like-minded communities

One of the most useful things about MyBlogLog is the way it allows you to network with other blogs that are related to yours. For every blog listed on MyBlogLog, a community exists that you can join to interact directly with other fellow members. Networking within communities is a good way of exposing your blog to a larger volume of people that ultimately will drive more traffic to your site. There are three main ways you can connect with MyBlogLog users:

1. Communities. Finding and joining these communities is easy: by default, MyBlogLog adds you to the communities of websites you visit often. When you sign up for an account, the site also prompts you to enter keywords of topics you're interested in. Think of keywords that are related to your industry or business, such as *designer shoes* if you're a website selling designer accessories. From here you'll be taken to a results set of blog communities that relate to that particular phrase. Each community's profile page contains a summary of the blog and related tags and allows you to interact with other MyBlogLog members who are part of the same community.

2. Member profiles. If you type in a query such as *designer shoes* and click on the "members" link on the results page that is returned, you'll be taken to a list of MyBlogLog members whose personal profile is related to your query. Clicking on any of these results will take you to that member's personal profile page, where you can leave a message or subscribe to the feed of his or her activity on MyBlogLog and other social media sites. Leaving a comment on the member's profile increases the chances of that blogger and his or her readers visiting your profile and, ultimately, your blog.

3. Adding contacts. Besides leaving messages on someone's profile page, you can add friends as contacts for your own personal profile page. You can do this either by adding any existing Yahoo! contacts you have or by inviting up to five contacts' e-mail addresses.

TIP 44 Add other activities to MyBlogLog

A fairly recent addition to MyBlogLog is the "New with Me" section that is visible on the home page of your profile. "New with Me" aggregates your recent activity on other social media sites such as FriendFeed, Delicious, Digg, Flickr, Twitter, Yahoo! Answers, and YouTube as a live stream into your MyBlogLog profile page. MyBlogLog can pull your activities on these sites into your profile by accessing your public RSS feeds linked to each of them. Besides enriching your profile on MyBlogLog, the "New with Me" section exposes your activity on other sites to your communities and contacts, which helps drive more traffic to your profiles on those social media sites. Related to "New with Me" is "New with My Neighborhood," which aggregates the recent activities of your MyBlogLog contacts, and "New with My World," which shows updates from all MyBlogLog users that contain content relating to tags you've created in your profile.

To activate the "New with Me" section, access your profile page and click the "Add your services here" link. The page that follows will list all the services that MyBlogLog interfaces with. For each of these, you'll be prompted to add your user name to the URL for that service so that MyBlogLog can access the associated RSS feed. To make this process simpler, MyBlogLog lets you enter a profile name that is similar to your profile name on your other services. This allows the site to automatically populate the associated URL for each service that contains your user name and find those feeds without you needing to enter them in manually.

Note that MyBlogLog can access only social media services on which your feed is publicly available. So, if your updates are protected on Twitter, for example, MyBlogLog won't be able to access your feed and pull it through into your account. Once a service has been added to MyBlogLog, you can remove it again by returning to the services page and removing your profile name or user name from the associated URL.

Add the "Recent Readers" widget to your blog

One of the most useful things about MyBlogLog is the "recent readers" widget. Including this widget on your blog allows you to keep track of other MyBlogLog readers who visit your site and to leave a trail to your blog when you visit others. When a member of MyBlogLog arrives at your blog, the member's photo and a link to the member's profile is included in the widget, which displays in your blog's sidebar on the home page. In this way, the recent readers widget is a kind of footprint that leaves a record of your visitors who are fellow MyBlogLog members. Whether you're visiting other blogs or tracking visitors to your own blog, the recent readers widget is useful in two main ways:

1. It allows you to keep track of who is visiting your site and then click through to their profile page, where you can leave a comment. In this way the widget allows you to interact with and build relationships with other bloggers who are interested in your content.

2. When you visit other sites that have the recent readers widget installed, the blog owner and their audience will be able to click through on your picture and link within the widget to visit your blog. In this way you can build traffic to your site simply by visiting other blogs that are a part of MyBlogLog.

To install the recent readers widget on your site, log in to your account and click on the "get widgets" link within your personal profile. From here, select the widget and then select the layout you'd like so that it fits in with the overall look and feel of your blog. Once you've finished, you'll be given code to paste into your site that will include the widget in your blog's sidebar.

If you're on someone else's blog that has a recent readers widget, clicking "view reader community" at the bottom of the widget will take you to that particular blogger's website community—which is another way of sourcing new blogs to visit and new blogger relationships to build. Especially if the blog you're visiting is in your industry, clicking this link is a useful way to see what others in the industry are saying.

TIP 46 Leverage MyBlogLog stats

When you create an account with MyBlogLog, you gain access to various traffic stats about your blog. Although these are not a replacement for the normal stats that you can access from within your blogging platform or on stats packages such as Google Analytics, MyBlogLog's stats can provide useful supplemental insights into your readers' behavior on your blog. One of the most useful stats that MyBlogLog provides is a record of which links your readers are clicking on from within your blog posts that result in their leaving your blog. By monitoring what readers are clicking on, you can see what content they're finding the most interesting on your blog. This allows you to change your content accordingly, by writing more about the subjects they find interesting and including more of the kinds of links they're likely to click on. Knowing what content your readers find interesting on your blog is also useful since you can write follow-up blog posts on the same topics that generate the most interest among your readers.

To see the traffic details for your blog, log in to your MyBlogLog account and click on the "My Sites and Services" link in the left navigation menu of the home page. From this page, click "Statistics" at the bottom to view an extensive view of your site stats. The "offsite click" tracking shows you where readers have clicked off your blog from a link you've given them. This section also shows you the relative popularity among multiple links on your blog so you can see how they perform relative to each other.

Besides the offsite click statistic, you can see regular statistics such as the number of readers you receive, the number of page views your blog generates, and what search terms visitors are entering in to arrive at your site. Note that MyBlogLog gives you statistics for only the last five days. But, as mentioned previously, you can access a more comprehensive version of these stats for a longer time frame by using the stats included in your blogging platform or in external stats packages.

TIP 47   Understand Technorati

Technorati is a search engine that accesses blogs' RSS feeds to index blog content in various formats, including text, photo, and video. As far as improving your blog's visibility and growing your readership are concerned, Technorati is a useful site in which to include your blog.

When you join Technorati, you're given a profile page that shows your blog's ranking (relative to other blogs on the network), tags related to your content, and snippets of recent blog posts you've written. As well as a place to showcase your own blog, Technorati is a good place to read about what others in your industry, including your competitors, are saying. There are two ways to find other blogs on the network: the first and main way is to enter related keywords into the search field on the home page and search on either blogs as a whole or on individual blog posts. Alternatively, you can browse through Technorati's various subject categories such as travel, music, and finance, under which related blogs are organized.

Besides its search engine, blog directory, and profile pages, Technorati features a "top 100" list, which includes the blogs it considers most important on its network. As well as this overall list, Technorati has a top 100 list for different subject areas. These lists are updated daily and are ordered by an algorithm called "Technorati Rank," which uses the previous month's blog data to evaluate the inbound links to a particular blog. This evaluation includes the quantity of links, as well as factors related to the link's source such as the site's age, relevance to your blog, and credibility. The more quality links that point to your blog, the more important Technorati will consider it to be and therefore the higher your Technorati Rank will be.

Besides affecting your visibility on Technorati, your Technorati Rank can affect things such as how much you stand to make on advertising via your blog and whether you qualify to host ads for certain advertising networks. A recent addition to Technorati is Twittorati, which contains tweets published by the authors of Technorati's top 100 blogs.

Join Technorati and claim your blog

Joining Technorati is a simple process that involves two steps: signing up for your account and claiming your blog to verify that you're the owner.

1. Signing up. To join the site, sign up for an account by clicking the "Join" link on the Technorati home page. From here you'll be asked to enter in your real name and your member name (both of which will appear on your public profile page), the e-mail address that you want associated with your account, and a password. Once you've entered these details, you'll be sent an activation link to the e-mail address you associated with your account. Once you click this from within the e-mail address, your account is ready to go and you'll be prompted to sign in.

2. Claiming your blog. Once you've created an account, you need to associate your account with your blog. This is done in a process known as *claiming your blog*, where you prove that you're the blog owner. Once a blog is claimed, it will be added to your public profile page as well as into Technorati's blog directory and index.

To start the claiming process, enter the URL of your blog on your profile page in the "my claimed blogs" section and then click the "claim" button. From here you'll be asked to give the details of your blog, including its title, URL, and description. You'll also be asked to identify tags and up to three categories that are related to your blog's subject matter, which in turn helps Technorati group your blog in the correct category in its blog directory.

After you complete the form, Technorati reviews your claim application and will contact you to confirm approval or give you further instructions, which usually happens within a few days. Previously the process of claiming your blog was done by providing you with a snippet of code, which you then added to your blog so that it could be found and verified by Technorati's engine. Technorati changed this system to one of manual review to make it difficult for fake or "spam" blogs to be included in its index.

TIP 49　Use Technorati tags

When you claim your blog on Technorati, you're asked to provide tags that relate to the overall theme of your blog. For example, if your blog is about used cars, you might enter tags such as *used cars*, *preowned cars*, and *used vehicles*. Since these tags relate to your blog as a whole, they tend to be high-level phrases rather than specific ones. As well as adding these general tags so that your blog can be found when people search on Technorati for these terms, adding tags for individual posts will ensure that your blog posts are visible for a broader range of search queries. For example, if you're writing a post about used Toyota cars, your tags for that post may include phrases that relate specifically to that post only, such as *used Toyotas*, *used Prius*, used *Toyota Corollas*, and *used Toyota vehicles*. In this way you're increasing the chances of your blog post being returned as a result for a search query such as *used Toyota cars*. Tags also are useful since Technorati tag pages tend to rank well on Google. So if your blog post is listed on more tag pages on Technorati, you'll drive more traffic to your blog indirectly via Technorati's presence on Google.

In the past, Technorati tags for individual blog posts had to be created either by manually adding a line of HTML code to your blog post that then generated the tag under the post or by downloading a plug-in to your blogging software that would generate this HTML for you. These days Technorati can interpret the standard tags that you create within your blogging tool itself by accessing your blog's RSS feed. These tags are called different things depending on which blogging platform you're using: in Blogger they're known as *labels*, while on WordPress they are known as *categories*. To ensure that Technorati can access the labels or categories you create, make sure your blog has a full RSS feed enabled rather than a short version. Short feeds usually syndicate only the URL or the URL and first paragraph of the post and not the full post or its associated tags. In most blogging platforms, you can change your feed preferences by accessing the settings menu in your blog account.

3

Microblogging

JUST AS its name suggests, microblogging is a shortened form of blogging, where multimedia updates that are usually shorter than a full-length blog post are published online. The key feature of microblogging is that people can subscribe to someone else's microblog and be notified when that person has published new content. These subscribers can then respond to the information or interact with other bloggers on the same tool.

Updates in a microblog are commonly made in text format but can also be made in other, multimedia formats, including images, audio, or video. One of the main advantages of microblogging is its flexibility: as opposed to being able to create an update using only your browser, as is the case with most conventional blogging platforms, most microblogging tools let you make and receive updates from your mobile phone or other portable devices. This flexibility makes microblogging tools a great way of sharing breaking news with others as it happens or to receive news as soon as it is published.

Microblogging is a good option for your business if you're new to blogging and want to start by creating updates that don't take as much time. They're also an efficient way to build up a community without a huge investment of time. Although a huge number of microblogging tools is available and the competition is stiff, only three are outlined in this section: Twitter, FriendFeed, and Tumblr, which together represent a good selection of the current most popular microblogging tools around.

Getting Started on Twitter

TIP 50 | Understand Twitter

As far as microblogging tools go, Twitter is currently the darling of the social media set. At its core, Twitter is a tool in which you can share short, text-message-length updates, or "tweets," with other people who are following your account and also read updates of people you are following, from your Twitter timeline—a continuously updating list of updates that you can see from the home page of your Twitter account.

As a business owner, you'll find Twitter a useful tool with which to build your brand by writing unique insights that you then share with your customers, partners, vendors, or other like-minded people in your industry. But beyond just brand building, Twitter is the ultimate crowd-sourcing tool, in that you're tapping into the collective knowledge of all Twitter users to find information, learn new insights, and keep up to date with what's happening on a particular subject. Most recently, Twitter launched its advertising platform to allow for paid exposure on the site: through "Promoted Tweets," businesses can pay for a particular tweet to be shown alongside related search results when someone searches on Twitter for a particular word or phrase.

One of the reasons Twitter is so powerful is that its extremely open software platform allows its data to be used by anyone. This means anyone can use its data to build his or her own third-party tool that incorporates Twitter functionality. As a result, you can use Twitter in many different ways—from your phone, from desktop applications, and even from other microblogging tools like FriendFeed. What's more, tools like TweetDeck and Twitter lists help you organize and manage your account so that you can separate your followers into themed groups that make sense to you.

TIP 51 Create your Twitter account

Twitter has a very simple and intuitive interface, which means that setting up an account shouldn't take long even if you've never used it before.

To create your account, go to www.twitter.com and click the "Sign Up Now" button. On the next screen you'll be asked to enter your name, the e-mail address you want associated with the account, and a password you will use to access it. The e-mail address that you use is how Twitter notifies you of events in your Twitter account (e.g., you have a direct message or a new follower request). For this reason, make sure the e-mail address you use here is one that you check often.

You'll also be asked to select a handle. Also known as a *handle*, this will be the name that other people will use to connect with you in their own feed by placing an @ sign before it (for example, *@jacksparrow*). Your handle also appears as part of the URL of your Twitter feed—for example, www.twitter.com/jacksparrow. When opening a Twitter account for your business, think carefully about what you want this handle to be—it will be an important part of your page's branding, and it will also affect how many people find you if they use Twitter's search function to find you by entering in your company name. For these reasons, most companies choose a handle that is close to their company name, such as *@microsoft* or *@google*. When you've thought of a handle, enter it in to the handle field, and Twitter will let you know whether it's available. Once you've secured one that's free, you're good to go. If you're including a brand as part of your handle, make sure that you own the copyrights to it.

There is no limit to the number of Twitter accounts you can have—many companies choose to have multiple accounts for different areas of their business (for example, @googlereader, @googlenews, and @google maps are all Twitter accounts that contain updates about specific Google products). If you're a small or medium-sized business that's never used Twitter before, one corporate account is probably enough.

Public vs. private accounts

New Twitter accounts are public by default. This means that anyone can see your Twitter page, whether they're following you or not, and anyone can choose to follow you without your prior approval.

If you don't want your updates to be seen by everyone, you can change your account setting from public to private. When you do this, your updates are protected so that only people who are following you can see your Twitter page, and any new users who want to follow you need to be approved by you first. A new user who wants to follow you will send you a follower request that you'll be able to see on your home page. You'll also receive a notification of this request in the e-mail account linked to your Twitter account. You can then click through to the user's Twitter page from the request note and then choose to accept or reject the user as a follower.

If you protect your account, the visibility of your tweets will also be limited in the following ways:

- They won't show up in search results.

- They won't be visible in the feed on the main "Everyone" tab.

- A direct reply sent to someone who isn't following you won't be seen by that person.

Usually private accounts are personal accounts set up by users who want to be followed only by people they know. If you're building up a business Twitter account, your aim is most likely to expose your brand to increasing numbers of people by building up your followers, in which case it makes sense to allow instant subscribing without your approval. Another advantage of public accounts is that your unprotected Twitter page can act as an advertisement for nonfollowers who may land on your profile page and then choose to subscribe to your feed based on the content they read.

TIP 53 · Customize your profile

Once you've set up your Twitter account, you can customize certain areas of your Twitter page via the "settings" tab in the top right navigation menu. By customizing your page, you can align it with your company branding and help it stand out from other home pages. These are the main areas of your Twitter account that you can change:

- **More info URL:** This element appears in the profile section of your Twitter home page. By adding the URL of your company website or business blog, you give people a next step to follow if they want to find out more about your business. This effectively capitalizes on your Twitter traffic by driving visitors who are already fairly familiar with your brand (via reading your feed) to your website. Since they've already interacted with your brand, there's a greater chance that they will eventually convert to customers or loyal readers if the URL you provide is for your blog.

- **Bio:** Add a sentence that sums up your business and explains you to people who are new to your page and aren't familiar with your brand. Keep it brief: in true Twitter fashion, the sentence can be a maximum of 160 characters. Writing a compelling online bio can be a key way of convincing nonfollowers to your page to follow you. Keep the tone of the bio light and personal and try not to be too formal or too sales heavy.

- **Location:** Including your location information means that you're more likely to show up in Twitter search results if someone is conducting a geographical search for products or services in your particular area.

- **Profile picture:** In a business Twitter account, the profile picture area is a great place to upload your business logo to reinforce your brand.

- **Background and colors:** Twitter lets you customize your colors and background, either by selecting from a stock selection of backgrounds or by uploading your own graphic. Like uploading your company logo as your profile picture, the background image you use is another opportunity to reinforce your company's branding through color or design. If you do upload your own background, make sure its design doesn't detract from the tweets on the page.

TIP 54 Begin tweeting

Once your account is set up, you can begin with a short update, known as a *tweet*, in the text box that asks, "What are you doing?" on your Twitter home page. Your update can be up to only 140 characters long—the same character limit for a normal cell phone text message—so you'll need to think of a succinct way to phrase your sentence so that it fits into the allotted space.

Once you've written your tweet, clicking the "submit" button under the text box publishes it to the general Twitter feed that everyone can see, also known as the *Twitterverse*. If someone is following you, your tweet will appear in the top of the feed (note that tweets appear in chronological order in your feed, with the latest tweet appearing at the top). If a Twitter user isn't following you, your tweet won't appear in his or her own feed but will appear in the user's search results if he or she searches on a subject that is related to your tweet.

It may seem like an obvious statement to make, but the contents of your tweets are critical to your success on Twitter. Especially if you or your brand isn't well known, how useful your tweets are to others is an important factor when someone is deciding whether to follow you. When you're deciding what to write, think about your followers: what would add value to them and get them to join a conversation? Use your Twitter account as a way to offer unique insights about your industry or share useful information rather than pushing your own brand. You can also use Twitter to link to useful resources that others in your industry have published, such as a newly released industry white paper if you're a market research firm.

Besides writing useful content, writing regular updates is the best way to grow your group of followers. You can remind yourself to do this by asking Twitter to "nudge" you if you haven't updated your status within a day. At the same time, don't "overtweet" either, as then you risk annoying and ultimately losing certain followers. As well as posting your own updates, you can "retweet" what someone else has said or respond directly to someone else's tweet. For specifics on how to reply, see Tip 59, and on how to retweet, see Tip 60.

Use URL shorteners

Because the character space for a Twitter update is so limited (140 characters or less), a long URL that you post as a link in an update can take up valuable space. To get around this, URL-shortening services such as Bit.ly (http://bit.ly) and TinyURL (http://tiny.cc) take your original, long URL and convert it to a shortened "alias" URL. When this alias URL is clicked, it redirects to the original URL you supplied.

For example, let's say you want to write an update that references your new holiday ideas section of your website. Your tweet might say something like "Just in time for the holidays—make your seasonal lighting special for your visiting friends and family with our lighting guide: www.mylighting store.com/holiday-ideas." If you wrote this tweet as is, it would exceed the 140 character limit. To solve this problem, go to http://bit.ly and paste in your long URL; you'll be given a shortened URL that masks the long one, such as http://bit.ly/3K2XPk.

There are many URL-shortening tools on the market, and most have value-added features that go beyond just shortening a URL. TinyURL, for example, gives preview functionality to your URL, so that those who want to click on the shortened link can see what they are accessing before actually clicking on the link. TinyURL also has a bookmark plug-in that you can install in your browser, letting you create a shortened URL without needing to visit its site. Bit.ly gives you traffic statistics relating to the URL you paste in, such as how many people clicked on the link and what location they're in. To see these stats, add a + to the end of the shortened URL provided and paste this into your browser. Remember that these statistics are an aggregation of all clicks to that long URL everywhere on the web—not just clicks from your update. If you want to see only stats for your specific URL, you can create a Bit.ly account, which will then give you referral data pertaining to your users only. Other URL shorteners, such as Doiop (www.doiop.com), allow you to add keywords to the end of your shortened URL so that they appear thematically related to the original URL you provided.

Include photographs in your tweets

As well as creating text updates and updates that contain links to useful resources, you can also link to images from within your tweets. Uploading and linking to photographs from within your updates is a way to enrich your tweet with context—this makes them more interesting for your followers, and you'll encourage new people browsing your profile page to become followers as well.

You can upload photos or videos to a variety of third-party sites that interface directly with Twitter. The current most popular photo-sharing tool for Twitter is TwitPic (http://twitpic.com), but many other competitors offer similar services, for example TweetPhoto (www.tweetphoto.com) and yfrog (http://yfrog.com). While sites like TwitPic and TweetPhoto allow you to only share image files, yfrog allows you to upload videos as well. This means you only have to use one site to upload media rather than having to use a separate site such as TwitVid (www.twitvid.com) if you want to share video content as well. Besides photographs and videos, you can also share other types of files such as documents or sound files using tools such as FileTwt (www.filetwt.com) and TwitFS (http://twitfs.com).

With most of these media-sharing tools, you simply log in to the site with your Twitter details and then upload the picture, video, or file from there. You can also give your file more context through things like location tags and text captions. Some tools, like TweetPhoto, give you extra functionality including statistics about who's viewed, favorited, and commented on your photos; the ability to geo-tag your photo if you upload it from a GPS-enabled phone; and integration with other social media sites such as Facebook, MySpace, or LinkedIn. Once you've uploaded your image, video, or other file, you'll usually be given a short URL for the location of your picture so that you save space in the 140-character limit of your update when you link to it from within your tweet.

It's worth noting that at the time of writing, Twitter was considering allowing capabilities for rich media like photos and videos to be uploaded directly from the Twitter interface. If this happens, specialized Twitter image and photo uploading sites like the ones mentioned above may eventually become redundant.

TIP 57 Understand what followers are

Once you start tweeting, you'll see the tweets of people you're following in the home page feed of your account. Tweets appear in chronological order, with the most recent feeds appearing at the top of the page and older tweets appearing lower down. At the beginning of a tweet, you'll see the person's handle, which is always hyperlinked. If you click on the name, you'll be taken to that person's Twitter home page. Those who are following you will see your tweets in their home page or on any third-party Twitter application they're using.

As opposed to other social networks, following works asymmetrically in Twitter. This means that even when people are following you, you don't have to be following them back for them to see your updates. If you decide for any reason that you don't want to follow someone anymore, you can simply visit that user's Twitter page and click "unfollow" from the dropdown function button underneath the profile picture. When you unfollow someone, your name will disappear from his or her list of followers, and your tweets will no longer appear in his or her feed. Twitter also won't notify those you stop following.

The default follower setting on Twitter allows anyone to follow you without prior approval from you. If you'd prefer to approve your followers first and not have your Twitter feed visible to everyone, you can change your settings to protect your updates by clicking the "Settings" link in the top right navigation menu once you've logged in. At the bottom of the page, you'll see a checkbox that you can check if you want your updates to be protected. If you do protect your updates, the follow system remains asymmetrical: although any new follower requests for your feed have to be approved by you, you can still follow anyone else whose updates are unprotected without their approving you first.

If the constant stream of tweets in your feed seems overwhelming, third-party applications such as TweetDeck (see Tip 74) can help you organize your feed into categories you define.

TIP 58 Find people to follow

Once you've started tweeting, the next step is to find people to follow on Twitter so that their tweets will show up in your timeline. This is a good way to get followers for your own account, since each person you decide to follow will receive an e-mail notification telling them that you're now following them, along with a link to your account and statistics about you.

The easiest way to start following someone else is to click "follow" under the profile picture of their Twitter page. However, unless you know the person's handle, you won't be able to find the user's page. Twitter solves this problem by allowing you to find people to follow in several different ways, which you can access by clicking the "Find People" link in the top navigation menu from your home page:

- **Find on Twitter:** This function lets you search for people or businesses by entering a first or last name or business name. From the search results, click the "follow" button to the right of the person or business you want to follow.

- **Find on other networks:** This function pulls through the contacts from your AOL, Gmail, or Yahoo! Web-based e-mail accounts that are already on Twitter. To get started, enter in your e-mail log-in details (your e-mail address and password) from any of these Web-based accounts and select those you'd like to follow from the list of contacts returned. The contact list will default to selecting to follow everyone in your address book—but if you don't want to follow someone, just deselect the checkbox next to that person's profile picture and handle.

- **Invite by e-mail:** This function lets you add in e-mail addresses of clients or friends to invite them to follow you. Note that these recipients don't already need to have a Twitter account to receive your invitation.

- **Suggested users:** Twitter explains its "suggested user" list as being similar to staff picks in a bookstore: the list contains accounts of people or companies (usually high-profile ones) that Twitter feels are interesting or useful to follow. Twitter uses certain criteria to compile this list, such as how many followers the people have, how high-profile they are, and what their profile says. From there Twitter product teams look at the account to see whether it's a good account for a new user to follow and whether the person who owns the account is famous or would appeal to a lot of people. Just as with finding people from other networks, you'll have the option to check or uncheck people on the list that you'd like to follow or not follow.

Reply to followers

Twitter works best when you engage both with the people you're following and the people who are following you. By doing this, you expose your updates to a wider group of people, which increases the number of followers you have for your account. Besides direct messaging, there are two ways you can let people know you're talking specifically to them on Twitter:

- **@ replies:** An @ reply involves beginning your tweet with @ plus the handle of the person you want to respond to. For example: *@susanporter Interesting stats—wonder if those translate to outside the US as well.* You can either type this in manually or click the gray arrow (called a *swoosh*) below someone's tweet, which automatically populates your update box with @ and their handle. When you write an @ reply to people, they can view it in a sorted list of replies that is linked to from their home page. You can see this sorted list on your own account by clicking the link that says @ plus your handle in the right column. Viewing a sorted list makes it easier to see who is talking directly to you so that you can respond accordingly.

- **Mentions:** Whereas with an @ reply you start the update with @[handle], with a mention you simply include the @[handle] part anywhere in a tweet. Mentions are a way to link to someone else's feed from yours, which effectively endorses him or her by exposing the user's feed to your followers. Mentions are also a good way to comment on a business or a product so that it will be noticed both by the company itself (provided it's on Twitter) and a large group of people (your followers).

When someone does a search for his or her handle, any tweets that mention the user in this way will be returned in results. The main difference between an @ reply and a mention is that with an @ reply only users who are following both the sender and the recipient of the tweet will see it. With a mention, anyone will see the tweet, follower or not. If your account is protected, any @ replies or mentions you send to people who aren't following you won't be seen by them.

Retweet

If you read someone's update that you find interesting and want to share with your own followers, you can "retweet" the update so that it is seen by all your followers as well. To retweet someone's update, copy and post the text into your update field and then place "RT @[handle]" at the beginning of the update. When you retweet, it's correct Twitter etiquette to keep the exact words of the original tweet that was written.

For example, if you are following @susanporter and she posts *@susan porter Chicago direct marketing conference will take place on 10-14 October 2010*, you can retweet this in your own feed by writing *RT @ susanporter Chicago direct marketing conference will take place on 10-14 October 2010.*

Many third-party applications like TweetDeck (www.tweetdeck.com) and Tweetree (www.tweetree.com) make it easy for you to retweet by including an icon on their interface that you click, which then creates the tweet again. Then you click once more to submit the update so that it's reposted on your feed. If you are going to retweet, make sure the majority of your tweets are your own original updates so that your brand is still being seen as adding unique value to its followers. You can also add your own insights in a retweet by adding a comment between the *RT* and the *@[handle]*. However, since all tweets are limited to 140 characters, you may not have space to do this.

Third-party Twitter Web applications such as Tweetmeme (http://tweet meme.com) and Retweetradar (www.retweetradar.com) let you see the most popular retweeted content across Twitter. By using the search function within these tools, you can see the types of tweets in your industry that are generating the most retweets and try to write updates that are similar so that your content is reposted by others. Having your own content retweeted by others is a good way of exposing your Twitter account beyond just your own followers, since your update will be seen by all the followers of the person who is retweeting as well.

TIP 61 Direct messaging

A direct message, also called a *DM*, is a private tweet sent to another follower so that only the two of you can see it. Direct messages are a good tool to use if you want to share information with someone on Twitter that you don't want to be seen by all followers—for example, your e-mail address or phone number. Think of Twitter's direct message function as a private e-mail account within your Twitter account. As with e-mail, a direct message is seen by only the sender and recipient, but it differs from e-mail in three main ways:

1. The character limit on a direct message remains 140, like a regular Twitter update.

2. Direct messages aren't organized in threads, so when replying you'll need to refer to the previous message to provide context.

3. Once you've sent a direct message, you can delete it, in which case it will also disappear from your recipient's in-box. In this way a direct message stays in your control even once it's been sent.

The first way to create a direct message is to click the "message [handle]" link on the right column of the Twitter page of the follower you want to contact. From here you simply type in your message and then click the "Send" button below the text box. You can also direct-message someone via your own status update box by using the "d" direct message command. To do this, type *d [handle]* followed by your message, for example *d @susan porter Please can you send me your e-mail address and contact number?* To view your direct message activity, click the "Direct Messages" link in the right column of your profile page.

Note that you can send a direct message only to someone who is following you. If someone who isn't following you sends you an @reply request for information, for example, you can request that the person follow you to reply via direct message. These restrictions are in place to prevent spammers from contacting you; the only direct messages you'll receive will come from people you're voluntarily connected with.

TIP 62   **Mark favorites**

Especially if you've built up a large number of users that you follow from your business account, Twitter can be overwhelming as you try to keep up with your feed, which is constantly updated with new content from your followers. Especially if you are away from your feed for several hours or days, you can easily lose track of a tweet that you found interesting or that contained a useful link or that you wanted to respond to directly.

To solve this problem, you can keep a tweet easily accessible so that you can read or respond to it later by marking it as a favorite. To mark a tweet as a favorite, click the gray star that appears if you hover your mouse to the right of the tweet you want to mark. Once you've clicked it, the star turns yellow and appears permanently alongside the tweet. When you want to come back later and find all the tweets that you've chosen as favorites, click on the "favorite" link in the right navigation link of your profile page, which will bring up your favorites list.

Note that your favorites are not a private list—anyone who's looking at your profile can see them by clicking the "favorite" link from your home page. But, if you mark as a favorite a link from someone whose profile is protected, anyone else who is not an approved follower of that user will not be able to see the link in your favorites list.

If you want to remove a favorite link from your list, click the star alongside it again so that it turns back to gray. As soon as you do this, the link will be removed.

Another way to mark a favorite is by entering the command "fav" plus the handle of the person in question. For example, if you type *fav travelwriter* into your update box, the Twitter user Travelwriter's latest tweet will be marked as a favorite by you and added to your list.

TIP 63 Use Twitter search

One of the most useful parts of Twitter is its search function, because it allows you to narrow down tweets from all over the Web into just one particular subject in real time. If you want to see what all Twitter users (besides just the people you're connected to) are saying about a particular topic, access the main search function either by going to http://search.twitter.com or by entering a keyword phrase into the search box in the right column of your Twitter profile page.

Once you've typed in a keyword, the results page will look like your main Twitter stream, with tweets organized in chronological order, except that they'll all be related to the keyword phrase you entered. Also, these results won't just be limited to the tweets made by people you're following, as is the case with your main tweetstream.

If you're searching from the main Twitter search page, you can click "advanced search" under the text box to enter more specific criteria for your query, such as searching in a particular language, within a specific geographical location, date range, or on tweets that are positive or negative in nature. The positive/negative feature is a great way to keep track of what others are saying about you when you're doing a search on your own brand name.

If you think you'll do the same search more than once, you can subscribe to those particular results by clicking "save this search" at the top right of the search results page for a specific query. This gives you a continual stream of results on the same keywords. For example, if you're a store selling tech gadgets, you can keep a continual search stream for "tech gadgets" to see new products on the market or hot topics that are being talked about.

An interesting feature of Twitter's search function is the ability to see what the most popular topics of the moment are among Twitter users. You can see this by viewing the text links under the search box or in the right column of your Twitter home page. Some of the topics will contain hashtags—for more about how these work, see Tips 65 and 66.

TIP 64 Create lists

Creating Twitter lists is a good way to sort people you're following and other Twitter users into groups that make sense to you. For example, on your business Twitter account, you may want to sort tweets into lists like customers, partners, or industry experts. Lists make it easier to keep track of different types of information in your Twitter feed, such as news related to your industry versus what your competitors are saying. You can create up to twenty lists of five hundred users each who are in turn able to see that they've been added to your list. You can also subscribe to lists that others have created. Overall, lists are a great way to expose your Twitter account, and your brand, to a larger number of people in your industry.

To create a list, click the "New List" link in the right column of your profile page. You'll be asked to name your list with a phrase related to the list's subject, such as *photography news*. This will then form part of your list URL, such as www.twitter.com/jacksparrow/photography-news if your handle is *jacksparrow*. You'll then be asked whether you want the list to be private or public. By default, a list is public, but you can choose to make it private if you don't want anyone else to see it. You can add people from your follower list, or you can add them to the list of your choice by clicking the "Lists" dropdown box on their profile page.

Your existing lists are linked to from your profile page under the "Lists" section. To view the lists you're following and lists of yours that others have subscribed to, click the "View all" link under the same section. On this page, you'll also be able to see lists you've been added to that were created by others. Another way to see what lists you're on is to click the "Listed" link alongside your number of followers on your profile page.

A key point about lists is that you can subscribe to someone else's list without needing to follow the individuals contained within it. In the same way, if you create your own list, you don't necessarily have to be following the people on it. This means that you can keep track of what a wide variety of users are saying while at the same time keeping your main tweetstream manageable in size.

Leveraging Twitter

TIP 65 Find and track popular hashtags

If you've been on Twitter for even a short while, chances are you've seen tweets that contain a word with a hash symbol (#) before them, such as *#government* or *#showbiznews*. These are known as *hashtags* and, similar to the tags you may add to blog posts to categorize them under a particular topic, they work by aggregating all thematically related content in one place. Overall, hashtags are a powerful way of tracking, participating in, and sharing information on a particular topic with other Twitter users—particularly those users you're not following and/or who aren't following you.

When someone enters a search query into Twitter, posts appended with related hashtags will be returned as search results. For example, if you do a search for landscape gardening, you may see tweets that have hashtags appended at the end of them, such as *#landscape* and *#gardening*. Clicking on each of these will bring up all the current tweets related to that topic. Similarly, if you write content on landscape gardening, such as a new blog post or e-book, you may mention it in a Twitter update and then append your tweet with *#landscape* and *#gardening*.

Particularly for a business Twitter account, hashtags are an excellent way of exposing your product, service, or brand to an audience that may be interested in topics related to your industry. Hashtags are also a good way to get your updates to appear in search results for people who aren't your followers but may then choose to subscribe to your updates.

Besides brainstorming your own words and then searching for related hashtag themes using Twitter's search function, you can also use sites like Hashtags.org (http://hashtags.org), Twubs (http://twubs.com), and Tag alus (http://tagal.us) to identify popular hashtags on a particular subject. From this research, you can learn what the hot topics of the moment are within your particular industry so that you can contribute to those conversations as well. Each of the sites mentioned above have different strengths; Hashtags.org, for example, gives up-to-the-hour information on a topic in the form of statistics and graphs, while Twubs lets users contribute their own tweets, photos, or videos around a particular hashtag topic to give it more context.

TIP 66   Place hashtags in your tweets

1. Find the hashtag. The first step is to come up with a good name for your hashtag. Even if you come up with a phrase that relates to your content, if other people aren't using it, your tweets under that hashtag won't be exposed to significant numbers of Twitter users. To find a hashtag, you can either enter keywords into Twitter search, or you can use sites such as Hashtags.org (for more on brainstorming hashtags, see Tip 65). Once you've found a popular hashtag that relates to what you're writing about, do another search to see what's already being said under that topic. This is a great way to see that you're adding value rather than just repeating what everyone else is saying. It can also be a good way of seeing what your competitors are talking about.

2. Watch your character count. Once you've decided on a popular hashtag that's related to the content of your tweet, you're ready to incorporate it. While there is no character limit to the hashtag you choose, it will be counted toward the 140-character limit in your update. Some people manage this restriction by including the hashtag as part of the post instead of adding it at the end; for example, *Download our new #gardening e-book to see how to grow your own green fingers*. However, this can be a jarring experience for your readers and may be interpreted as a message about the hashtag itself (in this case, gardening) rather than as a message tagged to be about gardening. For this reason, most people add hashtags at the beginning of their update; for example, *#gardening Download our new e-book to grow your own green fingers*. This makes it easier to read and immediately identifies its subject.

3. Don't overuse them. A quick way to annoy people reading your update is to overuse hashtags within your tweet so that it's clunky and difficult to read. Using too many hashtags also looks like you're doing a hard sell of your product or service, which Twitter audiences have little patience for.

4. Give context. Don't assume your readers know what your hashtag means. If it's not immediately obvious (check with a friend outside of your industry), provide an explanation about it in the words that surround it.

TIP 67 Tweet your company blog posts

If you have a company blog, your company Twitter account is a great channel on which to publicize it, by linking to recent blog posts from your Twitter updates. You can either do this manually, by commenting on a new blog post you've written and then linking to the post in your update, or create an automated Twitter update that pulls through a link to your latest blog post soon after it's published. If you want to pull links in automatically, a variety of third-party applications that interface with Twitter can help you do so quickly and easily. One example is Twitterfeed (www.twitterfeed.com), where you enter your blog's RSS feed URL (for more on blog RSS feeds, see Tip 11) into the interface. From there Twitterfeed periodically checks your blog feed and posts an automatic Twitter update with a link to your latest blog post when the blog feed is updated with new content.

If you do choose to update your Twitter feed automatically with notices of new blog posts, or even if you do it manually, make sure these aren't the only kinds of updates you make. It's not a good idea to use Twitter purely as a promotional tool for other sites you may have without engaging with your followers or adding new or interesting insights of your own. If you use your Twitter account simply as a way to promote your blog or website, you risk annoying your followers at best, and losing them at worst, since you're not giving them unique content. Either way, being too self-promotional via your Twitter account can damage your brand's reputation among Twitter users.

If you're using Twitterfeed, a good way to ensure that your blog updates aren't posted too often is to adjust your frequency settings. You can change these so that, for example, Twitterfeed posts only automatic updates containing a link to a new blog entry once a day or even once every other day. Doing this gives you lots of space and time to add in your own useful Twitter updates that will dilute the automated ones. This gives you the best of both worlds: you don't have to manually post updates to your blog each time, but your Twitter feed stays full of unique and useful content for your followers.

TIP 68 Publicize your account

Like most social networking tools, the more active you are on Twitter, the more exposure your account will get, which in turn will impact your success with the tool. The most obvious way to stay active on Twitter is to get into the habit of posting regular updates—say once or twice a day. When you do this, you quickly build up a significant volume of tweets, which means you'll appear more often on your followers' timelines. Also, the more you tweet, the greater chance you have of your updates being retweeted by others. This again means more exposure for you among your followers as well as among the users following them.

As well as posting regular updates, interacting with your Twitter followers is a good way to publicize your Twitter feed to their followers. The easiest way to let people know you're replying directly to them in an update is to use an @ reply, which is when you begin your tweet with @ plus the handle of the person you're responding to. You can also use a mention, which is where you include @ plus the handle anywhere in your tweet. For more information on replies and mentions, see Tip 59.

Once you've started publicizing your account within Twitter itself, you can start thinking of ways to market your account on external sites as well. An easy place to start with this is to place a link to your Twitter page anywhere else where you have a Web presence. This can include places like your website, your company blog, your Facebook page, your LinkedIn company profile page, or on any other social media profile pages you may have. On certain social media sites such as MySpace, Facebook, and blogs on Blogger and TypePad, you can add a Twitter Badge to the site. This badge is a widget that pulls your tweets through into the page on which it resides, which makes it a kind of advertisement for your Twitter feed on other places where you have a steady readership. A Twitter Badge is also a good way of sharing your updates in places like your blog where you may be talking about related content. To get the code you need to install the badge, go to www.twitter.com/badges. Note that your tweets need to be unprotected for you to install this widget.

Listen and learn

Twitter is an excellent business reputation-monitoring tool because it gives you a cheap, simple, and convenient way to monitor what people are saying about your brand in real time, anywhere in the world. Monitoring your brand on Twitter is most effective if it's done over an extended period of time so that you get a fuller and more balanced picture. Also, getting into the habit of listening regularly to what's being said about you means you're in a better position to respond quickly if a problem arises. Follow these steps to monitor your reputation on Twitter:

1. Search. Save Twitter searches on your brand name (on http://search .twitter.com), as well as for other related keywords such as your competitor's brand name and generic words describing your industry or product. For example, if you're Jetblue, you might save searches for "Jetblue," "Southwest Airlines," and "budget airlines." Saving multiple searches in this way helps you keep track of what's being said about your industry in general beyond just your brand, which can help you identify trends and business opportunities.

2. Gauge the sentiment. Track whether the tweets about your brand are negative, positive, or neutral overall. If you find this process too overwhelming, consider using a Twitter monitoring tool such as SocialTALK (http://socialtalk.com), CoTweet (http://cotweet.com), or Radian6 (www .radian6.com).

3. Respond. Start by addressing negative tweets through @ replies. If you can, offer an immediate solution to a user's problem. If you can't do this, at least let them know that you've acknowledged their complaint and are taking steps to fix the situation.

4. Look at your response effects. Evaluate the effects of responding to negative tweets. Do the user's tweets come around to being positive, or do they stay negative? Are other people on Twitter mentioning the fact that you're attempting to solve the problem? If done correctly, solving a consumer's problem publicly can result in a more positive sentiment about your brand than there was before the problem arose.

5. Track. Keep a note of the questions customers asked, how you responded, problems that arose, and your solutions to them. Either do this manually or by using tools mentioned in point 2.

TIP 70 Don't spam

Twitter's increasing popularity has meant that the site's spam guidelines have become more stringent over time. Even if you have good intentions, you may be performing actions on Twitter that violate its terms of service, which can result in your account being suspended. Make sure you're not at risk by following these guidelines:

- Don't post duplicate updates to your account as a way to ensure more people see your tweet throughout the day. Besides being a spam technique, doing this is also a fast way to annoy your users and damage your brand's reputation.

- Only create multiple Twitter accounts if it makes sound business sense. While a clear boundary between different products may warrant this, don't create multiple similar accounts in order to increase the overall volume of your tweets.

- If you do have multiple Twitter accounts (for example, Google has different Twitter accounts for its different products such as *@googlemaps* and *@googlenews*), only post your update once in the most relevant account you own. For example, Google should post a notice about an update to Google Maps only to their *@googlemaps* account.

- Don't send unsolicited direct messages (DMs) unless you have permission to do so or if someone sends you a direct message first. Of course, there are exceptions to this: some types of business Twitter accounts, for example, run promotions where they send specific voucher codes to individual Twitter users via a direct message.

- Be careful when following or unfollowing users. Although these are normal Twitter functions, repeatedly following and unfollowing people (known as "follower churn") or following or unfollowing a large volume of people at once can trigger Twitter's spam flag for your account.

- Don't post unrelated information around a hashtag to gain more visibility for your tweet.

- Don't use Twitter just to drive traffic to your website or blog—make sure you include value-added updates too (for more on this see Tip 54).

- Don't send large numbers of duplicate @ replies. If you do want to respond to multiple Twitter users, make your replies personalized, or stagger your responses.

- Don't post links that are misleading: your post should give users a good idea of what they can expect to find should they click through a link included in your tweet.

TIP 71　Use real time to your advantage

Twitter's real-time nature means that you can reach current and potential consumers anywhere in the world at any stage of their engagement with your product or service. There are several other ways you can use Twitter's real-time nature to your advantage:

- **Catch problems early.** If you're continuously monitoring what's being said about your brand (see Tip 69 for more about this) and are responding as soon as an issue arises, it's less likely that a problem or negative sentiment about your brand on Twitter will gather momentum.

- **Solicit feedback.** If you're developing a new product or service, Twitter can be a good way to get immediate feedback about it from your customers before its official launch. Based on the feedback you get, you can then make changes that speak directly to your customer's needs and opinions. Also, by involving consumers in your product development, they're more likely to be happy with the outcome, which in turn will make them more loyal to your brand.

- **Crowdsource.** Your Twitter followers represent access to instant expertise and opinions over a wide range of subjects. This means that the site is a great resource not just for marketing your business, but for getting quick answers to problems or questions you may have about day-to-day business processes. For example, you could ask your followers about the best places to source a particular raw material or where to find statistics on a particular topic.

- **Find topics to talk about.** Trending topics, hashtags, and Twitter searches are a good resource for finding new material to research and topical subjects to blog or create podcasts or video commentaries about.

- **Help your customers.** Twitter's immediacy allows you to streamline your consumer's experience of engaging with your product or service. For example, if you're holding a conference and you need to change the venue at the last minute, Twitter can be an effective way of communicating this up-to-the-minute information to conference attendees. Retail stores, for example, can use it to announce late changes to store hours or traffic conditions for customers on their way to a store sale.

TIP 72   Get your employees involved

If you're starting a Twitter account for your business, chances are that many of your employees will already have a personal Twitter account. Leveraging your employees' existing presence on Twitter is a good way to publicize your business account, especially if you're still building up followers. By asking your employees to link back to your account through @ replies or mentions, you increase your chances of attracting new followers, since your account will be exposed to all your employees' followers as well. In return, link back to your employees' accounts if they write an update that relates to your business, by using an @ reply or a mention.

Encouraging interaction among your employees with your business account not only exposes your brand to more potential Twitter followers but also creates a sense of camaraderie among your employees. This can extend to making Twitter a powerful platform for group problem solving and idea generation within your business. A good way to round up your employees into group discussions on Twitter is to create an employees list, which they can subscribe to in order to stay up to date with current discussions. (For more on creating lists, see Tip 64). Besides increasing your brand's exposure, interacting with your employees showcases a healthy company culture to external Twitter users who are reading your updates.

An individual Twitter account typically looks very different from a business account, since most of the updates will be personal and some may be fairly controversial. One option for managing this identity issue is to ask employees to create two separate accounts—one where they discuss work or industry-related issues and one for personal use. Bear in mind that your employees may not all be open to doing this: especially if they're longtime Twitter users, they will have already built up a significant number of followers on their main personal account and won't want to put effort into creating and maintaining a new account where they need to build up followers from scratch. A better strategy may be not to link to accounts where employee updates are especially controversial.

TIP 73 Use mobile applications

Along with accessing Twitter via the site or from a desktop application (for more about these, see Tip 74), you can access the tool using your cell phone. Just as you'd send a text message, Twitter allows you to text an update to your Twitter account, which is then shared with your followers just as it would were you writing the update from within the site itself. Using Twitter on a mobile phone is a great way to share news and stay connected when you don't have access to a browser. For example, if you're at a conference, you may use Twitter from your phone to broadcast your comments on a particular speaker you're listening to or to give details for a new product as the manufacturer announces them at the same conference. Overall, Twitter is an excellent way to broadcast news to a wide range of people much more quickly than you could create a full-length blog post.

Before you can use Twitter on your cell phone, you need to add your phone number to your Twitter account. You do this by sending a text message to Twitter, which will reply asking for your handle. Next you'll be asked to verify your Twitter password, after which your account will be linked. If you don't already have a Twitter account, you can do this by phone too—instead of replying with your handle, reply with "SIGN UP." From there you'll be asked to choose a handle via your phone, after which you'll be able to begin tweeting. Within the United States, you can tweet from your phone by sending a text message to 40404. Twitter doesn't charge you, but your cell phone provider will charge you as it would for a standard text message. Be sure to consult your carrier to double-check that your text-messaging plan covers Twitter updates as well.

If you have a smartphone with Internet access, such as an iPhone or BlackBerry, you can download mobile Twitter applications that give you more functionality than just sending plain text updates as explained earlier. For a BlackBerry, you can download the official Twitter app at http://appworld.blackberry.com/webstore/content/8160, which offers features such as automatic URL shortening, photo uploading, searching, and adding people to follow. For the iPhone, you can download the free "Twitter for iPhone" app in the iTunes app store, which gives you similar functionality to that contained in the Twitter for Blackberry app.

TIP 74 Use desktop applications

Ironically, one of Twitter's main strengths is its openness in allowing people who are not employed by Twitter to add to its core functionality. Twitter does this by making its software and data completely open to developers, which means that anyone can make a tool that interfaces with the site. As a result, a whole host of third-party tools exist that build on basic Twitter functionality in a new and meaningful way; these tools let you do more in terms of organizing and managing your Twitter account than you can do if you're just accessing Twitter from within your browser.

Many third-party applications, like TweetDeck (www.tweetdeck.com), HootSuite (www.hootsuite.com), and Twhirl (www.twhirl.org), are downloaded onto your desktop and log you in automatically to your account when you turn your computer on (provided you're connected to the Internet). Desktop applications also generally don't tax your computer's memory usage, as most of them are low on memory usage and are light to download.

A major advantage of using a desktop application to access Twitter is that it allows you to organize your tweets easily into different groups that you can define. For example, TweetDeck lets you create a group called *clients* that contains only updates made by your followers who are also your clients. This makes it easier to keep track of events or conversations in your industry. You can also create columns for dedicated Twitter keyword searches, which continually update with the results of that particular search. For example, if you're a reseller of Converse sneakers, you may want to create a search result column on the keywords *converse sneakers*.

Besides interfacing with Twitter, TweetDeck lets you link up with your Facebook account: you can pull in status updates of your friends, and you can update your own status and upload pictures and videos to your Facebook page. For this reason, TweetDeck is a good way to manage multiple social media channels your business may have.

If you have multiple Twitter accounts, both Twhirl and HootSuite allow you to separate each account into a different window that allows you to stay in control of all your accounts in one place. This can be particularly useful if you have a personal Twitter account and are also managing a business account.

TIP 75 Understand Promoted Tweets

In their first step towards generating revenue, Twitter launched its advertising platform, known as "Promoted Tweets," in April 2010. A Promoted Tweet is a tweet that a business pays for to be shown at the top of a search result for a query related to that tweet's content. Only one Promoted Tweet is shown on every search results page, and it's clearly marked as sponsored.

For business owners, Promoted Tweets represent a more effective way to cut through the noise of a normal tweetstream when trying to communicate with Twitter users. The main difference between Promoted Tweets and other social advertising platforms such as Facebook Advertising is that Promoted Tweets are tweets rather than ads. In other words, rather than simply advertising a product or service, they serve the same purpose as a normal tweet would for a business on Twitter—a way to start or continue a conversation with a potential customer. For example, Starbucks could ask users for their opinion on a new coffee they've launched, or Sony could ask users for their feedback about a new movie. Like an organic tweet, users will be able to retweet, reply, or favorite a Promoted Tweet.

By matching tweets to keyword searches and by promoting tweets instead of ads, Twitter ensures that users see promoted messaging that is engaging and relevant to the content they're looking for. In fact, a Promoted Tweet needs to be even more valuable than a normal tweet in order to be effective: although the Promoted Tweets system currently runs on a cost per thousand impressions (CPM) payment model, Twitter plans to introduce a "Resonance Score" that will impact its visibility and cost. This score will be determined by how much users interact with the Promoted Tweet in terms of retweeting it, favoriting it, replying to it, or clicking through on a link included within it.

Promoted Tweets are being introduced in phases so that Twitter can monitor its reception by users and its usefulness to advertisers. At the time of writing, only the first phase had been launched, which involved only a few selected businesses including Virgin America, Sony Pictures, and Starbucks. Depending on how it's received, Twitter plans to expand the program at the end of 2010 to show Promoted Tweets in users' timelines, and to allow Twitter clients and other partners to display them as well.

FriendFeed

TIP 76 Understand FriendFeed

Acquired by Facebook in August 2009, FriendFeed is a content aggregator, which means that you can post different content on the site, including text, videos, photos, or music, which is then shared with other FriendFeed users. Like other microblogging platforms, FriendFeed has a text box where you enter text updates, while underneath are links that allow you to upload photos and other files. When you create an update on FriendFeed, it is then published and made visible to your news feed, as well as the news feeds of others who are your friends. In the same way, other people make updates or upload files, and your news feed then includes that update. Updates contained in news feeds are shown in chronological order, with the latest update appearing at the top of the page.

FriendFeed's unique selling point is the wide range of social media platforms with which it can interface. By supplying FriendFeed the details of accounts you have on other social sites including Twitter, Facebook, Flickr, Blogger, YouTube, Digg, and more, FriendFeed updates your feed with updates you make on each of those separate sites. For example, if you upload a photo on Picasa and then post an update on Twitter, these actions will show in your FriendFeed account and will be visible to your FriendFeed contacts.

The other powerful thing about FriendFeed, which is common with many other social media tools, is the community that you can tap into for information, insights, or business connections. These connections can be made in several ways: you can add friends you know who are already on FriendFeed, or you can search for them using a keyword phrase. FriendFeed also suggests users that you can add as friends that they think are interesting in some way. You can also join groups in which members post on a particular topic. By tapping into this broad community of users, a FriendFeed account can be an effective tool to increase exposure for your business, whether you're interacting with fellow industry members, sourcing new clients, or building the brand of your business through the resources you share.

TIP 77 Understand FriendFeed vs. Twitter

FriendFeed is similar to Twitter in that it allows you to write updates that are published to a feed that is then visible to your followers or groups of which you are a member or others who search on a topic that you're writing about. There are a few major differences with FriendFeed that sets it apart from Twitter:

- You can connect to more than fifty services like Flickr, Facebook, Digg, and Twitter, so that you can automatically share content from those sites in your FriendFeed account.

- You can upload photos and other files from within your FriendFeed account.

- There is no 140-character limit for text updates.

What these differences essentially mean is that FriendFeed allows for richer posting of different media and gives you a better interconnection with other social media channels on which you have a presence. For example, if you want to share a photo with your Twitter followers, you first have to upload it to an external photo site such as TwitPic and then paste the link to the photo into your update. With FriendFeed, you simply upload the photo within your account, which you can then cross-post to your Twitter account as well. The absence of the 140-character limit on FriendFeed means that you can post a more substantial update that contains multiple resource links.

Another difference between FriendFeed and Twitter is that FriendFeed allows you to comment on updates, and as new users comment on updates, these are "floated" to the top of your feed of updates in real time. Multiple comments on a single update are displayed underneath the original post, which means you can view a threaded conversation. This creates more organized discussions on one topic and more streamlined information sharing. For example, if you're a business and you're asking a question about your industry, you can see all the input you'll get on this question in one place.

With these differences, it may appear that FriendFeed would be preferable to Twitter due to its broader range of functionality. However, the major advantage that Twitter has over FriendFeed is that it has a far larger audience and visibility. So if you're a business that wants to grow your group of followers quickly, you'll find more people in your industry on Twitter. For this reason many people maintain both a FriendFeed and a Twitter account and then cross-post to both.

TIP 78 Set up a FriendFeed account

To set up a FriendFeed account, start at www.friendfeed.com and click on the link that says "Sign up with your e-mail account." From here, you'll need to enter your full name and set up a user name and password for your account and an e-mail address that you want to be linked with it.

Once you've created an account, click the "settings" link on the right side of your home page, where you can change your account preferences and add a picture and a description. Since you're creating an account for your business, upload your company logo as your picture. When writing your account description, think of it as your "elevator pitch." Prospective friends (who may eventually become partners or customers) will read this first, so craft your description carefully to make it a light and engaging summary of your business.

Once you've set your account preferences, you can start adding friends to your account. FriendFeed lets you do this in several ways:

1. Find your friends: This is a search function where you can enter the name or e-mail address of someone who is already on FriendFeed. You can also search for people and businesses on FriendFeed who are in a specific industry. For example, searching *health insurance* will return results of companies or individuals within the health insurance industry who already have FriendFeed accounts.

2. Automatically find people you know: This allows you to add as friends the contacts you already have on other sites, including Twitter, Facebook, Yahoo!, Gmail, and Hotmail.

3. Add recommended friends: These are people or businesses that are popular on FriendFeed or that FriendFeed considers interesting or useful to have as friends.

FriendFeed lets you create friend lists, which is a good way of organizing your contacts into different buckets. FriendFeed suggests that you sort your friend lists into "personal," "professional," and "favorites," but you can create your own groups as well. Keeping your contacts in different groups makes your account easier to manage, especially if you have many contacts from different sources.

TIP 79   Create updates

Like Twitter, FriendFeed lets you publish updates so that they're shared with others by entering text into the box at the top of your home page and then clicking the "Post" button. Unlike Twitter however, you're not bound by a 140-character limit, and so your post can be as long as you want it to be. In addition, you can also post other content such as photos, text files, or music.

To upload a photo along with your post, click the "Photos" link underneath the update box, and find the location of the photo on your computer that you want to upload. Once you've selected it, it will upload and display as a thumbnail image below the text box. If you're satisfied, click the "Post" button. To upload another type of file such as a PDF or an MP3, click the "Files" link alongside the "Photos" link under the update box, and select the file for uploading. Once that's done, click the "Post" button. To avoid piracy issues, FriendFeed currently places a limit on the amount of MP3 files you can upload to three per day. Note that although you can include URLs of videos in an update (such as a YouTube URL), you can't upload the actual video file as part of your update.

Besides posting directly from within FriendFeed, you can also post content to your account from within your Web browser by installing the Friend-Feed bookmarklet into your browser toolbar. To do this, click the "Tools" link to the right of the search box on your account home page and then click "Bookmarklet." On the page that follows, drag and drop the "Share on FriendFeed" button onto your browser toolbar. Once this is done, you can post any Web page of a site you're currently viewing into your FriendFeed account as an update. For example, if you're reading an article on the *New York Times*, you can highlight part of the text that you find interesting and click the "Share on FriendFeed" button in your browser. This then opens a new window containing the title of the story and the snippet of text you highlighted. You can also drag images from the Web page into the post. Once you've finished creating the post, select the feeds to which you want to publish, and click the "Post" button.

TIP 80   Aggregate your feeds

In addition to adding your own updates into FriendFeed, you can pull into your FriendFeed account your activity in other social media tools such as Twitter, Tumblr, Picasa, Flickr, Facebook, and social bookmarking sites like Digg and Delicious. FriendFeed pulls in the updates from these tools by accessing your feeds from each site and then importing the information into your FriendFeed account. Allowing FriendFeed to pull through all your other feeds is a good way to manage all of your social media activities in one place, as well as to enrich your FriendFeed account with other types of content, such as photos, videos, and bookmarked articles.

To aggregate your other feeds into FriendFeed, you need to add what is known as an *imaginary friend*—this is as opposed to "real" friends such as other FriendFeed users you're connected with. In effect, an imaginary friend is a feed from another tool, which then allows you to follow people on other services and accounts from within the FriendFeed interface.

To aggregate your feeds from other accounts into FriendFeed, sign in to your account. If you don't have an account, you'll need to sign up at www .friendfeed.com, where you'll create a user name and password and link an e-mail address that you check often. Once you've signed in, click "Browse/ edit friends" from the "Friends" navigation menu on the right side of your home page. From here, click the link that says "imaginary friends" and, on the page that follows, click the "Create imaginary friend" button. You will be prompted to enter a name for your feed, so if you want to link your Twitter account, type in *Twitter*. From there you'll be given a list of services that you can link to your account. Select the Twitter link, after which you'll be asked to enter in your Twitter user name. Once this is done, you'll see Twitter under the "active services" list, and your Twitter feed will begin pulling through to your FriendFeed. Repeat this process for any other service you want to add—you'll need to have your user name or e-mail address that is linked to each service that you want to include.

TIP 81   Create groups in FriendFeed

FriendFeed groups allow multiple people to write updates, make comments, and post information on a particular topic that all group members can see. For example, the "Apple Room" on FriendFeed consists of more than six thousand subscribers who post information, links, and updates relating to Apple, and everyone who subscribes to this feed can see the updates that are made.

Groups are a powerful way to connect with other people in your industry or to showcase your knowledge in a particular niche. For example, if you sell comic books, you could join a comic book group where you can stay up to date with upcoming new releases, events, and news relating to the comic book industry, as well as give your input by reviewing new books that are released.

To create a group, click the "Browse/Create groups" link under the right column of your FriendFeed home page and then click "Create a group" in the top right corner of the group home page. You'll be prompted to name the group and select whether you want it to be a public, standard, or private group. The option you choose will depend on the purpose of your group. In a public group, for example, anyone can subscribe to the group and post updates, which makes it good for information sharing. In a standard group, multiple selected authors can make post updates, but anyone can view the group and comment on the updates you make. This type of group is good for building your brand and gaining exposure in your industry where multiple people in your company post updates. In a private group, only people you invite to join can see the group and post to the feed, which can be a good option if you want to discuss business issues only with other employees in your company.

Once you've created your group, you can invite others to join. If you don't want to create a group from scratch, you can subscribe to an existing group. To start, do a search on the keywords in your industry, which will bring up results of related groups. If you find a group you want to join, click the "Subscribe" button at the top of the group page, which will then add you as a member. Depending on the group settings, you'll then be able to make updates and comment on updates made by others.

Interact with others

Just as FriendFeed allows you to pull information and feeds from other tools like Facebook and Twitter into your FriendFeed account, you can share information on FriendFeed with these other social media tools. This is a useful way of leveraging the time that you spend on FriendFeed to translate into activity on other platforms too. There are several easy ways that Friend-Feed allows you to share information across other platforms:

■ **Cc to Twitter:** Whenever you post a new update, you'll be given the option to post the update on your Twitter account too by checking the "cc Twitter" checkbox underneath the update box. By copying a post you make on FriendFeed to Twitter, you'll be publishing the update for two audiences to see instead of just one.

■ **Add the FriendFeed Facebook application:** Once you've installed this, any updates you make on FriendFeed will be published as a Facebook status update on your Facebook account, which means it will appear in the Facebook news feed that your fans and friends will see. Adding this application also means you'll be subscribed to your Facebook friends who are also using FriendFeed. Connecting your FriendFeed and Facebook accounts is a good way to cross-promote content to both your Facebook and Friend-Feed connections, and it also saves you the time you'd take to post the two updates individually on each separate service. To add this application, search for it in the Applications section of your Facebook account. When you're installing it, you'll need to give Facebook permission to access your FriendFeed account.

■ **Use the share function:** Whenever you've made an update, Friend-Feed lets you click the "share" button below the post you've made. A new window will come up that gives you both the short and long URL versions of your post and the embed code for you to copy and paste the update in other tools. You'll also see quick link icons below the URLs to take you to Facebook, Twitter, Digg, Reddit, and Delicious in one click.

Tumblr

TIP 83 | Understand Tumblr

Tumblr is a lightweight, no-frills blogging platform, known as a *tumblelog*, that sits halfway between a microblogging tool like Twitter and a regular blogging tool like WordPress or Blogger. Although Tumblr and competitors such as Posterous don't offer as much functionality or flexibility as a regular blog, they are easier to maintain and create posts in, while at the same time letting you post more substantial updates than you can do with a microblogging tool like Twitter (which imposes a 140-character limit for text updates only).

Tumblelogs are a great option if you want to get your feet wet with blogging. They're also a great option to go for if you don't have a lot of time or other resources to invest in a business blog but still want to share your thoughts in text and multimedia to an audience within your industry. Even if you do already have a regular blog, tumblelogs like Tumblr can be a great supplement to it if you're blogging on the move since they let you post easily and quickly from your phone or via e-mail.

The rest of this section will focus on one example of a tumblelog: Tumblr. There are six types of content that Tumblr allows you to post: text, photos, videos, quotes, links, and instant-message conversations. You can also easily interface with other Tumblr bloggers; for example, if you read a post written in another Tumblr blog, you can "reblog" it to your own account if you want to share it with your audience too. In this way Tumblr harnesses the viral nature of blogging by allowing content to be spread quickly among users, which in turn gives you added exposure for your business to your own readers.

One of the most popular tools on Tumblr is the Tumblr bookmarklet (more on this in Tip 86), which allows you to quickly and easily post Web content to your account from within your browser. Apart from posting new content to Tumblr, you can import feeds from other places where you have a presence, such as Blogger, Twitter, Flickr, Digg, and Delicious. When you link these feeds, making an update on any of those sites means that it will post that update to your Tumblr account as well.

TIP 84 Start your Tumblr blog

Starting your Tumblr blog is a quick and simple process. You sign up for an account straight from the home page at www.tumblr.com. To create an account, you'll need to set up an e-mail address and password. From there Tumblr will automatically populate the URL field underneath it with the name linked to your e-mail account, in the format of http://[yourname].tumblr.com. This is editable, though, so if you're starting a business blog on Tumblr, you may want a name that is close to your business's name rather than your personal name.

Once you've entered your information, Tumblr will log you in to your account, at which point you can begin posting six possible types of content: text, photos, videos, audio, quotes, links, or instant-message conversations. These content types are shown on the tabs at the top of your home page.

To give your blog a title and description, to change its appearance to fit in more with your company branding, click the "Customize" link on the right navigation menu when you're in your dashboard. From here you can customize your blog's look and feel as much as you like, such as by changing the colors and fonts and uploading your own images. If you have the technical resources, you can even change the CSS coding behind the site to make it completely unique. Tumblr also gives you CSS code that you can paste into your website or other blog if you want to integrate your Tumblr blog somewhere else. On the same menu, you can also choose to send Tumblr posts to services like Twitter and Facebook.

The "Popular" menu item in the main top navigation menu shows you posts that are currently the most popular across the whole Tumblr network. "Goodies" contains useful applications you can download, such as the Tumblr bookmarklet (to allow you to post content when you're on another page on your browser) and the Facebook app, which lets you share your Tumblr posts to your Facebook account.

Your Tumblr blog is publicly viewable by default. If you want to create a private blog, you can do so by creating another blog from the main dashboard that is set to be viewable only by you and others you invite. Note that a private blog doesn't have a standard Web address or RSS feed like a public one does.

TIP 85 Integrate your RSS feed

Your Tumblr blog can integrate with other social media sites you may use such as Twitter, Facebook, or Blogger. Each time you post on one of these sites, you can have it cross-posted to Tumblr by importing the RSS feed from those services. By doing this, you can keep your Tumblr blog active even if you spend more time posting elsewhere, like Facebook or Twitter. Overall, integrating other feeds with your Tumblr account means that it can act as a central base in which to keep track of all the updates you make on other social media channels. This can be useful for marketing your business as well: instead of supplying customers or business partners with several different URLs for your blog, Twitter, and Facebook accounts, you could simply give them your Tumblr address, where they can then see all these postings in one place.

To add a feed from another site to Tumblr, click the "Customize" link from your home page and then select the "Services" menu item. The first two options in the dropdown box allow you to add your Facebook and Twitter details, while the third lets you add your RSS feed URL if you're using FeedBurner. The fourth option in the dropdown menu instructs Tumblr to automatically import your feeds from several other sites. To access this, click the dropdown box from the "Automatically import my feeds" section. You're given options to import your feeds from blog platforms such as WordPress, Blogger, and LiveJournal, as well as from a host of other sites like YouTube, Vimeo, Digg, and Delicious. You can also choose how you want the feed imported, such as the link only, the link with summaries, or only the photos. Once you've selected a service, you'll add your user name for that service or the feed URL into the text box below it for Tumblr to link it to your account.

When you add a new feed to Tumblr, note that you won't be able to import your blog posts or other content that is more than two days old. So, if you've had a blog for a while and you want to import it into Tumblr, you'll only see posts from two days before you added the feed. Also note that you can import a Twitter feed only if your account is public, in which case your updates aren't protected.

Add Tumblr widgets

Tumblr has a library of widgets and plug-ins that help make the blogging process even more convenient and that let you interface with other social media sites such as Twitter, Facebook, and Flickr. When you integrate these widgets in your Tumblr blog, you create a channel to drive more traffic to these sites to grow your audience base on each of them. To browse these widgets, click the "Goodies" link in the top main navigation area of the home page once you're logged in to your Tumblr account. Some examples of widgets you can install are:

- **Tumblr bookmarklet:** One of the most popular apps on Tumblr, this is a widget that you download and install into your browser. Once it's installed, you can simply click on the bookmarklet from within your browser if you come across an interesting piece of content to post it to your Tumblr account. This saves you the time and hassle of having to log in to your account separately in order to publish a post.

- **Facebook app:** Installing this widget lets you share your Tumblr content with your Facebook friends by incorporating your Tumblr activity into your news feed. This exposes your activity on Tumblr to your Facebook friends as well and helps drive more traffic back to your Tumblr blog.

- **iPhone app:** This app lets you post content including photos, text, and other media that you find online using your iPhone straight to your Tumblr account. This is convenient if you'd like to post while you're mobile and don't have access to a browser. The app allows you to post to multiple tumblelogs, and you don't have to log in each time you need to post as it integrates with your Dashboard when you install the app.

- **Twitter:** This widget pulls activity from your Twitter account through to your Tumblr blog. You have control over how this is displayed, such as by choosing the number of tweets you want to be shown. If you click on one of these tweets, you'll be taken through to your Twitter account. Besides helping drive traffic to your Twitter account, this app enriches your Tumblr blog with more frequent posts each time you write a Twitter update.

Use third-party Tumblr services

In addition to Tumblr's associated applications and widgets (see Tip 86), external companies develop tools that can be used in conjunction with it. To access the third-party application directory on Tumblr, log in to your account and click "Goodies" from the top navigation menu. From here, click the link to third-party apps on the right column of the page. Apps are organized into four main sections:

- **Apple mobile device applications:** With applications such as iPostr, iView, and TumblePhone, you can post photos and other media to your Tumblr blog from Flickr and other sources via a slick interface on your iPhone or iPod Touch. Like the Tumblr iPhone app, you can use these third-party applications to post to your blog without needing to have access to a browser.

- **Web applications:** Applications like AlertThingy and Ping.fm let you post to your Tumblr account as well as to other social media sites, including Twitter, FriendFeed, and Facebook. Applications like Blip.fm and Tumbltape help you organize audio files and share music playlists with your readers. A useful application for expanding your audience is Psolenoid, which links related posts together from different blogs (including Tumblr blogs). With this app, people reading a post on your Tumblr blog will get a link to a related post on another blog, which gives them a useful extra resource. Conversely, when other bloggers use Psolenoid, links to your posts that relate to their content will appear on their blog, which will drive more traffic to your Tumblr blog.

- **Desktop and mobile applications:** In most cases these are applications that you install on your cell phone or desktop so that you can post to your Tumblr blog without needing to visit the site in your browser. Examples include Tumblenote, MarsEdit, and Opentumblr. Others, like Dial2Do and Jott, use voice recognition software so you can create Tumblr posts using your voice.

- **Site widgets and browser plug-ins:** Widgets like Tumblr Badge let you easily add content to your blog, while the Tumblr Post browser plug-in lets you drag and drop content onto an icon within your browser without needing to log in to Tumblr itself.

4

Social Networking

FOR MANY people, social networking sites are a way to strengthen personal connections with friends and family, colleagues, or even potential employers. Beyond personal networking, though, social networking sites allow your business to engage with potential customers on an individual level. The nature of social network platforms also means that when people interact with your brand, their activity is broadcast to their own network, which means greater brand exposure for you. This increased exposure may not immediately translate into a direct sale of your product or service, but it may result in future sales to buyers who have already become familiar with your brand. Whether you're a small business that's new or a bigger business that's better established, social networking sites level the playing field: the main factor in successfully promoting your business is not how big you are or how much money you can spend but rather how effectively you can connect with your target market in a two-way conversation.

Social networking tools differ in niche and purpose. Some, such as Facebook and MySpace, are general networking tools through which friends and colleagues can interact, while other sites have a narrower purpose. LinkedIn, for example, specifically targets professional networking, while Ning lets people create their own social networks on a particular topic. Just as the purpose varies, so the best way to market yourself as a business differs from site to site. This section covers seven major social networking sites: Facebook, LinkedIn, Orkut, Plaxo, Ning, MySpace, and Meetup.

Facebook Pages

TIP 88 — Groups vs. pages

Both groups and pages on Facebook give Facebook users a way to interact in a single location about a particular topic. However, even though groups and pages are similar in this way, there are several key differences between them:

- **Visibility:** While only registered Facebook users can see group content, anyone can see a page—even people not registered with Facebook. Facebook pages also have visibility in search engine results pages while groups do not, which means that you're better able to drive external traffic to a page than to a group. Finally, a page allows you to add in your company brand name as part of your URL, which makes it easier for consumers to remember, and has better visibility on internal Facebook search results as well as external search results (like Google) for searches on your brand's name.

- **Messaging:** Groups allow you to send messages to members as e-mails in their Facebook inbox—though only up to 5,000 members. Pages, on the other hand, only allow you to send updates to fans, which show up as notifications on their profile page. Because an e-mail may be more engaging than an update, for some this is the one major disadvantage of a page over a group.

- **Information:** Compared to a group, a page lets you include more detailed information about your business and also lets you import other content into it, such as your blog and Twitter feed. In addition, pages allow you to include Facebook applications (such as event calendars), while groups do not.

- **Statistics:** Pages are linked to Facebook Insights while groups are not. This means that with a page, you can see statistics about your fans' interaction with your brand, which makes it easier to track the success of your promotional efforts on Facebook.

Since groups are more effective for informal groups of people discussing a short-term event or a niche topic, they can be a good way of creating a viral momentum. In general, though, the extra functionality and visibility of a page means that it is usually a better option if you want to create an official community on Facebook around your brand. The rest of the tips in this section will therefore focus on pages rather than groups.

TIP 89 Understand Facebook pages

Just as an individual might have a Facebook profile, Facebook pages are profiles for businesses that want to expose their product or brand. As with a personal profile page, any updates you make to your page's content will display in the news feed of those who become a fan of your business's Facebook page. Perhaps even more valuable to you as a business is that any interaction your fans have with your page will be displayed in their Facebook friends' news feeds as well. In this way your Facebook fans expose your brand to their personal contact circle on Facebook, which effectively makes them your brand advocates on the site.

There are three main areas of content on a Facebook page:

1. Sidebar. This area of the page contains the main summary information for your Facebook page. Depending on the settings you choose as the page owner, you can display elements here such as a profile image (usually your company logo), your business name, a tagline, the number of fans your page has, and links to the profiles of a random selection of six of your fans.

2. Central area. This is the most flexible area of a Facebook page since you can customize the content according to your own preferences and separate content sections into tabs. By default, Facebook pages have three tabs. The **wall tab** is a dynamic area in which you can post updates or new content and where your fans can post their own content. The **information tab** is a static content area where you can provide information about your business or brand, including things like your company's mission statement, an overview of your product or service, and your website details. Finally, the **boxes tab** lets you add various application modules that you can select and customize as much as you want to. You can also devote entire tabs to Facebook applications (for more on these applications and how you can include them, see Tip 92).

3. Right column. The right column is where Facebook displays advertisements that are related contextually to your page's content. This section cannot be moved or changed by you. For more on advertising with Facebook, see Tips 101–108.

Define a reason for your page

If you decide to create a Facebook page for your business, don't assume that everyone will want to become a fan of it just because they know your brand or even because they've stumbled across your page by accident. Since any business can create a page on Facebook, you will be competing with hundreds or even thousands of other pages in your industry alone. For this reason you need to ensure that your page can compete with other business pages in your subject area and that it in some way stands out from those of your competitors that also have a presence on Facebook.

With this in mind, the first step in ensuring that your page cuts through the noise of similar pages is to give people an incentive to "Like" your page, at which point they'll become a fan. The options for this are limitless and will depend on your specific product or brand, but the incentive should be something that will benefit them. For example, if you're a photography business, you could run a competition with prizes for uploading the best photographs, which people will be able to do only if they are a fan of your page. Or you could offer a product giveaway in return for the best fan answer to a question on a particular topic. Again, to participate and have a chance to win the product, the person would have to Like your page in order to be eligible. Alternatively, you could simply reward new fans immediately, such as by giving them sneak peeks at new products and events or giving them discounts on your product that only Facebook fans would be eligible for.

When you're deciding what type of incentive to give Facebook users in return for Liking your page, it's useful to identify the demographic you'll be targeting on Facebook. Your targeted Facebook demographic may well be different from your regular target market, in age, interests, technical ability, or other factors. Just as with any other marketing campaign, you should first be sure you know whom you're talking to, which will give you a better idea of what incentives will entice them.

TIP 91 Create your page

Creating a basic page on Facebook is a simple process that can be done in a matter of minutes. To get the feel for it, start by creating a very basic page and then enrich it later on with applications and customized tabs. To get a basic page set up, follow these seven steps:

1. From the Facebook home page (www.facebook.com), click the "Advertising" link in the footer at the bottom of the page. On the advertising page, click the "Pages" menu item, and from here click the green "Create a Page" button. On this page you'll be asked to provide the name of your business and the category that it falls under, such as health and beauty, pets, or real estate. At the time of writing, Facebook was not allowing businesses to change their name or category name once a page has been created, which means that if your business name changes, you'll need to create a new page from scratch. Many Facebook users are currently engaged in discussions around this topic in an attempt to get Facebook to change this policy.

2. Add a profile picture. In most cases, businesses will use their brand logo for this image rather than a photo. This profile image will be shown in full size when someone is on the wall or info tab.

3. In the Blurb box, add a short tagline about your company. It's worth taking the time to craft this sentence carefully; for many new visitors to your page, your tagline is one of the first things they'll read that tells them what your business is about.

4. Once these elements have been finalized, update your status box and upload images or other media to your page.

5. Update your settings. You can customize the order in which you want your tabs to appear. By default, Facebook orders your wall tab as the first thing people see when they land on your page, but you can change this to another tab, such as your info tab. You can also make the landing page look different depending on whether or not the person looking at it is a fan of your page.

6. As the administrator of your page, you can decide on how much freedom your fans have on your page, such as whether they can post content on your wall and what type of content they can upload: text only, for example, or photos and videos as well?

7. Once you've created your page, you'll see a "Like" button on the landing page, visible only to people who aren't logged into Facebook or who haven't already Liked it.

TIP 92 Use Facebook applications

A Facebook page is highly customizable thanks to the thousands of third-party Facebook applications that can be added as customized tabs to make your page unique. Some popular application tabs for Facebook pages include:

- **Discussion boards:** These let your fans interact with each other and with your business through discussions of your products, events, and other information you provide on your page.

- **Photos and videos:** These let you upload your own photos or videos, and you can choose to let your fans do the same. Facebook does not limit the number of videos or photos you can upload.

- **Events:** This application lets you tell your fans about upcoming events related to your business, such as shows, sales, or exhibitions. When users RSVP via this tab, this response is published to their news feed, and the event is added to their calendar.

- **Reviews:** These applications let your fans write reviews of your business and rate your products or services. These reviews and ratings are then posted on your page and in their news feed, which their own contacts will see.

- **Calendar:** Applications such as My Google Calendar allow you to add a public Google calendar to your page that you can use to communicate events such as new product launches, sale periods, and seminars.

You can choose from thousands of third-party applications by browsing the apps directory at http://www.facebook.com/apps/directory.php. You can also get ideas for application tabs to include in your page by browsing your competitors' pages at www.facebook.com/pages/?browse. If you have access to more advanced technical skills, you can also develop your own Facebook application tab that can be customized for your particular business (for example, a restaurant might create a table reservation application).

TIP 93 Keep your page fresh

Once you've created your Facebook page, it's essential to update it with fresh content to keep your existing fans returning and to attract new ones. Each time you publish a new wall post, photo gallery, or video, this update will be published to your fans' news feeds, which is in turn shown in the news feeds of their friends. This means that the more active you are on your page, the more your activity will be broadcast to your fans, which will prompt them to visit your page more often. Also, being visible in their friends' news feeds increases the chance that your fans' friends will also Like your page in order to become a fan, and potentially your customers. If they then have a positive interaction with your business, they're more likely to advocate your brand via word of mouth to others within their circle of influence—whether they do this on Facebook or on other platforms.

At the same time, however, it's important to get the balance right between keeping your content fresh and not updating too frequently so that your fans become inundated with your brand name in their news feed. As a general rule, updating your page's content once a week should strike a good balance between the two. As always, make sure that when you do add new content it's interesting and/or adds value for your fans.

To get in the habit of posting new content, create a schedule where you commit to posting new updates regularly, such as once a week. If this feels like a lot, consider sharing the load by having multiple administrators of your Facebook page, so that more than one person can update your content. New content doesn't have to be limited to status updates—it can be anything from uploading photos of new products or including information on a calendar about upcoming events to uploading useful resources for your fans such as white papers, presentations, or articles related to your industry. Another easy way to keep your Facebook page fresh is to adjust your settings so that your activity on other social media sites such as Twitter is automatically pulled through into your page.

TIP 94 # How to get traffic to your Facebook page

While establishing a Facebook page is an excellent way of connecting your brand with Facebook users, you need to market it in the same way you'd market your blog or website to drive more traffic to it. The first step in publicizing your page is to update it often with fresh content (see Tip 93). Every time such an update is published in your fans' news pages, they are prompted to visit your page. When they visit your page and then interact with it, this activity is published in their news feed, which exposes your page to their Facebook friends as well. Besides updating your page often, there are several ways you can spread the word about your Facebook page so that your traffic and fan base increase:

- **Link to it:** Link to your page from other online channels you've already established, such as your blog, website, Twitter account, or LinkedIn profile. You can also link to your page from personal media such as your e-mail signature or at the end of a PowerPoint presentation document that you feature on your blog or website.

- **E-mail people about it:** Send an e-mail to people you're already connected with, such as your Facebook friends, e-mail contacts, and business partners, telling them about your page. In the e-mail, mention how they can benefit from Liking your page to become a fan, but don't be too pushy.

- **Use Twitter:** Whenever you create and upload new content to your page, write a Twitter update about it that contains a link to your page.

- **Acknowledge new fans:** When someone Likes your page, or when an existing fan posts on your wall, acknowledge him or her by posting a message on the fan's wall.

- **Use Facebook advertising:** Consider buying Facebook advertising to promote your page by signing up at www.facebook.com/ads. For more on advertising with Facebook, see Tips 101–108.

- **Leverage real-life events:** If you're planning an event related to your business, use Facebook's events application to invite your fans to attend. When they RSVP, this action will be published in their news feed, which can be seen by their friends as well, thereby creating further exposure for your page.

TIP 95 Analyze your stats

Just as you track the performance of other marketing channels such as your blog or website, you should track the effectiveness of your Facebook page against your marketing goals. The overall measure of your Facebook page's effectiveness differs depending on the nature of your business and your goal for your page. For example, success could mean increasing the number of fans, or it could mean getting a large number of fans to interact with the page, such as by commenting on the wall or uploading content. Other measures of success may be driving a large portion of fans to your website from your Facebook page.

Once you've identified what your goals are, you can start monitoring activity on your page in this context. Based on how your fans are behaving, you can make changes, such as by increasing a certain type of content on the site or rearranging the tabs to make it easier for them to post comments and content on your wall. Facebook's built-in Insights tool lets you do this by giving you data and statistics that relate to your fans' engagement with your page. For example, you can view statistics on the number of page views and unique users you have over a certain time period. You can then tie this data back to other external actions and events related to your business, such as launching a new TV advertising campaign or holding an in-store sale. You can also track your users' actions on the page, such as how many of them leave a comment or view a photo gallery as a percentage of the total visitors to the page. In this way you can monitor the ratio of fans that view your page but don't interact with it and think of ways to improve this ratio. The Insights tool also tells you other things about visitors to your page, such as their age, gender, and geographical location.

To get the most out of your Insights statistics, keep a running record of the dates when you've added content and what that content is. You can then match these actions back to your number of unique users to help you identify which changes or additions to your page are providing the most return—whether it's an increase in visitors to your page or more user interaction.

Work with existing pages and groups

If you're a fairly well-established brand, there may already be a group on Facebook that's dedicated to your company. In many cases these groups are created by Facebook users who have no affiliation with your company other than the fact that they like your brand. If you're thinking of creating a Facebook page and find that related groups already exist, don't see this as a threat. Rather, take it as a compliment that people are aware of your brand and like it enough to create a Facebook presence for it. Instead of trying to compete directly with these groups by ignoring them, or even trying to take them over, use the creators' brand loyalty to your advantage. Acknowledging their existing groups in a positive way on your own official Facebook page can be an excellent way to strengthen your brand's presence on the site.

One example of this done well was Coca-Cola, which found that a Coca-Cola page had already been created by two independent Facebook members. The page had grown so large in popularity that it had become the biggest branded company presence on Facebook. Instead of insisting that the fans hand the page over to Coca-Cola, the company's strategy was to reward the two page creators instead—by flying them to Atlanta to visit their company headquarters. By embracing the existing Facebook presence, Coca-Cola capitalized on the members' brand loyalty and were able to leverage this as a way to generate even more publicity for their brand. In this way the two independent Facebook members became part of Coca-Cola's overall marketing strategy.

If you find that your business already has a brand presence on Facebook, follow Coca-Cola's lead and create your own page; then acknowledge that existing page or group from your own. You can do this in several ways, such as by linking to the other page from yours or by posting on the other group page's walls and commenting on the content uploaded. By doing this, you'll come across as a secure brand that's not threatened by competition.

TIP 97 · Link to and from your page

Think of your Facebook page as part of your general marketing mix along with your online channels, like your business blog and website, and your offline channels, such as brochures, press releases, and print advertising. When you think of your Facebook page holistically in this way, it's easy to find opportunities to promote it besides via the Facebook site itself. By promoting your Facebook page in as many places as you can, you drive more traffic to it, which increases the chance of those visitors becoming fans of your page.

Ideas for places where you can promote your Facebook page:

■ **Your blog and website:** On your blog, include it on the right or left sidebar, and on your website include it in the "Contact Us" section.

■ **Your profiles on other social media sites:** Examples include your profile on LinkedIn, Flickr, Twitter, and YouTube.

■ **Your e-mail signature**

■ **Printed media:** Examples include your business cards, presentations, handouts, or white papers.

■ **Printed or online promotional materials:** Examples include press releases, print advertising, and advertorials.

In the same way that you link to your Facebook page from these places, you can also link back to your website or blog from your page's information tab. By linking to your Web page or blog from your page, you can capitalize on people who want to know more about your company but aren't fans of your page. Remember that to Like and therefore become a fan of your page a person already needs to have a personal Facebook account. Anyone who arrives on your page from somewhere else, such as a search engine, and doesn't have a Facebook account, won't be able to become a fan. By linking to your blog or website, you funnel such people to other places where you can connect with them further.

By interconnecting your Facebook page, blog, website, and other promotional media in this way, you will collectively drive more traffic to each channel. This has the net effect of exposing your brand to more people and building up a more diverse customer base.

TIP 98 Feed in your Twitter account

An easy way to keep your Facebook page updated with regular, fresh content is to pull your Twitter updates automatically into your Facebook page. You can do this by installing the Twitter application from within Facebook, which will then import your updates into a separate Twitter tab on your Facebook page. To install this application, follow these steps:

1. Log in to your Facebook account and search for "Twitter" in the main search box on your home page.

2. Click on the link in the search results to take you to the Twitter application page.

3. On this page, click the "Add to My Page" link in the left column.

4. A pop-up window will appear with your current list of pages linked to your account. Select the page that you want to pull Twitter updates into.

5. Your tweets should now appear on a tab of your page in real time.

As well as pulling your tweets through to your Facebook page, you can also push your Facebook page content (such as photos, updates, links, notes, and events) to your Twitter account. To export your content to Twitter, visit www.facebook.com/twitter and click the main Twitter icon in the middle of the page to start the process. You can select the type of content you want to send to Twitter (e.g., updates and photos but not notes and events). Your posts will truncate to fit into a Twitter update, and a short URL link will be included back to that content on your page. Combining your Twitter and Facebook updates in this way saves you the time of having to make updates twice if you have both a Twitter account and Facebook page as part of your social media strategy.

TIP 99 Feed in your blog posts

Just as you can pull Twitter posts into your Facebook page, you can also pull blog posts into your page by importing your RSS feed into Facebook (for more on RSS feeds, see Tip 11). Including blog posts is an easy way of keeping content on your Facebook page fresh, as well as promoting your blog to drive more traffic to it. To pull your blog posts into your Facebook page, follow these steps:

1. Blog posts are imported into the "Notes" tab of your Facebook page, so to access the settings for interfacing your blog, log in to Facebook and click the "Notes" tab in the Applications menu at the bottom of your page.

2. Select "Write a new note." From this window, you'll be taken to the page containing the notes settings.

3. Click the "Import a New Blog" link.

4. Enter the URL of your blog's RSS feed into the text box. If you don't know what the URL of your RSS feed is, you can find it easily by looking in the help documentation of the particular blogging platform you're using or by navigating to the RSS section of your blog. Note too that Facebook will allow you to import only one RSS feed at a time, so if you have more than one business blog, decide which you want to be your primary one and select that one as the feed that will be linked.

5. Check the box that confirms you are the owner of the content that is about to be imported. Facebook doesn't allow you to import feeds from blogs that you don't own or that you don't have permission to reprint elsewhere. If you're thinking of importing a blog that one of your colleagues owns, for example, you need to get permission first.

6. Click the "Start Importing" button. You'll then be given a preview of the feed to check that the right blog posts are being pulled through.

7. Once you've verified that it is the correct feed, click the "Continue" button.

8. Once this is done, your RSS feed will begin importing to your Facebook page. This means that each time you write a blog post the notes section of your page will display a post summary and a link to that particular blog post.

TIP 100 Use a Fan Box on other sites

Once you've set up your Facebook page, a Fan Box widget is a useful way of advertising your fans' activity on your page in other locations such as your blog or website. Cross-promoting your Facebook page in other locations lets you convert your site or blog visitors into fans of your Facebook page and vice versa.

One of the most useful things about the Fan Box widget is the inclusion of a "Like" button on the widget itself, which means that users don't actually have to leave the page they're on and visit your page, or even log in to Facebook, to become fans. As well as showing fan updates, the Fan Box widget displays a list of other fans, including any of that person's Facebook friends who are already fans.

To set up the Fan Box widget, log in to your Facebook page. Once you're logged in, click the link that says "Add a Fan Box" in the left navigation menu. From here you can choose what content you'd like to include in the widget and the dimensions you'd like it to have to fit in with your blog or website's existing layout. Although the dimensions of the Fan Box can vary, the minimum width of the widget is 200 pixels and the maximum height is 554 pixels.

Once you've finalized the settings for the Fan Box, Facebook will give you a snippet of JavaScript that you cut and paste into the HTML code of your blog or website. Where you choose to display the widget on your blog or website is up to you and depends entirely on the purpose of your Facebook page: if your page is used mainly for communicating news to your fans, the widget is probably best suited to a news-related page of your site or a subscription page where someone can subscribe to your blog via RSS. If your Facebook page plays a more central role in your marketing and encourages a lot of fan interaction, you can include it in the home page of your blog or website. Once you save the code to your blog or website and publish the changes, you should see the widget displayed.

Facebook Advertising

TIP 101 Understand Facebook ads

Facebook advertising can be an effective way to drive traffic to your Facebook page and increase your brand's visibility on Facebook in general. Anyone can sign up for Facebook advertising—you don't have to have a page to do so—and there is no set cost for an ad. Instead you specify a maximum amount that you are willing to spend on the ad, either on a "per click" or "per thousand impressions" basis. In other words, you can choose to pay each time someone actually clicks on your ad or for every thousand times that your ad is shown to a Facebook user. You can also decide how much you want to spend per month on your ads, which can be up to $30,000. As far as placement goes, Facebook shows your ad in places where it is contextually relevant to the theme of the ad. This could mean placing it alongside profile pages, pages, or on groups. For example, if you sell ballet shoes, your ad might appear on a Facebook page for a ballet school in your area or in the ad space of the profile of someone who belongs to a dance academy. Whichever page it appears on, your ad will always be shown on the right-hand column. Depending on the page, up to three ads may show at once; in these cases where more than one ad appears, it's not possible for you to decide whether your ad appears in first, second, or third place.

Facebook ads are usually most effective when their main aim is to drive traffic to a company's presence on the site (such as its page) rather than to sell a product or drive people to the company's external website. For example, instead of just advertising your website or blog, you can create ads for a specific event your company is organizing and then link the ad to the events tab on your Facebook page. Generally, as with other online advertising, the more closely related your ad is to the destination page a user lands on after clicking on the ad, the more successful your ad will be. Facebook advertising also allows you to target your ads so that they appear only to audiences you specify, such as those of a certain age or in a particular geographic location.

TIP 102 | Create your Facebook ad

Creating a Facebook ad is quick and easy. It's usually a good idea to start with one or two ads, track how they are performing, and then create more ads when you can gauge what works best for your particular business. The steps for creating a Facebook ad are:

1. Click on the "Advertising" link in the footer of the Facebook home page.

2. From this page, click the green "Create an ad" button.

3. On the next screen, you'll be able to design your ad. Note that a Facebook ad consists of three main elements: the destination URL, the title, and the body of the ad.

4. The destination URL is the Web address of the page where you want your users to land when they click on your ad. If you're sending users to your Facebook page, you'll put that URL in here; if you're sending them to your website, you'll use your Web address. To make your ad as effective as possible, you should always ensure that the landing page is closely related to the content of the ad in terms of subject matter. For example, if your ad talks about an event you're hosting, you should point people to the specific event details on your Facebook page. If you already have your Facebook page and you're logged in as its administrator, you'll be able to select it from the dropdown menu when you're creating the ad.

The title of your ad should be a catchy summary of your ad that doesn't exceed twenty-five characters (including spaces). Your title should grab your audience's attention and entice them to read the rest of the ad as well as click through to your destination URL.

Your ad's body copy should relate to the title of the ad so that the two work as a coherent whole. Ad body can be up to 135 characters in length, including spaces. As you write your ad, you'll be able to see a preview of it on the right side of the page. Body copy should be informative while also containing a call to action for the users reading it, such as encouraging them to click through to your page or respond to an event invitation.

You can also upload an image in your ad. Note that the image can't be more than 110 pixels wide and 80 pixels tall and 5 MB in size, and its aspect ratio should be either 4:3 or 16:9.

TIP 103　Decide which audience to target

Your Facebook ad will generate the most return if you make sure you're exposing it to people who are most likely to be interested in your brand, product, or service. Although showing your ad to anyone on Facebook may generate a lot of impressions, the ratio of clicks to impressions will not be very high, and the cost of your ad relative to the return it gets is likely to be high.

Luckily, Facebook makes it easy to target your ad to specific groups of users through ad targeting. Once you've created your ad, Facebook will give you several choices about the groups of users you want to see the ad. You can target your ad based on a wide variety of factors such as the user's age, gender, geographic location, or education level. You can also target your ad to appear for certain keyword searches, and you can decide whether or not it should be shown to people who are already fans of your Facebook page. Based on the criteria that you select to target your ad, Facebook shows you an estimated number of people who would be exposed to your ad. From this number, you can estimate how much running your ad will cost.

Your Facebook ad will be more effective if you use targeted ad copy in conjunction with Facebook's demographic targeting features as outlined above. For example, if your ad is targeted to women between the ages of twenty-two and thirty in San Francisco, mentioning their age group, gender, or the city of San Francisco in the ad copy itself will make the ad copy more relevant to the people viewing the ad, which makes it more likely that they'll click through to your ad's destination URL.

If you find that despite selecting targeting criteria your ad is still under-performing, it may be that the target group you've selected is too narrow. You can solve this problem by widening your targeting criteria, such as expanding the audience from San Francisco residents to all users in California.

TIP 104 — Understand Facebook advertising cost models

Facebook offers two cost models for its advertising:

- **Cost per thousand impressions:** Also known as *Pay for Views*, this cost model is based on the number of impressions your ad generates—the number of times it is shown to Facebook users when they are on the site. As opposed to traditional impression-based advertising models, where you're charged a set amount for a certain number of views, Facebook's cost-per-thousand-impressions model allows you to set the amount of money you want to spend for every thousand views of your ad. How much you bid to spend per thousand views relative to other advertisers will then determine how often your ad will be shown to Facebook users. The current minimum CPM (cost per thousand impressions) is $0.02.

- **Cost per click:** With this pricing model you specify the amount of money you're willing to spend if someone actually clicks on your ad. You're not charged each time someone simply sees your ad, only when someone actually clicks on it. The cost-per-click model also works on a bidding system, where the more you're willing to pay per click relative to what other advertisers are willing to spend, the more your ad will be shown to Facebook users that you specify in your ad targeting. Note that the minimum cost per click for a Facebook ad is $0.01.

For both of these cost models, Facebook provides you with a "bid estimator" that shows you the range of bids that currently exist for your particular type of ad and ad subject. The cost model you should go for in a Facebook ad depends entirely on your business and the type of ad you create. If you're running an ad campaign for a new business where your main aim is to expose your brand, then having a user perform a specific action (such as buy a product or sign up for a newsletter) may be less important. In this case, a cost-per-thousand-impressions model may work better for you. If your ad's success depends on how many people click on it, such as when you're advertising an event on your Facebook page that people need to respond to, paying only when someone clicks on your ad will make more sense.

TIP 105 Decide on a campaign budget

How much you're willing to spend each time someone sees your ad or clicks on it is linked closely to how big your budget is for your entire Facebook advertising campaign. Looking at it in reverse, the daily budget that you set will determine how much you can bid in terms of cost per click or cost per thousand impressions. (For more on Facebook's cost models, see Tip 104). So what should your daily budget be? Facebook helps you work this out to some degree by giving you budget estimates that relate to recommended minimum bids for ads that are similar in subject to yours. In reality, the only way of actually seeing what works for you in terms of the return you get for the money you spend is to test varying budgets once your ads have started running.

Ad budgets in Facebook are set at a campaign level, and the minimum investment is $1 a day. For example, if you have a campaign that contains several ads, and your daily budget is $1, that money will need to cover all the ads within that campaign. If you have five different campaigns, each with a daily budget of $1, you'll have a total budget of $5 per day for your account.

It's worth noting that Facebook lets you set only a daily budget for your ads as opposed to one that's set monthly. This actually works to your advantage: by having a daily budget, you ensure that your ads are spread out and run all month long, even if they run for only a short period each day. If you were to set a monthly budget, your ads would run constantly until the budget ran out, which could be only a few days into the month. In that case your ads would not run for the rest of the month unless you were to increase your budget.

Facebook guarantees that you'll never be charged more than the amount you set as your daily budget. If you find that your budget is running out too quickly, or that your ads aren't generating a lot of impressions, you can change your campaign budget at any time. You can also pause or delete ads in a campaign, which means you'll stop being charged for them.

Decide on your ad scheduling

Once you've decided on the cost model for your ads, your minimum bids, and your maximum daily budget, you'll need to decide for what time period you want your ads to run.

When you first create an ad in Facebook, your settings are defaulted to show your ads continuously, with no end date. Throughout the days that your ads are active, they'll be shown to your targeted Facebook audience until your budget runs out for that day. Your budget will run out when your ad reaches a certain number of impressions if you're paying per thousand impressions or a certain number of clicks if you're paying per click. Each day your budget is reset, and your ads will stop running only when you pause or delete the campaign. To help you target ads toward more specific events, or as a way to test ads, Facebook gives you the option to show your ad during a specific time frame only. You define this time frame when you create the ad by specifying a specific start date and time and end date and time.

Whether you want to run your ads continuously or for a specific time period depends on the type of ad you're running. You might want an ad for general branding purposes to run continuously, although it could become costly if you spend your daily budget each day until you decide to pause or end your campaign. Obviously it makes more sense to pick a specific start and end date when advertising a time-limited event. In that case, be sure to run your ad long enough in advance of the event to give it maximum exposure.

Choosing a specific time frame to show your ads is useful if you have a small budget or when you want to test ad variations against each other, such as ads with different copy or different landing pages. By running the ads for specific time periods, you can separate them into distinct test buckets that you can then compare.

TIP 107 Measure your ad performance

Facebook has a built-in reporting interface that helps you see how effective your ads are in terms of both impressions and clicks, as well as which Facebook users are engaging with your ads. From the main dashboard you can view high-level statistics such as your ad campaign's total spending, clicks, impressions, and click-through rate. Known as *CTR* for short, your ad's click-through rate is the number of clicks it accrues as a percentage of total impressions.

If you want more granular data, you can access more detailed statistics in reports that you can download. To access these, click the "Reports" tab in the Ad Manager (www.facebook.com/ads/manage). From here you can select three types of reports:

1. Advertising performance. This report contains the most basic and important information about the performance of your ads. You can see several metrics that gauge the performance of your ads, including the amount of money you've spent, the impressions and clicks you've generated, and the associated click-through rate of the ads. Note that you can also see statistics for unique impressions, unique clicks, and unique click-through rates. As opposed to these regular numbers, you can see the unique numbers for each. In other words, if the same user sees your ad multiple times, or clicks on it more than once, the unique click-through statistic will count this only once, since it's the same visitor performing the same action.

2. Responder demographics. This report tells you about the age, region, country, and gender of the Facebook users who are clicking on your ads. You can also see impressions and clicks for each of these brackets to compare the effectiveness of your ads between different demographic groups.

3. Responder profiles. This report tells you about the type of Facebook users clicking on your ad based on the interests they specify in their personal Facebook profile. In the "interests" column, you'll see an aggregate of interests—for example, dancing or films—that multiple users have specified who are then clicking through on your ads. You can also see the books, music, and TV shows that are popular with multiple users who are engaging with your ads.

TIP 108   Optimize your ads

Ad campaigns work best when they are constantly being honed, pruned, and updated in response to how they are performing. By analyzing your ad statistics in Facebook's Ad Manager (www.facebook.com/ads/manage), you can test different ad formats and targeting options against each other to keep improving your ads so that they have the best performance possible. There are several ways you can optimize your ad campaigns:

- **Relax your targeting:** If your ad is not generating a large number of impressions, your targeting criteria might be too narrow, in which case you need to broaden the demographics of the groups exposed to your ad.

- **Shift your budget:** Consider increasing the budget for campaigns that aren't performing well and decreasing the budget on those that are. Note that because budget is set at the campaign level, if you pause an ad in a campaign that has multiple ads, the budget will still feed to the other ads within that particular campaign.

- **Increase your maximum bid:** By increasing your maximum bid, you increase the chances of your ad being shown more often. This is especially the case where other businesses' ads are competing for the same target audience.

- **Test your ads against each other:** Also known as *A/B testing*, this method allows you to compare similar ads to see which one performs best (whether in terms of click-through rate or number of impressions). Making small changes to otherwise identical ads means you're able to isolate the variables that are affecting performance. For example, you could use different images in two ads but the same ad copy or use ad copy that's worded slightly differently in each to see which one is more effective. You can also test ads against different demographics. For example, you could have the same ad targeted to women aged twenty-two to thirty as well as to women aged thirty to forty and then compare the stats for each. In this example, you'd be able to identify which age group is responding better to your business proposition.

LinkedIn

TIP 109 Set up your company profile

Having a company profile in LinkedIn is a good way to reach not only potential employees but potential clients and partners as well. Through elements like LinkedIn groups and the site's question and answer section, you can interact with other people to show off your expertise in a particular field, which helps to build your reputation as an expert within that industry.

To set up a company profile, you'll need to first have a personal LinkedIn profile. Once you have one of these, log in using these details. If you don't have a personal profile, you'll need to create an account from scratch, where you'll enter your first name, last name, e-mail address, and a password that you select.

Once you've logged in, access the Companies page (www.linkedin.com/companies) from the main navigation menu, and click the "Add a Company" link on the top right of the Companies page. From here you'll need to enter your company's name and a company-based e-mail address. This step checks that your company doesn't already have a profile on LinkedIn. If your e-mail domain (e.g., the "mycompany.com" part in an e-mail address that is joe@mycompany.com) is tied to an e-mail domain for an existing company profile on LinkedIn, you'll be able to click on the existing company name to edit the profile—provided you have editing privileges. If your company does not already have a profile, LinkedIn will send a confirmation e-mail to the address you entered, which will send you a link to your new company account. This step confirms that your e-mail address exists and sets your e-mail address as the administrator's e-mail address.

Once in your account, you'll be able to start entering your company details, such as your website URL, a description of your services, your industry, the number of employees you have, and your geographical location.

Once you've provided this basic information, you can add your company logo. You can also change your settings, such as specifying employees who have editing privileges to update your company's profile. LinkedIn automatically pulls in employees that have listed your company as their employer.

TIP 110	Add a "Share on LinkedIn" widget

Once you've created your company profile, the next step is to market it so that you can increase its visibility and traffic. Besides promoting it internally by being active on groups and other discussions, encourage your employees to include your company name in their profile, which will then link to your page. You can also publish content on LinkedIn from elsewhere using the "Share on LinkedIn" widget. Incorporated on your company blog or website, the widget lets your visitors share your site's content with their own networks and connections on LinkedIn.

Users who see content they like can click the "share" button alongside it, which opens a window that gives them the option of sharing the content with a specific LinkedIn network or with their existing connections on the site. Once they've done this, your content appears in their LinkedIn news feed, which creates more exposure for your business since their feed will be seen by all their contacts as well. The ability for users to share your content to their own circle of influence on LinkedIn is another incentive for you to write interesting and unique content on your blog or website.

The steps for installing the widget are as follows:

1. On your home page, click the "Developers" link in the tools menu in the navigation footer, and then click the "Get Started" link under the LinkedIn Widgets section.

2. Click the "Get the Code" link under the "Share on LinkedIn" section of the page.

3. The widget produces a URL encoded with parameters including URL, title, summary, and source, which are populated when a user shares that piece of content. On your site you should include a URL that contains the parameters in the following format: http://www.linkedin.com/shareArticle ?mini=true&url=[articleUrl]&title=[articleTitle]&summary=[articleSummary] &source=[articleSource].

4. Paste the URL into the source code of each page on which you want the widget to appear. The link should then be populated dynamically with that particular page's article, URL, and title.

TIP 111 Join groups

LinkedIn groups are a good way to connect with other people in your industry, as well as to develop a reputation as an expert in a particular area. For example, if you sell photography equipment, you can use groups on LinkedIn as a platform on which to discuss different equipment options with fellow members who are likely to be in your industry and to comment on and review new products on the market. LinkedIn gives you two options for groups: you can either find an existing group in which you can participate or create a new one. A good starting point is to participate in existing groups, since chances are there will already be a large number of fellow group members with which you can interact.

To browse groups you may want to join, log in to your LinkedIn account and click the "Groups" link in the top navigation menu of your home page. On this page, click the "Group Directory" tab, and then enter keywords that relate to the groups you're looking for, such as *photography equipment.* You can also select a category of the type of group from the dropdown list to narrow your options; in this case you'd select "Corporate Group." After you've found a group you'd like to join from browsing through the search results that are returned, click the "Join this Group" button. You'll be asked to choose the settings you'd like for receiving group announcements and messages.

Once you've joined a group, you'll see various tabs in the top navigational menu that allow you to join existing group discussions, start new ones, submit related news articles, view related jobs, or post new ones.

If you want to start a new group, instead of clicking the "Groups Directory" tab on the Groups home page, click the "Create a Group" tab alongside it instead. From here you can select a new group name and description, and you'll be able to select your access settings for members. Note that your new group won't go live immediately—your application first needs to be approved by a LinkedIn administrator.

TIP 112   Ask and answer questions

LinkedIn's Answers section allows any LinkedIn member to write a question for other members to answer or for any LinkedIn member to answer a question asked by someone else. In addition to being a great knowledge-gathering tool for your industry, asking questions is a good way to connect with potential clients and partners in your industry, and answering questions is a good way to build a reputation as an expert on a particular topic.

You can choose those you'd like to ask a question to, such as the whole LinkedIn network or only selected connections. When asking a question, note that you'll have a greater chance of initiating a useful discussion if you ask content-based questions (e.g., "What are the best ways to market a photography equipment business?") than, for example, if you ask for contact details or use the forum as a way to blatantly advertise your business. A user who thinks a question is inappropriate can flag it, and if enough users flag the same question, it will be removed and reviewed. If this happens too many times, you may be blocked from asking or answering questions in the future. If you do want to recruit or advertise something, LinkedIn gives you the option to disclose this via checkboxes.

The Answers section awards what it calls *expert status* to certain members who are judged to be experts in a particular subject area. You can view a list of experts in particular topics via a link on the Answers home page, and you can identify someone as an expert in a topic by the white and green "expert" star that is visible on their profile.

This is an invaluable distinction as a way to improve your brand presence on LinkedIn. To gain expert status, you need to have your answer selected as "Best" by the person who asked the question—the more times this happens, the higher up you'll be in the list of experts in that particular area. To gain expert status quickly, stick to a narrow subject area and answer only questions for which you're confident you have a good answer. Note that giving a "private" answer (one that can't be viewed by others) won't count toward building expertise.

Leverage your personal profile

If you don't yet have a business presence on LinkedIn, chances are you may already have a personal profile for yourself. As well as being an effective way to connect with people linked with your own personal career, your personal profile can be a way to promote your business on the site. With a few modifications, your personal profile can become a networking tool for potential clients and partners:

- **Talk about the benefits, not the features, of your past experience:** When writing your profile, don't list just the previous companies you worked for or with and the responsibilities you had in each role. Potential clients who are reading your profile are more interested in how your experience and abilities could benefit them via your current business, so slant your profile accordingly. For each role, write about the value you added to the company and the unique skills you gained from each job. The key is to list the general benefits of your experience that a potential client could use from you now.

- **Change your default title:** LinkedIn uses your latest role as the default title for your profile. This title is more important than you may think in terms of first impressions, because it appears as part of your profile summary to people who view your profile but who aren't yet your connections. In the same way you modify your profile to list benefits, use your title to convey the main benefits you can offer a future client rather than the last job you had. For example, rather than keeping your title as "copywriter," change it to something such as "Writes value-added, action-oriented copy for corporate websites." A title like this will provide a potential client with greater incentive to click through to your public profile or to add you as a contact.

- **Link to your business profile:** If you have a business profile set up, link to it from your personal profile by adding it to the information. You can also use status updates in your personal profile as a way to keep your connections informed about events and updates related to your business.

TIP 114 Use LinkedIn search

Besides marketing your business with a professional and personal profile, LinkedIn can be used as a tool to proactively find potential partners or future clients. The easiest way to do this is to use LinkedIn's built-in search function.

You can access the search function in the LinkedIn header of any page you're on while you're logged in. Besides searching on people, you can search on companies, groups, people, jobs, your LinkedIn e-mail account, or the Answers section. If you know the name of the person you're looking for, search for the person's name to find his or her profile and request the person as a connection. If you want to find contacts within a specific company, use the company name as the search term. From here results will show you employees with their company, and you can view their profiles to see their role within the company and how long they've worked there. You can also find references for a particular person using LinkedIn's reference check tool. This is a good way to find a balanced opinion about someone else that you may want to partner with in the future.

If you don't know any specifics about the people or companies you want to connect with, use a general keyword search like *photography equipment suppliers* or *online marketing agencies* to see people and companies in those industries. From there you can submit a request to add them as contacts. LinkedIn also gives you the opportunity to add a short message—make this as personal as possible, especially if they don't know you at all.

Your success with adding people as connections is likely to be greater if you have a connection in common. LinkedIn shows you whether and how you're connected to the people whose profiles you're viewing in the right column alongside their profile. You can then request an introduction from the contact you have in common—which provides more context than if you were just contacting them with no common connection. You can also use this introduction technique to full effect by looking through the contacts of people you're connected to and then requesting an introduction from there.

Orkut

TIP 115 | Understand Orkut

With the phenomenal growth of social networking in recent years, it's no surprise that Google wanted to be part of the action. As its own answer to social networking sites like Facebook, the search engine giant launched Orkut in 2004. At the time of Orkut's launch, Facebook hadn't yet opened its interface to developers or allowed businesses to establish a presence through channels like pages. Once this changed, though, Facebook quickly overtook Orkut in terms of market share in the United States. Orkut has nevertheless managed to carve a niche as the dominant social network in certain other countries: while only around 17 percent of Orkut's users are from the United States, over half are from Brazil and around 20 percent are from India.[1] This means that if you're a marketer with a potential customer base in Brazil or India, Orkut can be an excellent platform on which to promote your business. Even if your target audience is predominantly in the United States or Europe, Orkut can be a good supplement to other campaigns you may have on Facebook or Twitter.

Like most other social networks, Orkut lets users create a personal profile through which they can connect with other users who have similar interests. One area in which Orkut differentiates itself from other social networks is that you can join communities (or create your own) that center around a particular topic. Although the site is used primarily for personal networking, Orkut communities are a good place to expose your brand since you can select a highly targeted audience with whom to interact. By providing useful content and resources to people who are likely to be interested in your product or service, you increase the chance of an Orkut user's becoming your customer. Orkut also allows you to advertise on communities using built-in advertising programs like Google AdSense and Orkut Promote. As with other social networks, a marketing strategy that is successfully executed on Orkut can help turn users not just into customers but into brand evangelists who spread the word about your business within their own circle of influence.

TIP 116 Join Orkut

When Orkut launched, you needed to be invited to join by someone else. The idea behind this requirement was that it would ensure a user base that was highly active in its networking. These days Orkut is no longer invite-only; all you need to join the site is a Google account, which you'll already have if you use other Google services such as Google Groups or Gmail.

Once you've logged in to www.orkut.com, your first step is to customize your personal profile: to do this, click the "Profile" menu item from the main navigation menu, and then click the "More info" link in your summary profile area. Orkut breaks your profile information into three sections: "Social," "Professional," and "Personal." On the "General" tab, add information about yourself (or your company), such as your name and country location. The "Social" and "Personal" tabs let you add personal information about yourself, as well as things like your interests and hobbies. Since you'll be marketing your business, you may not want to fill all this out, but you should still fill out the basics as a personal user. On the "Professional" tab, include a link to your company website and a description of the services or products you offer.

Once your profile has been filled out, the next step is to add friends by clicking the "Find friends" link in the "My friends" section of your profile page. Orkut lets you find friends in several ways:

- Search on the names of people you know who are already Orkut members.

- Add people from your Google contacts who are already Orkut members.

- Send an e-mail to your Google contacts or friends who aren't on Orkut. For both of these options, Orkut will send an e-mail on your behalf that invites them to join the site and become your friend.

TIP 117 | Add scraps and updates

Two elements of Orkut can make your profile more interesting to look at: adding updates and adding scrapbook elements. Text-based updates on Orkut are similar to a Facebook status update or a Twitter update. To add an update in Orkut, fill in the text box just below your name on your main profile page. From here, it filters into the tab that says "My updates" farther down your page. Similarly, you can see updates of your friends in the adjoining tab that says "All." Updates are a good way to populate your Orkut profile with notifications about your latest blog posts or links to news or promotions that you talk about on your website. You can also use this area to link to interesting resources that relate to your industry or business and that your Orkut friends would find interesting.

If you want more functionality with your updates, you can add "scraps," which are rich updates that can include video, photos, audio, or flash widgets. You can add scraps to your own scrapbook or to someone else's—in both cases, they're visible to everyone else viewing that profile. To add a scrap, click the "scraps" link either in the left or top navigation of your profile page (or someone else's if you're posting to their profile). Enter the scrap you want to write or upload videos, photos, audio files, or flash widgets of your choice. You can upload images or videos from your own computer, or you can add a Picasa gallery or the URL of the gallery if it is on another photo-sharing site such as Photobucket. If you want to post rich content, you can use embedded HTML by pasting the HTML tags straight into the text box. Orkut lets you preview a scrap before it's posted, so you can make changes before publishing it.

Just as you can restrict the visibility of information you fill out in your profile, you can limit who can write in your scrapbook—for example, only you, only your friends, friends of friends, or your whole network. For business purposes it's best to keep this as open as possible by allowing your whole network, or at least your friends of friends, to post.

TIP 118 Engage users on brand community pages

Orkut communities allow groups of Orkut users with similar interests to congregate and communicate around a specific subject. For a business, joining communities is a good way to network with other people in the industry or with potential customers. You can also create communities of your own, which is a good way of establishing yourself as an expert in a particular subject area. It's a good idea to join and participate in existing communities before creating a new one so that you build up your network and become familiar with the Orkut environment. To find communities, click "Communities" from the main navigation menu and then search on related keyword phrases, such as *Web development* if you're a Web development firm, in the search area on the right of the Communities page. You can also browse communities in the categories listed on the page—"Automotive," "Business," "Computers and Internet," and so forth.

Be sure that any input you give in communities is genuinely useful so that you're associating your brand with being useful rather than just promoting yourself. In the same way, when you create a community, you should ensure that your aim is to add value to other Orkut users in an area for which you can provide expertise. For example, if you're a Web development company, use your group to provide hints and tips and training on Web development, rather than as a way to push your services.

To create a community, click the "Create Community" button on the Communities page. You'll be prompted to give a name to your community, choose a category for it, and describe what the community is about. Once your community page has been created, you can engage with your users through things like initiating polls and forum topics or posting about upcoming events linked to your business. Besides inviting friends to join your community, you can link your community with related ones to expose it to a wider group of people who may want to join. To do this, click "Add" under the related communities section on the right navigational menu of your new community page. From here you can search on communities and then click the "Add" button alongside communities that relate to yours.

TIP 119 Enroll in Orkut Promote

Orkut Promote is Orkut's free advertising program, which lets you promote your product or service to other users on the site. The most useful aspect of Orkut Promote is that it harnesses the viral nature of social networks by letting users spread your promotion to their friends if they find your ad interesting. The key concept here is that users get to decide whether your ad will become viral, based on their own tastes, interests, and receptiveness. For this reason it's crucial to create a quality ad that will have the best chance of being spread among users. The more interesting users find your ad, the more people will see it, and the more chance you have of building new customers. Orkut Promote is also highly cost effective—provided you already have an Orkut account, advertising on the platform is free to use.

To get started, click the "Promote" link in the left navigation menu of your profile page. From there you'll be taken to the page where you'll create your ad. The first element you'll need to think of is the title of the campaign—for this, think of something catchy and informative that grabs your users' attention and prompts them to click through on the ad. The next element is the description field, which is the main body of the ad. Besides text, you can add photos from an Orkut photo album or a video from YouTube. Note that only images you've uploaded that you've set to be viewable by everyone can be used as content for the ad.

Once you've created your ad, click the "Create Promotion" button, which will automatically send the ad to all people you're friends with. These friends will then see the ad in the top right of their profile. If they like the ad, they can click the "Spread" link on top of the promotion, which then automatically sends it to their friends, who can in turn share the ad with their friends. On the other hand, users who don't think your ad is interesting can click the "Trash" button: doing this removes the ad from their profile permanently and replaces it with a new one.

TIP 120　Track and improve your ads

If you're taking the time to create an advertising campaign on Orkut Promote, you should be tracking your ad's effectiveness so you can work out the return you're getting on your time investment. The easiest way to use this is to analyze Orkut's built-in stats linked to Promote that tell you how users are seeing and responding to campaigns you're running. To access these stats, click the "Promote" button on the left navigation menu of your profile page. From there the Promote page is divided into two tabs: "Create a Promotion" (for more on setting this up, see Tip 119) and "My Promotions." On the "My Promotions" tab you'll see key metrics related to each campaign, such as the number of unique users who viewed, clicked on, or trashed your ad. Arguably most important is the "Reach" statistic, which shows you how many people your campaign has reached as a result of people clicking the "Spread" button when they see your promotion.

By analyzing these statistics, you can work out which of your ads are most effective in getting people to engage with your brand. Perhaps some of your campaigns are being seen by a lot of people but not many people are clicking on them, or maybe lots of readers are seeing your ads but then a large proportion are trashing them. The stats help you identify campaigns with a high reach and click-through rate, and these are the ads that you should aim to replicate.

So how do you create a campaign that others will spread? The key is to come up with an ad that is interesting and relevant to your users. Researching your target demographic can boost your chances of serving them with an ad for a product or service they're likely to be interested in. Another way to increase your ad's reach is to add friends on Orkut with whom your brand already has a relationship, such as your blog readers or newsletter subscribers. In these cases people who are already familiar with your brand are more likely to spread a campaign if they see it. Remember too that Orkut is extremely popular with audiences in Brazil and India—so ads targeted to these countries are likely to be more successful than ads targeted to American audiences, for example.

Plaxo

TIP 121 Understand Plaxo

Plaxo was launched in 2001 as an online address book tool that allowed you to keep your contacts' details consistent and up to date no matter how many separate address books you had. Plaxo does this by syncing with your separate contact lists such as your Web-based e-mail contacts, your Outlook contacts, and your cell phone address book. Any updates to their details made by contacts in your address book who are also Plaxo members will automatically be updated in your Plaxo address book.

In recent years Plaxo has expanded its core address book functionality to include a business networking tool known as Pulse. Although the address book tool is still very much a part of Plaxo, the addition of Pulse now means that the site is more of a social network where you can add Plaxo users as "connections." You can then share media like text updates, links, photos, and blog posts with your connections. You can also publish your activity from other social media sites such as Flickr, Facebook, LinkedIn, and You-Tube; similarly, you'll be able to see your connections' activities on these sites within Plaxo as well.

Although Pulse has similarities to social networking sites like Facebook and MySpace in that you create a personal profile and build up connections, there are three key differences:

1. The site is more business-focused, so it helps you make connections with others in your industry rather than just with consumers.

2. The site aims to help you strengthen real relationships with people you actually know, rather than building a network of virtual friends.

3. The average Plaxo user is forty-two years old, which means users are likely to be key decision makers with a certain level of influence in their industry.

As a business owner, then, you'll find Plaxo is more useful as a personal business networking tool through which you can connect with potential business partners or clients on a one-to-one basis, rather than as a platform on which to advertise your business to potential customers.

TIP 122 Set up your Plaxo profile

The first step in setting up your Plaxo profile is to sign up for an account at www.plaxo.com. You'll be asked to give your name and e-mail address and select a password. Once you've verified your e-mail address, you can log in to your account, where you'll be prompted to start adding people you know as connections and address book contacts. Plaxo helps you do this by importing your existing contacts from other Web-based address books like Gmail and LinkedIn.

Once you've added your connections, click the "See Full Profile" link to the right of the home page when you're logged in. This page allows you to edit the personal information that you'll share with others, including your contact information, work experience, and links to your company website and/or blog. To fill in each part, click the "edit this section" link at the top right of each information box. Since Plaxo is best used as a personal business connection tool, it's best to upload a picture of yourself for your photo rather than your company's logo.

Plaxo gives you a lot of flexibility about which information you want to make visible in your profile. The site also recognizes that you have different kinds of connections with whom you'd want to share different information, and so it lets you separate your connections into groups such as "Business" and "Family and Friends" so you can make certain profile information visible to some groups but not others. (Note, however, that a connection can be in more than one of these groups.) For example, you can make your birthday visible to your friends and family but not to your business connections. To change your visibility settings, click the dropdown box under each section of information, where you can choose which group you want to be able to see that piece of information.

Plaxo also creates a public version of your profile, which is visible in search results for people who see you but aren't a connection or to those who type in the URL you've selected for your profile. To see what's visible in your public profile, select "Public" from the "See what you're sharing with" dropdown on your profile page. If you prefer, you can also disable your public profile so that only Plaxo connections can see your information.

TIP 123 | Use the Plaxo address book

Although Plaxo's online address book may seem like a fairly basic service, it's an essential one: your contacts are at the core of your marketing efforts since they are your primary way of spreading your brand's message, generating leads, and building up your customer base.

When you create your Plaxo account, you'll be prompted to import contacts you have on other lists, including your Web-based e-mail accounts such as Gmail, Yahoo! Mail, Hotmail, Outlook, or Apple Mail or on sites like LinkedIn. Then, when you modify or delete a contact in your Plaxo account, you can sync this back out to all your other address books on the sites mentioned and even to your cell phone. To access your address book later, click the "Address Book" main menu item from the home page once you've logged in to your account.

Besides letting you sync information between different address books, Plaxo leverages the interconnections its users have between them by suggesting users you may know that you'd want to add as connections. Note that there is a distinction between a Plaxo "contact" and a Plaxo "connection." A contact is someone who is just in your address book; a connection is someone you've chosen to interact with using Pulse. When people who are both connections and contacts make a change to their contact details, this new information filters down to your address book too, so that their information is updated automatically in your account. Plaxo's address book is a good way to ensure consistency with all your contact information across the many different address books you may have. The site also serves as an effective backup in the case of theft, damage, or data corruption, since the data is all stored remotely on Plaxo's servers.

If you want access to more advanced functionality in your address book, you can sign up for a Plaxo Premium account (for which you'll pay a monthly fee), where you can do things like sync to Microsoft Outlook, reduplicate your contacts, and have access to automated backup and recovery functionality.

TIP 124   Add connections

Once you've added contacts to your Plaxo address book, you're ready to start adding connections via Pulse, the site's social networking functionality. Plaxo makes a firm distinction between an address book contact and a connection on the site:

- An **address book contact** is a personal contact that is usually imported from another address book like Microsoft Outlook. Address book contacts remain private so that only you can see their details, and you can add up to 10,000 contacts.

- A **connection** is someone in your address book who is also on Plaxo and with whom you choose to share media like photos, blog posts, or links that you post on the site or other social media sites. They need to also accept you as a connection, which means you'll see anything they share on the site too. You can have up to 1,000 connections.

Because of this distinction, you can use Plaxo as both a private address book tool and as a networking tool. Plaxo encourages you to only connect via Pulse with people who you actually know so that your Stream (the timeline of media shared by your connections) is more manageable and useful. You can separate your connections into friends, family, or business so you can share different information with different groups of people (e.g., your Flickr photos only with your friends, or your blog posts with just your business connections).

To add a Plaxo connection, click the "Connections" dropdown menu item from the "More" tab on the home page once you're logged in. On this page, you can add connections in several ways: via webmail accounts such as Gmail, with people who Plaxo thinks you might know, or via your Plaxo address book. Once you've selected people to invite, click the blue "Connect" button at the bottom of the page.

Once someone has accepted your invitation, you'll be able to see the media they've shared in your Stream (for more on this, see Tip 125). To view all your connections, click the "View Connections" link at the top of the Connections page. On this page you can categorize connections as friends, family, or business contacts, and you can also delete connections. Note that if you do this, they'll remain a Plaxo address book contact unless you delete them from there as well.

TIP 125 Use Pulse

Pulse is Plaxo's social networking part of the site. With this functionality, you can add connections (for how to do this, see Tip 124) and then share media with them directly through the site or via other social media sites you engage on, like Flickr and Facebook. The media you share (blog posts, photos, links, status updates, etc.) are then published in your Plaxo connections' Stream, which is a timeline of media shared by all of their connections. Likewise, you'll be able to see everything your connections have shared in your own Stream. Because Pulse allows one to upload media both from within Plaxo as well as via other social media sites, it becomes a useful central point from which to keep up with all the social media activity that your friends, family, and business contacts are engaging in.

To begin using Pulse, click the "Stream" tab from the Plaxo home page once you're logged in. Start by adding a status update to your Plaxo account by filling in the text box on the right of the page below the sentence that says, "What are you doing?" If you want to upload messages, photos, or links, click the three corresponding links at the top left of the Stream page. A pop-up window will then appear with tabs for each of these content types, as well as two more for sharing product reviews or polls. Once you've selected your desired content tab, click the "To" text field to select recipients for your update, for example your friends, your family, or Plaxo Groups to which you belong. Then, upload your media by selecting it from its location on your computer. When you've finished, click the blue button at the bottom of the tab.

Back on your Stream page, you can filter your Stream to see only updates from certain groups of people. For example, to change your view so you only see updates from your family, change the defaulted filter bar on the left of the page to "Family." If you want to be able to publish updates to Pulse via other social media websites, you'll need to allow Plaxo to pull in these feeds (for more on how to do this, see Tip 126).

TIP 126 Enable feeds from other services

With Plaxo's Pulse social aggregator tool, you can pull feeds into your Plaxo account from other social media sites you're engaging on such as Facebook, Twitter, YouTube, or blog platforms like Blogger. This means that every time you make an update on one of those sites, the update will be published to your Plaxo connections as well. In this way, adding external feeds to your Plaxo account allows you to expose your other social media activity to more people, which in turn drives more traffic to those sites. In a business context, it also helps you to make richer connections with your Plaxo business contacts.

To add feeds to your Plaxo account, click the "Edit this section" link on the Websites section of your profile page. From here, enter in a user name that you commonly use so that it can quickly find your feeds on different social media sites and then click the "Find My Sites" button. Note that you have to have a public account with a particular site to see your connections' updates on it and vice versa—for example, if you're not part of Twitter, you won't see your connections' Twitter updates in your feeds. Similarly, if your Twitter feed is set to private, your Plaxo connections won't see your updates in their own feed.

Once your feeds are enabled, you'll see them published in chronological order along with your connections' updates (for more on using Pulse to view your connections' updates, see Tip 125). Since Plaxo lets you define your connections differently (such as "friends and family" or "business"), it also lets you choose which groups of people see which feed. For example, you could arrange it so that only your friends see your Flickr account updates, while everyone including your business contacts sees your Twitter updates. In this way you can create a different profile for each type of person looking at your account—a profile with a personal slant for family and close friends or a more professional profile for your business connections.

TIP 127   Create groups

Plaxo groups are an effective way of sharing resources and gaining knowledge on a particular topic, whether among your own employees or with people in other companies. They're also a good way of connecting with other Plaxo members who aren't part of your extended network. For example, if you join the "investment management" group, you'll see a list of group members with links to their profile pages. From there you can ask to connect with them and so extend the connections you have on the site. As a member of a Plaxo group, you can share information such as photos, videos, messages, and your own social feed with other members on the group, who can then comment on the information you've posted.

Plaxo lets you either join an existing group or create a new one. To find existing groups, do a keyword search for terms related to the subject you're interested in. For example, if you offer investment management services, search with keywords like *investment management* to browse related groups from the search results that are returned. From here you can ask to join the group, at which point the moderator will need to approve your request. To create a group, follow these steps:

1. Click on the "Groups" link under the "More" tab on the home page of your profile.

2. In the left-hand column, click "Create a Group." You'll be prompted to choose a name and URL for your group and add a description and photo for it.

3. Next, decide who will see your group. If you make it private, only people you choose to invite will be able to see it. If it's moderated, you have to approve the members first. If you make it public, anyone will be able to see or join the group.

4. Click "Create Group."

5. From here, select who you want to invite to the group—you can select both Plaxo connections and address book contacts, or you can invite people by e-mail.

6. Click "Invite to Group," which will send an invitation to the selected recipients to join the group.

Ning

TIP 128 Understand Ning

Ning, from the Chinese word meaning "peace," is one of the newest additions to the social networking space. Ning's key difference from general social networking sites like Facebook and MySpace is that it allows people to create their *own* social network around a specific subject. When you create your own network on Ning, you can customize its structure, design, and features to suit your own specific needs. To date, Ning has just under two million social networks and around forty million registered users.[1]

As a business owner, creating a network on Ning lets you establish yourself as a leader in your industry, as well as permitting you to network with other industry members and expose your brand to a target audience likely to be interested in your product or service. Within your company a Ning network lets your employees interact with each other and share resources and ideas on current projects. Ning networks contain a customizable interface into which you can include add-on widgets like event calendars and multimedia elements like video uploads and photo galleries. You can also include interactive tools like forums, groups, and chat, which enable members to communicate with each other directly. As in any other social network, each Ning member has a profile page from which to share updates and make connections with other Ning members and communities. Each member's profile page also features an activity stream of other members with whom the member is connected.

Ning offers both a free and a premium service: a free account gives you basic functionality, while a premium account costs a monthly fee in return for extra features such as the ability to have your own domain name for your network (e.g., http://networkname.mycompany.com instead of http://networkname.ning.com), access to more storage space, and the ability to remove ads and promotional links from your network. In July 2010, Ning will be phasing out free accounts to a paid service only. You'll be able to select from three pricing models depending on the functionality you'd like for your network.

TIP 129 — Create your Ning network

Before you set up a Ning network, think carefully about the strategy behind it. Who will your audience be, and how will the network benefit them? What specific value will your network give them to keep them as loyal members? This could be helping them connect with each other, providing a forum for discussions, informing them of industry-related news and events, or providing them with resources. By associating your business with a network that adds value, you'll do your brand more of a service than using the network purely as a place to sell your product or service. More recently, Ning has removed the ability to search and browse existing networks in an effort to combat spammers. This means that now the only way to view a network is to be invited and then join it or to know the URL of the page. Therefore, building membership numbers on Ning these days depends solely on word of mouth from existing members, as well as external marketing efforts.

Once you've created your Ning account, log in and click the "Create a Ning Network" button. You'll need to choose a name and a URL for your network, and on the next page you'll enter a description, language, and country, and make the network publicly accessible or private so only you and people you invite can see it. On the next page you can add features to your network that will make it more interesting and interactive for your users, such as forums, blogs, photos, videos, events, chat, and music. Finally, you'll be able to customize your page's theme in terms of color and design. If you prefer, you can import your own images to use or make changes to the style sheet so that you have complete control over the layout and appearance. Once you're happy with your layout, click "Launch."

Once this basic setup has been completed, click the "Invite" link to add members to your network, either by importing contacts from your existing address books or by adding in e-mail addresses manually. Now you're ready to begin adding content such as photos, videos, and events. Once your network is set up, you can make further changes to it by clicking the "Ning Networks" link in the top right of your home page when you're logged in, and then click the "Manage" link under the network you want to edit.

Collaborate with other industry members

While creating a Ning network is easy enough, building a significant member base is more challenging. One way to deal with this challenge is to join forces with other people in your industry to help build up the network by either managing it together or providing useful content to members. Collaboration between industry players has several advantages:

■ You pool your resources in terms of contacts you invite to join. This is possible since you're tapping into each person's network to invite people, rather than just your own.

■ You can promote your network on each person's website and blog instead of just your own, which increases its exposure and drives more traffic to the network, which in turn increases the numbers of people joining as members.

■ You're seen as a neutral, value-added resource center rather than a place for one company to promote itself, which can encourage more people to join as members.

■ You have a larger amount of content that is more varied, which further adds value to your members.

There are several ways you can partner with others in a Ning network. You could approach partners you work with on a regular basis or clients you work with to partner with you, or you could join forces with your competitors to start a network to provide a forum for consumers within your industry. One example of a Ning network that involves several different groups within a single industry is Barista Exchange (http://baristaexchange.ning .com). Created by coffee barista Matt Milletto, Barista Exchange has evolved into an interactive portal that covers all aspects of the gourmet coffee industry. Through the network, coffee consumers can interact not only with other baristas but also with growers, resellers, equipment suppliers, and even coffee shop owners. As a result, the content spans a variety of areas, including coffee shop reviews, coffee recipes, news and trends in the industry, and advice about buying coffee and coffee equipment. By collaborating on one network, each different sector of the industry (such as the coffee shops and the equipment suppliers) gets more exposure for its businesses than were it to create a separate network. For more on marketing your Ning community, see Tip 133.

TIP 131 · Encourage the conversation

A social network is most effective in building and retaining a membership base when there is regular interaction between you and your members, as well as between members themselves. Asking for member input instills a sense of empowerment, which makes them more likely to become loyal to your brand and to spread the positive word about it to others. In addition, participating in discussions with members on your network lets you build your reputation as a business that listens and responds to its customers, whether their input is of a positive or negative nature.

The first way to encourage interaction between members is to include functionality that facilitates discussions within your network interface, such as by including groups or chat functionality. To facilitate a conversation between members and your business, you could ask for feedback and reviews on your products or services or suggestions for how you could improve on your current offering. Another way of encouraging users to be active participants in your network is to ask them to upload their own content, such as photos or videos. You can frame this proposition within the context of a competition, where you provide incentives for them to submit content in the form of prizes or discounts. If your business is hosting an event, make use of an event calendar and ask your members to RSVP on the network and comment on any information you give them about the event itself.

Besides using your network as a forum in which members can submit reviews or make suggestions about your business, you can use it as a place for them to report faults or problems with your products. If someone does start a discussion or leave a comment that has a negative slant, respond immediately and honestly on the network (i.e., as a follow-up comment or discussion post). By responding publicly, you address the problem while letting other members know that you're dealing with the situation. It's also a good idea to follow up directly with the customer about steps you're taking to remedy his or her situation—a personalized, proactive response allows you to better contain any negative connotations the person may have developed about your brand.

Manage your
network effectively

Once you've set up your network, and as your membership numbers grow, the amount of activity in your network will increase. To avoid spam and keep control of the content that is posted, Ning lets you moderate content to deal with spam or inappropriate postings. To share the load of this task, Ning also lets you assign administrative privileges to members of your network so that they can moderate content and to help enforce your network guidelines. Unlike you as the network creator, network administrators can't make high-level changes to your network such as deleting it or taking it offline, and they won't have access to your network information or analytics.

To promote a member of your network to an administrator, click the "Manage" link alongside the network you'd like to manage once you're logged in. Under the "Your Members" section, click the "Members" link. Check the box next to the name of the member you'd like to promote and then, from the "Actions" dropdown box, select "Set role: Administrator."

Administrative roles on Ning have several levels, which is useful if you want to allow someone to monitor certain sections of content rather than the whole network. For example, you could allow an administrator to manage only one particular discussion or forum category or a particular blog or photo album. To change these settings, click the "Manage Roles" section from within your Members page. From here you can name the administrator role, which you may want to be similar to the forum discussion that you're giving them control over. If you're giving them control over a specific piece of content such as a forum discussion, click the link that says "Add Content Item." From here you'll enter the URL of the location of the specific piece of content, such as an individual forum, photo, or video. Once this role is created, click "Save." After this is done, you can navigate back to the members page and select the person you want by checking the box next to his or her name and then clicking the "Actions" dropdown.

TIP 133 Market your network externally

Unlike general "catchall" networks like Facebook and MySpace, anyone can create a social network on Ning. Therefore networks similar to the one you want to create probably already exist, which means you face competition for members on your own network. In addition, you can't browse networks within Ning due to spam regulations. So, how do you publicize your network to drive traffic to it, amid competing sites that may be similar?

- **Advertise it on your other websites:** For example, if you own a paper-making company, and you've created a social network that talks about the art of paper making, link back to the network from your blog and from your company website.

- **Use a premium account for your own domain name:** If you sign up for a paid Ning account, you can have your network on your own domain name (in other words, *http://networkname.mycompany.com* rather than *http://networkname.ning.com*). Having your own domain name increases visibility for your URL on Google search results for your network name. Therefore, when you name your network you may want to think of a noun that is commonly used in searches for your business.

- **Newsletters:** If you already have people who've opted in to receive news from you, include a blurb about your new network in your newsletter along with a link to the network.

- **Guest blog:** Research who the key bloggers are in your particular industry and then offer to write a guest post for them that contains unique content that would be useful to their readers and that relates to the content and theme of your network. At the end of the post, include a link back to your network, which will help build credibility for your network to increase search engine rankings and will encourage their blog audience to visit your site.

- **Other social networks:** If you have a Facebook page, include a link back to your network alongside links back to your website and blog on the page, and if you have a Twitter account, write updates of the latest activities on the network and include a link back to the site. Be careful to keep a balance with this: don't use your Twitter or Facebook account solely as a way to promote your network, so be selective about the network activities you promote on these sites.

MySpace

TIP 134 Decide whether MySpace is right for your business

Although at one point it was the most popular social networking site in the United States, MySpace has more recently been overtaken by Facebook in terms of market share: as of September 2009, Facebook had 95.497 million unique visitors in the United States, as opposed to MySpace's 65.652 million.[1] MySpace's concept is the same as that of any other social network in that anyone can create a Web page ("my space") to network and connect with other users. One major difference between MySpace and Facebook, however, is that the former is not set up to be a "walled garden"—that is, your MySpace profile is defaulted to be publicly viewable, where anyone can see it and interact with it, even those you don't know as friends. In recent years MySpace has added news stream functionality, where status updates that you make are broadcast to your friends' profiles and vice versa.

As a business owner, there are two main ways you can market your brand on MySpace: you can set up a profile to connect with potential customers, or you can use MySpace Advertising to expose your brand to them while they're interacting on the site. As far as setting up a profile goes, businesses that fall within the entertainment industry or that target a younger demographic tend to see the best results from their efforts. One notable example is the music industry: many upcoming bands and solo artists use MySpace Music as a way to promote themselves and get their music exposed to potential new audiences long before (and even as a way of) securing a record contract. MySpace Music allows artists to do things like upload MP3 audio files of their songs, upload their own music videos, and promote upcoming gigs and tour dates on their profile, which are then broadcast to their fans on the site.

The large number of MySpace users means that exposing your brand to only a small percentage of these users can result in a significant increase in brand awareness and traffic to your blog or website. Investing in the time to market yourself on MySpace can therefore be worthwhile—provided that the typical MySpace user is in line with your target demographic.

TIP 135 | Set up your profile

To set up a personal profile, click the "Sign Up" link on the top left of the MySpace home page at www.myspace.com. After filling in your details, MySpace will pull through the address book of the e-mail address you used to sign up with (if it's a Web-based e-mail address like Gmail or Yahoo! Mail) so you can add as friends the contacts that are already MySpace members. Next you'll be prompted to start adding videos, music, or applications for your home page. You can do this either now or later by clicking "Skip this step." Edit your profile (which you can also access by clicking the "Edit Profile" link from the Profile tab on your home page) by entering information such as your interests, geographical location, marital status, schools you're linked to, and other general information about yourself. In the "Companies" section, you can add details about your business, while in the "Networking" section you can add your job title and industry, which will help with networking with others in your same industry later on. Make sure the information you include in your profile is well written and genuine—an unauthentic profile will negatively affect any business networking you undertake on the site. Think of MySpace as a place primarily to network and meet friends, the connections through which will help spread your brand to interested users.

Once your profile is set up, you can customize its look and feel by changing themes and layouts or adding or hiding modules shown on the page. You can also synchronize updates that you make on other sites like Twitter to pull into your profile, which helps you cross-promote any activities you're writing about across your audiences on both sites. To set this up, click "MyAccount" button in the top right of the page and then click "Sync." Click "Get Synced" to choose to feed your MySpace updates to your Twitter account or your Twitter updates to MySpace.

If you're a band, create an artist profile rather than a personal profile, which will allow you to upload MP3s, videos, and tour dates, and it will be listed in your particular music genre for fans looking for your kind of music. To create an artist's profile, click the "Music" tab and then the "Artist Signup" link in the top right corner.

Find friends

As with other social networks, friend connections are the primary way to network with others on the site, by e-mailing, chatting, or leaving comments on each other's content such as blogs and photos. For you as a business owner, friend connections are the main way to reach out to potential customers and expose your brand to groups of people who may be interested in your product or service.

The first way to add friends is to find people you already know who are MySpace users. There are several ways you can do this, all of which are accessed by clicking the "Find Friends" link under the "Friends" tab of your profile. You can search by user name, pull through existing contacts from Web-based e-mail accounts, or e-mail them directly and invite them to join.

Once you've added people you know, you can extend your friend networking to people you may not know directly but who fit your brand's target market. MySpace lets you use very granular criteria to narrow down the kind of user you're trying to add; for example, finding only females over the age of thirty in the city of Seattle. To start this process, click the "Browse" link under the "Friends" tab from the home page of your profile. On the "Basic" tab, you can select people based on gender, age, and geographical location, as well as the purpose of their profile. On the "Advanced" tab you have even more specific choices of people to search on, such as income, education, and whether or not they have children.

Once you've found someone you want to add as a friend, click "Add to friends," after which that person will need to approve or deny your request. To increase your chances of being approved, you can message the person when you request that he or she become a friend and mention something specific to the person's profile—such as interests or geographic location. It's important not to start the hard sell as soon as someone has been added as a friend—focus first on establishing trust, which means taking the time to connect and letting the new friend become familiar with your profile before you attempt to market to him or her.

TIP 137 | Create fresh content

While developing connections on MySpace is important in exposing your brand to your target market, keeping those connections returning to and engaged with your profile is essential. The most effective way to do this is to post fresh content regularly. Not only does your profile become more interesting, but each time you create new content your friends are notified via their news feed, which then encourages them to visit your page. Besides making text updates and uploading photos, videos, or music, there are two main ways of adding regular content:

- **The MySpace blog:** Your MySpace account comes with a built-in blogging tool—access it by clicking the "My Blog" link under the "Profile" tab. If you already have a business blog, you can post the same post into your MySpace blog with a link back to your blog URL, which will drive your readers to your external blog while creating fresh MySpace content at the same time. You can control who sees your MySpace blog; for example, you can make it private (the "Diary" option), public (the "Friends" option), or a "Preferred List," which is where you specify people who can view it. If your friends subscribe to your blog, they'll be alerted via e-mail whenever you publish a new post. MySpace also lets you customize the look and feel of your blog to your own preferences, from uploading a custom header to incorporating your own style sheet. To access these settings, click the "Customize Blog" in the left link menu underneath your profile photo.

- **Bulletins:** These are short messages you can write that are posted to your friends' profile pages. Bulletins are a good way to market an event relating to your business, such as a sale or a discount coupon, or inviting them to an in-store sale. If you do write bulletins, write them as if you're talking to a friend rather than a customer, with an emphasis on adding value rather than pushing your business outright. Bulletins are posted to your friends' private bulletin boards on their own profile, so you can customize them to be personalized to specific groups of MySpace friends such as your personal friends, fans, customers, or potential partners. To create a bulletin, click the "Bulletins" link from the "Friends" tab and then click the "Post Bulletin" link.

TIP 138   Join groups

A good way of exposing your brand to MySpace users is to participate in groups. If you join or create a group on a topic related to your industry, you'll be able to participate in forums and discussions that will help establish your reputation as an expert in that particular field.

It's useful to start by joining an existing group before attempting to start one yourself. This gives you a feel for the conversations that are already happening in your industry and establishes your reputation as a knowledgeable resource. It's also easier to begin networking with an existing group of people than to try to build up your own network from scratch. To access groups, click "Groups" under the "More" tab of your MySpace profile home page. You'll see a list of groups by category, such as "Business & Entrepreneurs" and "Places and Travel," so browse through the category that's related to your business. For example, if you're a realtor, the "Real Estate Networking" group could be a good place to show off your knowledge and showcase yourself as an expert in the real estate industry, which may ultimately result in gaining new business leads from fellow group members down the line. Alternatively, you search on related keywords in the text box below the list. Once you've found a group you want to join, click the "Join Group" button near the top of the page.

As a group member, you can post bulletins just to the group, read other bulletins people have written, and contribute to or create new discussion topics. When posting anything on a group, be sure that your content adds value rather than serves solely as an advertisement for your business or product. For example, if you offer tax services for small businesses, you could write a topic that compares the different tax e-filing systems that are available—this is related to your industry and adds value by providing an insight to a decision that group members commonly have to make when filing their tax returns. By including a link to your website at the end of the forum topic, you can still allow someone to follow up with you if he or she wants to use your services. One last point: make sure other group members haven't already posted the resources you share.

TIP 139   Add value

Although there are many legitimate businesses on MySpace that attempt to build relationships with other MySpace users to secure them as customers down the line, there are also many businesses that create spam MySpace pages that don't add any value to users and that link to scam websites. Over the years MySpace has become extremely sensitive to this, and so it's in your best interest to make sure you're following best practices when interacting as a business on MySpace, to avoid being labeled a spammer and having your profile deleted. Even if you don't get penalized, sending spammy messaging to MySpace users or having a spammy profile damages your brand's reputation on the site and elsewhere. Above all, you risk negating the time you've spent building up your brand's exposure on the site and wherever else your brand has a presence.

For the reasons mentioned above, when creating your profile, make sure you focus on adding genuine value to others through the knowledge you have rather than using the MySpace platform solely as a way to push your product or service. This principle applies to every activity you do on MySpace, whether it's blogging, participating in or initiating group discussions, posting bulletins, or leaving profile comments. If you comment on someone's profile, be sure to add something meaningful and personalized for that user, rather than a generic message that's a thinly veiled advertisement.

By providing your MySpace friends with something useful each time you interact with them, you make it more likely that they'll visit your profile or click through to your blog or website from your e-mail signature. If someone voluntarily seeks out your product or service in this way, all while having a good impression of your brand that you've developed on MySpace, you're more likely to convert that visitor to a customer who remains loyal over time. On the other side of the fence, you can avoid spam comments being posted to your own profile by changing your settings so that you have to approve all comments before they're published.

TIP 140 Use MySpace Advertising

Besides establishing a profile presence on MySpace, you can advertise your business via MySpace banner ads. These are served across the MySpace network to a targeted audience that you select, based on demographics such as age, gender, geographical location, interests, and occupation. Anyone can create and run a banner campaign on MySpace; the only requirement is a minimum daily budget of $5 and that the advertiser be based in the United States.

When creating an ad, you can either use the free MySpace template or upload your own ad so long as it's in a standard format accepted by the site. The destination URL of the ad should be determined by what you're trying to achieve—if you're just looking to expand your brand reach, you can send someone to your website or blog URL. In other cases, you may want to use MySpace to advertise a particular event or piece of information on your MySpace profile—in these cases, you'll want the person to click through to your profile page.

MySpace Advertising has two cost models: cost per click (CPC) and cost per thousand impressions (CPM). Cost per click is where you pay a predetermined amount when someone clicks on your ad, while cost per impressions is when you pay a certain amount for every thousand times your ad is shown (for a more detailed explanation of these costing models in the context of Facebook, see Tip 101). Which model you choose depends on whether you're using ads for branding purposes or whether click-through to a destination is the main goal (for the latter a CPC model would be better). Like other advertising models, MySpace ads let you determine your budget (beyond the daily minimum of $5) that you can change at any time and your ad's start and end dates. Defining specific dates for an ad is useful if you're advertising something with a limited time period, such as a sale or special event.

Like any other advertising platform, the critical success factor for MySpace Advertising is marketing your ad to the right demographic. This involves knowing at the outset who your target market is and then testing and honing your ads to be even more effective in compelling viewers to take action. The rest of the tips in this section explain how to do this effectively.

TIP 141 | Create your ad

1. Go to http://advertising.myspace.com or click the "Advertise" link on the footer of any page on MySpace and click the "Get Started Today" button.

2. Write a title and text for your ad using the built-in template generator. The title should be engaging and catchy, and the text should entice your user to a call to action or should provide information about your product if your ad's goal is branding.

3. Upload an image to your ad and select a background color for it. You can also choose from one of three dimensions for the shape of your ad.

4. Decide on a URL for your ad, which is the destination you want to send visitors when they click on your ad. If you're looking to increase your profile page, this should be the destination URL. If you want to drive traffic to your website, enter your site's URL.

5. Decide on your target audience in terms of age, gender, geographic location, etc. You can also choose to market to people based on criteria such as relationship status and the interests and occupations they've listed. For example, you may want to show your real estate ad to someone who has listed property development as his or her occupation.

6. Choose a daily budget (again, a minimum of $5 a day) or a lifetime budget that is the budget for the entire campaign. You can adjust these amounts at any time. Although it's worth starting off with a small budget, try to find a middle ground between cost effectiveness and having a big enough budget so that your ad shows to a critical mass of users.

7. Select your costing model—either CPC or CPM, depending on the nature of your ad (for more information, see Tip 101). For both models you'll be prompted to select a bid amount, which will determine how often your ad is shown relative to other competitors' advertising to the same audience.

8. Select your schedule: either have your ads run indefinitely with no end date or put in fixed start and end dates for your campaign.

9. Click "Continue," where you'll be prompted to sign up for an ad account if you don't already have one, and then add your billing information.

10. Review your details and place your order to have your ads approved by the MySpace editorial team.

TIP 142   Learn from your advertising analytics

Once your ads are running, MySpace gives you several free reports to monitor their performance, which you can access on the "Reports" tab of the "MyAds" interface. You'll be able to see key metrics such as clicks, click-through rate (CTR), impressions, and total ad cost relating to all your ads. Monitoring these statistics helps you make adjustments to your budgets, bids, targeting criteria, and ad content so that they become more effective over time relative to the money you're spending on them. For example, if an ad isn't getting enough impressions, you could try widening the targeting criteria of the people being shown your ad, while if a campaign isn't generating enough click-throughs, you could change the ad copy so it has more of a call to action.

Besides monitoring the statistics for each ad in these reports, you can use MySpace's conversion-tracking functionality to track the behavior of people after they've clicked on your ad. The term *conversion tracking* means monitoring the relationship between the number of people who click on the ad and the number who "convert" into customers or fulfill some other action such as downloading a white paper, signing up for a newsletter, or filling out an inquiry form. Conversion tracking is the most useful way of seeing the actual effectiveness of your ad in terms of compelling users to perform a certain action that benefits your business.

To get started with conversion tracking, go to https://advertise.my space.com/conversionTracking.html or click "Conversion Tracking" in the main navigation menu of the "MyAds" interface. On this page you'll be provided with a snippet of code to paste in the HTML body (i.e., the content between the *<body></body>* tags) of the page on your site that is served once the action takes place, such as a confirmation page after someone has placed an order. Conversion tracking works by using cookies, which are trackers that monitor users' actions from when they click on the ad. If a user completes the specified action and lands on the page on which the code appears, MySpace reads the cookie's stored information and records that a conversion has taken place. Once the code is added in, you can test the conversion by fulfilling a test order yourself. You should then be able to see it recorded in the conversion column of your reports.

TIP 143   Experiment based on stats

From your report statistics, you'll be able to see which ads are performing better than others. There are several different levers you can use to experiment with an ad to improve its reach and effectiveness:

■ **Test ad creative:** If your ads are generating impressions but not click-throughs, consider changing your ad's creative, i.e., its content. This could mean making a stronger call to action, a catchier title, a better graphic, or a more targeted URL. The best way to test your changes is to run similar ads in separate campaigns alongside each other where you change one element each time. Doing this lets you isolate a particular variable to see how it's affecting the ad's overall effectiveness. For example, if you run two identical ads except for a different title, you can isolate the title and see how it affects the click-through rate. If one title works better than the other, you can pause the ad that's not performing as well and run only the most successful one from that point on. To do this in MySpace, create two separate campaigns and give them similar names—e.g., "Brand Test 1" and "Brand Test 2." From here, compare their effectiveness by looking at the report statistics for each campaign.

■ **Lower or raise the budget:** If your ads aren't getting a lot of clicks or impressions, you could try raising your daily or lifetime budget so your ad shows for a longer amount of time each day.

■ **Lower or raise your bid:** If your ads are underperforming, try raising the amount you're paying per click or per thousand impressions. Raising your bid will let you appear above competitors' ads and therefore help increase click-through. In the same way, if your ad has a very high click-through rate, you could try lowering the CPC gradually to make the ad more cost effective.

■ **Broaden your target demographic:** If your ad isn't generating a lot of impressions, you could try broadening the demographic for which your ad is shown. For example, if your ad is targeted to female MySpace users between the ages of twenty and twenty-five, you could try expanding this age group from twenty to thirty-five. Alternatively, if you're happy with your impressions but want to improve your click-through rate, make your ad more targeted by narrowing the age or other targeting criteria.

Meetup

TIP 144   Understand Meetup

Despite being eclipsed in recent years by higher-profile names such as My-Space and Facebook, Meetup remains one of the oldest social networking sites in existence. The biggest difference with Meetup and sites like Facebook is that Meetup's ultimate purpose is to help people organize face-to-face meetings—in other words, the online social networking aspect of it is a means to an end as opposed to its entire reason for existence. By placing the emphasis on "real world" networking, Meetup gives you a better chance of establishing long-lasting, influential relationships with your target market and potential business partners than if you were only to interface with these individuals online. Having said this, the site is still a good conduit for driving traffic to your website and exposing your brand to a highly targeted online audience.

There are three main ways to participate in Meetup:

1. Find existing groups to join in a particular geographic location and subject area (for example, accounting services within San Francisco or within the greater Bay Area).

2. Establish your own group and then invite others to join. For $20 a month, you can host up to three groups of your choice on the site. Through these groups you can organize meetings, oversee RSVPs from members, share event details and calendars, and post photos and other media related to an event. You can also customize your group page in terms of its look and feel so that it remains consistent with your company's branding.

3. Sponsor an existing Meetup group. Provided the subject of the group relates to your business, sponsorship can be an effective way of increasing your brand's exposure on the site without needing to become a group member or establish your own group.

Perhaps most important, the first two options give you the opportunity to interact with other Meetup members on a one-to-one basis. This allows you to make meaningful personal connections within your industry—whether they're potential clients, business partners, or employees.

TIP 145 Search for existing groups

Even if you've joined Meetup.com to start your own group, it's a good idea to spend time browsing or joining existing groups before you create your own. Participating in existing groups will help you start networking on the site before you attempt to build your own member base and can help you identify how to differentiate your group so that you avoid competing for audience share with other groups. In fact, many Meetup members only join existing groups and don't create their own—in doing so, they are still able to network with others in their industry but avoid the time they'd invest in managing their own group.

You can find existing groups on Meetup in several different ways:

- Search by keyword. For example, if you're in the tourism industry in Florida, type in *Florida tourism* to see a results page of related groups.

- Browse through topics such as "Arts and Entertainment" or "Internet and Technology" to see all Meetup groups related to that particular subject.

- Browse through groups in your geographic location, such as within your city or district.

Whichever method you use, you'll be able to read the group page along with its member base, notes, and details before deciding whether or not to join it. Although there is no limit to the number of groups you can join, joining fewer groups rather than many will make for more targeted networking, and you'll be more likely to make meaningful connections that result in real business benefit.

Although you can search and browse existing groups without joining the site, you need to register to join or create a group and interact with its members. When you register, you'll be asked to complete a personal profile that will be publicly viewable by other Meetup members. Your profile is your opportunity to outline your business and expertise for others on the site and to provide a way for members to contact you directly if they want to find out more about the products or services you offer.

Create a new group

Although it's free to join an existing Meetup group, creating a group will cost you $20 a month. For this fee you can create and manage up to three groups of your choice. If you think your group will be active over a long period of time, you can sign up for a discounted six-month subscription that will cost you around $12 a month.

To create a group, you'll first need to join the site and create a personal profile. Once you've done this, log in to your account and click the "Start a Meetup Group" link in the top menu of your account home page. You'll be prompted to fill out information for your group profile, such as a group name, home page headline, group description, and URL. Since you're using Meetup to market your business, keep your group name as close as you can to your business's name to keep your branding consistent. However, you should also try to include some common keywords in your group's profile information that people would enter as search terms to find your group on the site (e.g., *bed and breakfast owners*), because the primary way that people will find your group is through Meetup's internal search tool. If your group features prominently in these search results through the inclusion of relevant keywords, you'll be attracting people to your group page who have been actively searching for a group like yours. This means they're more likely to join your group and attend your offline events, and are also ultimately more likely to be interested in the product or service you're offering.

The Meetup domain also has great visibility on search engines like Google, so use your targeted keywords when selecting your group's URL as well (for example, *http://www.meetup.com/bed-and-breakfast-owners-seattle*). This will make your group page visible on external search engine results as well as the internal Meetup search tool.

Besides helping you appear in related search results, a group profile is how people browsing your group page will decide whether or not to join. So, while including keywords is important, make sure the copy on your page is readable and engaging: first and foremost, your profile should be appealing to your human visitors rather than to search algorithms.

TIP 147 Hold regular meetups

Creating a group on Meetup is a good first step, but it's important to keep it active to build your membership. You can organize and then advertise on Meetup a variety of different activities to increase group activity and drive traffic to your website:

- **Networking events:** This is probably the most obvious reason for a meetup. You could advertise a networking event as a way for people to meet others in their industry where your company is the facilitator. Besides giving you the opportunity to connect with people you can potentially work with, you're giving members an incentive to attend the meetup as a way to form new business partnerships themselves.

- **Seminars:** You could hold a meetup to teach people a specific skill in a workshop environment, such as how to fill out your tax return if you're an accounting software company or how to use a digital camera if you're a photography website. If you hold training sessions, you can use your Meetup account as a place to store resources related to the training such as downloadable presentations, white papers, and exercises. In this way your Meetup page becomes far more than just a notice board—it becomes a useful resource for group members.

- **Sponsorship:** As an alternative to creating your own group, you can offer to pay the monthly site fee in exchange for providing services at the group's meetup. The group you sponsor could be in line with your business's industry so that your product becomes associated with that event. At the meeting you could give out fliers or brochures that talk more about the product or services you offer. For more on sponsorship, see Tip 149.

- **Presentations:** If you have access to someone influential in your industry, you could hold a meetup where your group sponsors the speaker to deliver a presentation to the audience and then post the video or notes from the presentation on your group page afterward. In this way your brand becomes associated with the useful presentation being delivered. You can also ask the speaker to link to your brand as a sponsor from his or her website, which will drive traffic to your site from the speaker's.

TIP 148 Promote your group

The first step in promoting your group internally is to make sure you include relevant keyword phrases that someone would be searching to find your group in search results (for more about how to do this, see Tip 145). Next, promote your Meetup group by including it as part of your online marketing mix consisting of your blog, website, Facebook page, Twitter account, and Flickr album. You can do this in several ways:

- **Link to it:** A simple first step is to provide a link to your Meetup page from your website in a place where you talk about events, such as your "Press" section. You can also include a link to your group on your Facebook page or when you write a blog post or Twitter update about an upcoming event.

- **Install the Meetup Facebook application:** This application is installed on your Facebook profile or page (for more about Facebook pages, see Tip 89) and lets you pull through information such as upcoming dates and RSVP functionality for Meetup events. By installing this app on your Facebook page, you're leveraging your Facebook fans to become members of your Meetup group and to attend your future events.

- **Meetup badges:** These pull through functionality from your Meetup page, such as a list of upcoming meetings or a countdown to your next Meetup, which is then displayed within a widget on your blog or website. You can also set your widget to display any upcoming meetups that are related to your industry or that are in your geographic vicinity. Widgets can be installed on any website and work on most major blogging platforms including Blogger and TypePad.

- **Create promotional materials:** Meetup lets you create marketing materials such as business cards, postcards, T-shirts, and invitations that you can print out and distribute at your events. Since these materials contain the URL of your Meetup group, they are a way of using your offline events to drive traffic back online to your Meetup group page and to encourage attendees to attend future events that you advertise on your group page.

Sponsor a group

Along with joining existing groups or creating your own, you can market your business on Meetup through the site's sponsorship programs. By sponsoring a group, you gain brand exposure on that group page and at the group's offline events. The main advantage of sponsoring a Meetup group is that your brand is automatically exposed to a targeted audience, the members of which are more likely to be interested in your product or service. There are a variety of ways you can sponsor a group, including:

- paying the group's monthly Meetup fee

- providing facilities or a venue for the group to meet in

- catering the event

- providing your product or service at a discounted rate (provided they're related to the subject of the meetup)

You can choose to sponsor more than one group—for example, if you sell fishing equipment, you could sponsor all fishing Meetup groups in the country. To get started with sponsorship, click the "Sponsor Meetup groups" link in the footer of the Meetup home page. You can find groups to sponsor in two main ways:

- **Find your own groups:** Click the "Find meetups" button and begin searching by topic or by location. From here, on the Meetup page you'll see a link that says "Sponsor our Meetup group," which indicates that they're looking for sponsors. Click this button to connect directly with the organizer. This option is best if you have a small budget and are sponsoring fewer than fifty groups.

- **Get Meetup to connect you:** If you're looking to sponsor fifty groups or more and have a budget of at least $5,000, you can get Meetup to help you find related groups. To do this, click the "Get in touch" button, which will let you e-mail Meetup directly. Meetup will not only connect you with potential groups but can also help with the details of the sponsorship, including messaging and finances. If you choose this option, you'll have access to statistics showing you the effectiveness of your sponsorship throughout the campaign.

5

Social Bookmarking

SOCIAL BOOKMARKING has its roots in the Internet browser's ability to bookmark a Web page so that you can refer back to it later. Social bookmarking adds a community aspect, allowing you to store your bookmarks in a remote location and then share them with other people and find bookmarks that others have stored. In addition, some social bookmarking sites like Digg and Reddit operate on a democratic voting system where its users decide which bookmarked content is useful and which isn't. In this way, the site's user base directly affects how much exposure a piece of content gets on the site, which in turn affects how much traffic will be driven to the link's destination.

Besides the obvious benefit of allowing you to share and find useful information with others, social bookmarking has many advantages for businesses looking to market themselves online. As a business owner, you can use social bookmarking tools to network with others in your industry, keep up to date with the latest news and trends, source new business or research opportunities, monitor what your competitors are doing and saying, and track what's being said about your own brand. Social bookmarking can also be an effective medium for promoting your business. For example, if a piece of your content such as an article from your blog or a white paper becomes popular on a social bookmarking site, it is exposed to hundreds of thousands of users. If those users click on the article, they land on your website, where they'll interact with your brand. Depending on how successful you are at retaining those site visitors, social bookmarking thereby becomes another avenue by which to collect new customers who will pay for your product or services.

Delicious

TIP 150 Understand Delicious

First founded in 2003, Delicious was acquired by Yahoo! in 2005 and has since become one of the most popular social bookmarking tools available for discovering and sharing content on the Web. Unlike when you use your browser to bookmark pages, links bookmarked on Delicious are stored remotely so that you can access them from anywhere. Within your user account, links are stored in a tag structure where you assign keyword phrases, known as *tags* (for more on these, see Tip 30), as a way to group content in your account into themes.

Like other social bookmarking tools, Delicious lets you share links with other Delicious users or with the general public. This social aspect of sharing content makes it an extremely useful tool for marketing your business in that you can bookmark links as a way to drive traffic to your blog or website. Success on Delicious is all about having great content. The more interesting your link is, the more it will be shared with other readers, which means more traffic to your site. If a Delicious user with a large network of contacts on the site shares one of your links that he or she finds useful, the chance that your article will be bookmarked and shared goes up. In addition to the initial traffic that a link generates, you'll receive repeat visitors from Delicious users who return to their bookmark page later and click the link to your website or blog again. Besides generating traffic from your own links, sharing useful links that aren't yours helps to build your reputation as a value-added resource, which helps when it comes to posting your own content.

Besides easily being able to share links with one another, Delicious users can search on existing tags that others have created to find interesting content, or they can subscribe to feeds of content about popular tags. Like other social bookmarking sites, if your link becomes popular on Delicious, there's a good chance it will gain traction on other sites too. For example, if your page becomes popular enough, social news aggregators such as popurls (www.popurls.com) may feature it, which creates another way for people to see your link and further increases your content's exposure online.

TIP 151   Create your account

To get started with Delicious, sign up at http://delicious.com by clicking the "Join Now" button at the top right of the page. If you already have a Yahoo! account, you can sign in with that; otherwise, you'll be prompted to create an account. You'll be asked to select a user name, which will form part of the URL of your Delicious account (e.g., if your username is *jacksparrow*, your account URL will be *http://delicious.com/jacksparrow*). By default, your Delicious updates are shared with all your Delicious contacts and on other Yahoo! services. If you want to change this setting, click the link that says "Manage who sees your Updates." You'll be taken to another page where, by unclicking the "Share my Updates" checkbox, your updates will be kept private. The disadvantage of making your account private, of course, is that your bookmarking activities won't be exposed to others, which negates the use of Delicious to promote your brand and business.

Next you'll be given the option to download the Delicious bookmarklet. This is a useful extension that installs itself within your browser and lets you tag content as you're browsing. The bookmarklet consists of two parts: one part lets you add tags to your bookmarking site, and one part takes you to your page on Delicious. When you're on a page that you want to tag, just click the "Bookmark on Delicious" link in your browser's toolbar. From here you'll be asked to input a tag relating to the content (for example, the tag *property prices* for an article about property price trends in California). Note that you can add multiple tags for one piece of content. On the "Tags" tab below, Delicious will show you popular tags that may be related to the article or blog post you're reading. The "Send" tab lets you send the article to other users on Delicious or to your Twitter account or lets you manually enter e-mail addresses of people with whom you want to share the link.

View the tags you've created on your Delicious account by clicking the "My Delicious" link on the toolbar. If you click on a particular tag, you'll see all the articles you've marked within that tag category. The main part of your Delicious account is organized into tabs. "Home" shows you popular bookmarks across the whole Delicious network, while the "Bookmark" tab lets you manage the bookmarks you've created and see other popular and recent bookmarks across the network. The latter ability is useful because you can enter a tag in the search field that will bring up only articles relating to that keyword phrase. "People" lets you see and manage the people within your Delicious network (for more on networking, see Tip 153). Finally, "Tags" lets you manage the tags you've created, as well as the subscriptions you have to popular tags.

TIP 152 | Start bookmarking content

Once you've created your Delicious account, you're ready to start bookmarking content. Even though Delicious is a useful way to drive traffic to your blog or website, it's important to see the site as a place to add value to other Delicious users by providing interesting content rather than as a platform via which to market your business. Enhancing your brand by being a useful, unbiased resource to other Delicious users in a particular subject area is a more effective long-term strategy in achieving success on the site. On a practical level, the majority of content you bookmark on the site shouldn't be your own. A good rule of thumb is to submit one piece of your own content for every ten pieces that aren't your own. Some people prefer to have friends or other Delicious users submit their content instead of doing it themselves and then do it for them in return; if you do this, again be sure the bookmark you're saving is genuinely useful and unique. Since you're using Delicious to benefit your business, you'll want to save bookmarks that are thematically related to your industry.

You can bookmark a link on Delicious in two main ways:

1. Once you've logged in to your Delicious account, click the "Save a new bookmark" link at the right of your page. On the page that follows, paste the link to the article into the text box and click "Next." The page that follows will let you add details about the link you're posting, including a title, notes, associated tags to go with the content, and a "send" field, where you can send your link to other Delicious users, your Twitter account, or specific e-mail addresses. If other Delicious users have already submitted the link you're trying to bookmark, the site will recommend tags for you to use that other people have already associated with it.

2. Install one of the various Delicious bookmarking tools at http://delicious.com/help/tools (for more on these tools, see Tip 155). These tools are installed into your browser so that you can bookmark a page without needing to visit Delicious. When you're on a page that you want to tag, click the "Bookmark on Delicious" link on your browser's toolbar, where you'll be prompted to enter the same information as in point number 1.

TIP 153　Network with other users

After you've created an account and begun to bookmark articles, you should start adding other Delicious users to your network. These could be people you already know, such as your friends or colleagues, or people you don't know but whose content you're interested in within your industry. Adding people to your network is useful for two main reasons: you can view the bookmarks they've created, which is good for finding new content and keeping up to date with trends and news, and you can send your bookmarks to other people in your network, which is useful for spreading the word about your content and driving more traffic to your site.

There are two ways you can add people to your network:

1. When you're on their bookmarks page (provided it's public), you can click the "Add to my network" button from the top right of the page.

2. If you know their user name, type it in the top right of your network page and then click the "Add" button.

You can see all the people that are part of your network and all the tags they've collected by clicking the "My Network" link of the "People" tab. At this point you may want to organize the people you've added into network "bundles." This is a way of grouping similar categories of people; for example, you may want to split your contacts into influential bloggers, customers, and personal friends. To create a network bundle, click the "Settings" link at the top right of your Delicious home page and then click "Edit Network Bundles."

A good way to increase the number of users who are part of your network is to include a network badge on your blog or website. When displayed on your site, the badge displays your Delicious user name, how many links you've bookmarked, and provides a link through which to add you to someone else's network. To include the badge in your site, click the "Settings" link at the top right of your Delicious home page and then click the "network badges" link under the blogging section. You'll be supplied with a snippet of code that you'll need to paste into the code of your blog for it to display on the site.

TIP 154 Write Delicious content

The key to success on Delicious is having as many people exposed to your content as possible so that they click on your link and convert from Delicious users to visitors on your blog or website. How successful your content is in achieving this depends largely on how interesting or useful others on Delicious consider your content. Having content that is unique in some way helps it cut through the noise of other, similar links on Delicious so that more people bookmark your link for future visits and more people pass it on to other Delicious users. So, how can you make sure your content lends itself to this?

The first rule is to provide content that's genuinely useful and value-added, rather than content that's simply trying to advertise your business. For example, if you're an interior designer, an article on the top design trends of 2010 is much more likely to appeal to Delicious users than an article that advertises your interior design services. Besides truly valuable insights, types of content that tend to do well on Delicious include how-to articles, resource lists, and entertaining or funny pieces. Articles presented in a format different from text (such as a video or podcast) also tend to do well. Another key factor in the success of your content on Delicious is writing a catchy title. This is what will separate your content from other links on the same page—a title that is interesting or compelling will encourage more users to click on it and bookmark it, thereby increasing its visibility on the site. For more on encouraging users to bookmark your content, see Tip 155.

It's worth bearing in mind too that the average Delicious user is likely to be fairly tech-savvy, so if your business is tech-oriented your article has a better chance of doing well on the site. If you're not in the tech industry, you could try taking a tech-related angle, such as how technology use is affecting your particular industry. Even if your article has nothing to do with technology, though, if it appeals to a wide enough base of users it's possible for it to reach the front page.

Encourage users to bookmark your content

An article on Delicious needs to be bookmarked several times by Delicious users before its visibility increases on the site. There are several ways you can encourage this:

- **Install "Bookmark on Delicious" buttons on your website:** These buttons make it easy for people to bookmark an article while they're visiting your blog or website. To access the code for these buttons, go to the Tools section of your account (http://delicious.com/help/tools) and then click the "'Bookmark this on Delicious' buttons" link. Delicious will then provide you with the code that needs to be pasted into your website. Once the code is included on your site, a Delicious icon will appear below each blog post that a visitor can click on to bookmark it.

- **Install the Delicious Tagometer badge:** Besides providing an easy link to tag the content, this badge lets your readers see how many others have bookmarked it. Popularity often provides an incentive for others to bookmark your article. To access the code for the badge, go to the Tools section of your account (http://delicious.com/help/tools) and then click the "Tagometer Badge" link. The badge is installed by pasting in code to your blog or website where you want the badge to appear.

- **Tag your article with keywords that are already popular on Delicious:** More people are likely to see your article if you use words they're already using to search for articles. To see popular tags that may apply to your content, click the "Popular" link in the "Tags" tab in your top navigation menu. Alternatively, you can search for tags by entering keywords in the search box at the top right corner of your home page.

- **Create more traffic to your blog or website:** If you e-mail the link to your network of friends, partners, clients, and colleagues or include the article link as a Facebook or Twitter status update, more people are likely to click on Delicious buttons you've installed around your content.

Subscribe to tags

Besides being an effective way to market your own blog or website content, Delicious can help you stay up to date with news and trends in your industry by knowing what popular bloggers, industry leaders, or even competitors are writing about. When you create a bookmark in Delicious, you create a tag for that particular content, which is a keyword phrase that you assign to that bookmark that categorizes it under a particular subject (for more on tags, see Tip 30). The most effective way to stay aware of articles relating to your industry is to subscribe to tags under a particular topic that other people have created. You can set up subscriptions to multiple tags that are related to each other to give you the widest breadth of content relating to your industry. Once the tags are set up, you'll receive a continuous stream of results that are updated automatically.

To set up a subscription to a tag, log in and click "My Subscriptions" under the "Tags" tab on the home page of your Delicious account. Click the "Add a subscription" button, after which a box will appear at the right of the page for you to add the tag you want to subscribe to. For example, if you're a tour guide company in New York, you may want to add tags like *new+york*, *ny*, and *nyc* to see all content posted that relates to those three keywords. Once you've specified these, you'll see all your subscriptions listed under each other in the right column of the page when you're in the tags page. Now, anytime someone bookmarks an article under any of those tags, the article will appear in your subscriptions page. It's a good idea to search on tags before you create subscriptions, so you can see the tags that are commonly in use.

To edit a subscription, hover your mouse over the tag and click the pencil icon to edit it. You can either change the wording of the tag, remove it, or restrict the bookmarks to a specific user, such as a competitor or influential blogger.

Mine Delicious for content ideas

As outlined in Tip 154, the key success factor to achieving visibility on Delicious to drive traffic to your blog or website is to make sure the content is interesting and unique. Interesting content encourages people to click on your link in Delicious and then bookmark the page, which makes for more repeat traffic later on. The best way to start thinking about the type of content that will be popular on Delicious is to see what articles already perform well on the site. There are several ways you can do this:

■ **Browse existing popular content:** A good way to start seeing what kind of content does well on Delicious is to view the most popular articles within a particular tag. To start this process, go to http://delicious.com/popular/ and type in a tag at the end to see the most popular articles in this section. For example, typing in *NYC* will bring up the most popular articles bookmarked under that topic. This search reveals that the most bookmarked article in this topic is a page that contains an aerial virtual tour of New York. If you're a New York City tour company, you may try creating similar content, such as an interactive map or photo gallery of the city.

■ **Subscribe to tags:** This is a good way of staying up to date with what's being written about in your industry (for more on how to subscribe to tags, see Tip 156). Doing this allows you to receive a continuous stream of content on a particular topic so that you can see what type of content does well or has already been written about. While you're on your tag pages, also look at the right of the page to browse through related tags; these may give you further examples of popular articles in a particular subject area.

■ **Look at people's top tags:** Another way to find popular articles is to browse the top tags of other Delicious users, such as influential bloggers, clients, or competitors in your space. Once you're on someone's profile page, look at the tag column on the right side of the page to see what his or her most popular tags are in terms of how many articles have been bookmarked under each one.

TIP 158 Be an influential user

- **Don't just push your own content:** The majority of the content you bookmark on Delicious should be content other than your own. By doing this you build your reputation as a Delicious user who adds value within your industry rather than using the site simply as a way to promote your own business.

- **Be consistent:** Get into the habit of spending ten or twenty minutes a day bookmarking articles that you find useful and that relate to your industry. Regular bookmarking will increase your visibility on the site so that others in your industry become more familiar with you. You'll also build your reputation as someone who adds value to the site, and this branding will carry across when you bookmark your own articles.

- **Stay focused:** If you're creating a Delicious account to market your own blog, keep the articles that you bookmark related to your industry so that your page maintains a consistent theme in line with your business. By default a bookmark is set to be public. If you want to bookmark content related to your personal interests, consider making those bookmarks private. To do this, check the "Mark as Private" box when you're filling in the tag and description for a personal bookmark. Doing this will add a gray lock next to the link on your page, which means that only you can see it. You can also click the "Edit" button underneath a bookmark you've already created and check the box from there.

- **Build up your network:** Spend time each day building up your network by reading what other users have written and then adding them as users to your network. If you commit a certain amount of time to this each day and add a few people, the task will become less overwhelming over time.

- **Blog regularly:** Writing content for your blog on a regular basis means you'll have more opportunities to include links to your content on Delicious, which will drive up the collective amount of traffic you're driving to your blog.

Digg

TIP 159 Understand Digg

Like most social bookmarking sites, Digg lets people share useful content with other people. Digg's key differentiator, however, is that it allows users to vote for or against a particular link that's been submitted, which in turn affects how many people see that content. When a user submits (or "Diggs") an article on the site, it appears on the "Upcoming Stories" page, where other users can view it and "Digg" it (i.e., vote for it) if they find it interesting or useful. Users who think the article isn't useful can "bury" it to vote against it. The more Diggs an article gets, the more visibility it will have on the site: if it receives enough positive votes, it will appear on the front page of the site or on the front page of a particular category. Digg is therefore a democratic voting system, where users collectively decide which content should get more visibility and which should get less. As a marketer, a blog post of yours that is deemed by others to add value will translate into significant traffic from Digg to your blog or website.

Besides being a traffic driver, Digg can help expose your brand to more people. Many Digg users are blog owners who use the site as a resource for new blog content. What this means is that if a blogger sees your article on Digg and bases one of his or her blog posts on it (and links back to your site), further traffic will be driven your site from that person's blog. In this way an interesting article on Digg has the potential to become "viral"— spread among increasing numbers of people over time.

Besides driving traffic to your own Web properties, Digg is an excellent way of networking with influential bloggers and other leading voices in your industry. It's also a good way of staying up to date with the conversations that are taking place in your industry between suppliers, partners, customers, or competitors. From these conversations you can tailor your business to provide services or products that meet the needs you've identified.

TIP 160   Customize your profile

The Digg community is about making personal recommendations for the benefit of others, so you should aim to build your reputation as someone who is on the site to add value (presumably your business has the same goal) rather than someone who's simply looking to drive traffic to his or her own blog or website. For this reason, your Digg profile should be personal rather than business-oriented, although you can add links to your website or blog from within it.

To begin editing your profile, click the "Profile" link in the top right of the Digg home page once you've logged in. Start by uploading an avatar to display on your profile by clicking the "Change Icon" link at the right of the page. While this can be any image and doesn't necessarily have to be a photo of you, steer clear of uploading your corporate logo for the reasons mentioned above. Next, fill out information about yourself by clicking the "Add Bio & Links" link in the "About" section on the right of the page. In addition to your name, geographic location, and a blurb about yourself, you can add links to your other online presences such as your website, corporate blog, and Twitter and Facebook accounts. Including these links means that people reading your profile are given an additional opportunity to engage with your brand or business elsewhere.

The rest of your profile section contains information about your activity on the site, including articles that you Digg or mark as a favorite and stats relating to your account, such as the number of friends you have, how many posts you've bookmarked, and how many times your profile has been viewed. The more active you are, the better this section will look, so set aside some time each day to bookmark articles or network with other Digg users. The "Settings" tab lets you choose which information others can see on your profile. Although you may not want to display everything, bear in mind that the more comprehensive your profile is, the more trust you'll build. Also on the Settings tab, choose "Customize topics" at the right of the page to filter your Digg articles to your particular industry.

TIP 161 Install the Digg toolbar

Once you've filled out your personal profile, you're ready to start Digging articles. The first way to do this is by submitting links from within the Digg site itself. To do this, click the "Submit New" link at the top right of the page once you've logged in. From here you'll be prompted to paste in the link to the article and to select whether it's a news article, a video, or an image. Once you've submitted it, Digg checks whether the article has already been submitted. If it has, it gives you the option to Digg it again, and if not, you'll be taken to the next screen, where you can organize the information in the submission and then submit it.

While it's easy enough to go on Digg and submit a story from there, it's even handier if you can submit an article directly from the browser while you're reading it, without having to navigate away from it. Many blogs and news websites have a Digg button installed under the article, which allows you to simply click on it to submit it, but many more don't. In instances where a site doesn't have Digg buttons installed, the easiest way to submit the article is to install the DiggBar. Besides letting you add content while you're on the page, the DiggBar allows you to read comments, find related comments, and share or e-mail the article or blog post with your contacts, other Digg users, or your Twitter account.

To install the Digg toolbar, click the "Resources" link in the footer of the Digg home page, and then click the "DiggBar" link under the Add-ons section of the Resources page. Or, you can just type http://about.digg.com/diggbar into your browser. On this page, you'll be prompted to click and drag the button into your bookmarks toolbar. Then, when you're on a page in your browser that you want to Digg, click the DiggBar. This loads DiggBar into the browser and provides a shortened version of the page's URL. From here you can access the toolbar's functionality such as Digging the article, seeing how many times it's already been Dugg, adding a comment, burying it, finding related news, or sending it via e-mail or to your Facebook or Twitter account. Note that the DiggBar will be accessible to you only when you're logged in.

Submit stories strategically

Whether you're Digging your own stories or someone else's (you shouldn't submit too many of your own—see Tip 167 for more on this), there are certain principles to bear in mind when submitting content:

- **Be discerning:** Any story that you Digg should add value to your friends or to the Digg community in some way, whether it's because the content is topical, unique, or a valuable resource. Although it's a good idea to be active on the site, when in doubt, submit fewer articles that you think are useful rather than too many that are of average or little value to your readers. If you're not sure about the types of articles likely to be popular among Digg users, look at the "Popular" tab, which lists the stories of the moment that have the most Diggs over the last hour, day, month, and year. When writing your own content with the hopes that it will be on Digg (or other social bookmarking sites), this can be a good way of seeing what is likely to be popular. In general, certain content types tend to be more viral in nature, such as resource lists or humorous posts. For more advice on writing viral blog content, see Tip 18.

- **Stick to a theme:** Preserve your company's personal branding by submitting Diggs on one topic only. For example, if you work in real estate, submit stories that relate to property in some way to build your reputation as a specialist in that area.

- **Submit to the right category:** If you submit a story to the wrong category, your article won't be displayed to the right target audience, so your click-through rate will be lower. You also risk irritating regular readers of that section, which can damage your Digg reputation. Try whenever possible to submit your story to the most specific category that you can (for example "Hardware" within the "Technology" category) rather than the "General" category: since the "General" category has the most articles submitted to it, your window of time during which to build up a significant volume of Diggs will be smaller.

- **Watch the time:** Submit articles when most Digg users are likely to be online, such as midmorning in U.S. Eastern standard time. This gives your article the largest audience possible, rather than submitting it when the United States or Europe is asleep.

TIP 163 Write a good title and description

When you submit a story to Digg, you're prompted to add a title and description to it to tell Digg readers more about its contents. Since your story will appear alongside other links on Digg, your title and description are the primary way of convincing readers to click through and read your article rather than someone else's.

When you import a story into Digg, the title becomes the default title of the blog post or article, which you can then edit. In many cases you can improve on an existing title so that it is more compelling and therefore encourages more people to click through and read the full text. For example, let's say you're bookmarking an article from the BBC about making the Internet more multilingual, and the title is "An Internet That Speaks to You." While this title may be adequate, a slightly modified version that provides more explanation, such as "An Internet That Speaks to You: Making the Net More Multilingual," can help to encourage more people to click on the article since they'll have a better idea of what it's about. Note that the title can be a maximum of sixty words.

Next, think about your description. The key here is to find the balance between saying enough about the article to generate interest and not revealing its entire contents. As a starting point, you could take the beginning paragraph of the article and elaborate on it but then not reveal the end of the article. By doing this, you're creating a "hook" that, together with the title, compels your readers to click through on it. If the writer of the article is well known, be sure to mention the author in the description as a way of adding to its credibility. Note that the description can be a maximum of 350 words.

Finally, Digg will let you append a photograph to your submission, which also encourages click-through. By default, Digg uses an image off the same page of the article, so if you're Digging your own blog post or article, this is a good reason to include an image in your blog post (for how to do this, see Tip 13).

TIP 164 Make it easy to Digg your content

Even if you become one of the highest-profile users on Digg, you should put effort into marketing the content you're submitting so that you encourage others to Digg it as a way of increasing its visibility. In previous years Digg had a "Shout" function that allowed you to submit a story and then send a "shout" about it. This was similar to a group e-mail, where you could tell two or more of your Digg contacts about the article and encourage them to Digg it. However, this function became a primary target by spammers, and it was removed from the site in May 2009. What this means now is that marketing a story to increase the number of Diggs needs to be done largely off-site by leveraging your existing network of friends, colleagues, clients, partners, and blog readers.

An easy way to encourage your blog readers to Digg your content is by including a Digg button alongside content on your blog or website. Installing this button allows visitors to click a button alongside content that automatically Diggs it—whether it's an article, a video, or an image. To add Digg buttons to your articles or blog posts, click the "Resources" link in the footer of the Digg home page. When you're on the Resources page, click the "Digg Button" link in the left menu under the "Publisher Tools" section. Alternatively, you can you can just paste http://about.digg.com/button into your browser. On the Digg Button page, you'll be given options for the style of button you'd like and a corresponding snippet of JavaScript to paste into the pages on which you want the Digg button to appear. Once it's installed, the widget can also show how many times the story has been Dugg by other users. If this number is high, it can encourage new readers to submit the story if they see that it's already popular.

Another way to encourage Diggs from your site is to include a widget that displays bookmarked articles from your Digg account. You can choose which stories you show in the widget, such as just your own stories, or stories that your Digg contacts have bookmarked, or the most popular stories on a particular topic. In addition to driving up the number of Diggs on an article, displaying your Digg bookmarks on your site enhances your visitors' experience by giving them more information related to the content they're reading. Access the code for the widget at the same URL provided earlier and then click the "Add a Digg Widget to your site" link.

TIP 165 Network with other Digg users

Besides being a good source of information for your industry, Digg is an excellent networking tool for your business. Making contact with other Digg users lets you build relationships with other people in your industry who may become potential partners or customers down the line. At the very least, networking on Digg gives you an opportunity to build your brand's reputation by exposing it to a wider group of people in a topic that you are an expert in.

Like other social networking sites such as Facebook or Twitter, Digg lets you add friends to your profile. Once people are added as friends, you'll be able to share content with them or keep track of upcoming stories they've Dugg. When you're browsing Digg, a green star alongside a story means that one or more of your friends have already Dugg it.

The first step in building friends on Digg is to be active on the site, both by submitting articles and by commenting on articles that others have submitted. Being active makes your profile more visible to others on your site, since your name (which links to your profile page) will appear alongside any activity you do on the site. As more people click on your user name and visit your profile page, you'll have more people requesting to be added as your friends on the site, and so your network will grow. For more on the advantages of being active on Digg, see Tip 166.

To proactively add Digg users as your friends, click the "Add Friends" link at the top right of your profile page once you're logged in. Digg pulls in contacts from your existing address books (such as from Gmail or Yahoo! Mail) who are already on Digg and lets you add them as friends. You can also search for existing Digg users by entering their user name, or you can invite people who aren't on Digg to be your friends by entering in their e-mail addresses manually.

In general you should try to add as friends other Digg users who are active on the site. They're likely to be of the most value to you because they'll be a constant source of new information and they'll Digg your stories when you submit them. It's worthwhile to have fewer active friends on Digg than a lot of inactive ones: fewer friends make it easier to monitor activity on the site and keep track of what's being spoken about in a particular topic.

TIP 166 Be active

Digg rewards people who share interesting and useful content with other users of the site on a regular basis. Many people don't see the site in this light and instead become Digg members just so they can submit their own blog post or story and then get their friends to Digg it. While this may get you some short-term exposure for your article, using the site solely to market your own blog or article won't build your reputation on the site to yield you long-term value. Being active on Digg allows you to raise your exposure in a particular industry and to your business's target market. As this happens, you'll be seen as a useful resource, which will allow you to build up your friends on the site. As you gain more influence, any articles that you do bookmark will be noticed by more people, which means you'll get more people clicking through your own articles that you submit. In addition, more people will look at your profile page and see previous bookmarks you've created. Also, the more people who view your profile page, the more people will click on the links within it to your blog and website.

Being active on Digg doesn't mean participating in the Digg community all day every day. What it does mean, though, is that you should commit a block of time each week for checking top and upcoming stories, submitting your own stories, and Digging stories that others in your industry have submitted. You should also spend time networking on the site, whether this means sharing stories with other Digg users, commenting on existing submissions, or finding a few new friends each week. Typically, it's easiest to network with someone once you've just Dugg their story, as they'll be more likely to add you as a friend in return for that action. On the other hand, Digg users will often unfriend people who are idle on the site—so being active is a way of preserving any connections you make. You can't build a large network on Digg instantly, but with a small commitment of time on a regular basis you'll gain influence and visibility over the long term.

TIP 167 | Be discerning

Building a favorable reputation on Digg means being discerning about the stories you submit. Whether you're submitting your own stories or someone else's, be sure that whatever you Digg is likely to be useful, interesting, or unique to other Digg users. Note that the Digg community doesn't like users submitting their own stories too frequently, since they want their site to be primarily a resource rather than a marketing medium. When you first sign up, therefore, don't Digg your own stories until you've submitted a significant amount of other content, you've built up a community of friends, and your stories are regularly being Dugg by other people.

When you've reached this point and are ready to Digg your own blog posts or articles, you should still be submitting external content so that the balance of stories you Digg aren't your own. A good ratio may be to Digg one story of your own for every ten or fifteen that aren't your own. This way you tip the balance to adding value to other Digg users first and publicizing your brand second. When you're submitting other content, keep it on topic to your industry so that you build your reputation as an expert in a particular area. When it comes to your own content, submit only the most useful of your blog posts so that you give them the most chance of being Dugg by other users.

Many Digg users feel that for your blog post or article to have a chance of making it to the first page of the site you shouldn't be the first to submit it. If you want to follow this principle, ask a friend or colleague to submit your article first and then Digg it afterward. From there, you can begin marketing it off the site by including Digg widgets on your site (see Tip 164 for more on this) and publicizing the URL in your Twitter or Facebook feed.

TIP 168   Use Digg advertising

The most recent addition to Digg is the ability for advertisers to promote their content on the Digg home page. As opposed to traditional banner advertising, Digg ads are run on a cost-per-click basis (for more on this structure in the context of Facebook, see Tip 104) and are in the form of sponsored articles that appear online with regular, unpaid Digg content. Although Digg ads are similar to regular content in terms of format, with a title, description, and thumbnail image, ads are clearly marked as sponsored. An ad could be linked to the same type of content you may see in a regular Digg story, such as news articles, video trailers, or product reviews, though it will obviously be content that is related closely to the advertiser's business. If you're marketing a product or a brand, Digg ads are a good way to get your message in front of tech-savvy individuals within a certain target market, since you can set your ad to appear within a certain subject category only.

As with regular Digg content, users can vote for (or "Digg") ads that they like and vote against (or "bury") ads that they don't like. In this way, users play an active role in ensuring that only relevant and useful ads are shown to them, rather than ones they feel don't add value. Implementing this voting system on ads gives you as an advertiser an instant way of seeing which of your ads are popular among users and which aren't. Once you know which ones are appealing, you can make modifications to your ads so that future creatives are more effective in soliciting a call to action from your audience. To make this voting structure even more effective, advertisers also have a monetary incentive to make their ads better: the more an ad is Dugg by users, the less the advertiser will be required to pay per click. Conversely, the more an ad is buried, the higher the cost per click will become, until the advertiser will eventually be priced out altogether.

Signing up for Digg ads is not currently self-service; to enroll and start your campaign, you have to first contact Digg's ad sales team. To do this, click the "Advertise" link in the footer of the Digg home page. On the "Advertise on Digg" page, click the link in the sentence that says, "Get your campaign started by contacting us." Alternatively, you can also reach the contact form page by pasting http://about.digg.com/ads/contact into your browser.

StumbleUpon

TIP 169 Understand StumbleUpon

StumbleUpon is a personalized social bookmarking tool that delivers pages to you based on your own interests as well as how popular that content is among other StumbleUpon users. StumbleUpon puts an emphasis on a personalized Web-browsing experience: as you use it over time, it learns what your preferences are and matches you up more closely with pages it thinks you would like. A key advantage to using StumbleUpon as opposed to a search engine to find sites is that you don't have to sift through vast amounts of information. On the flip side, you're not given as wide a choice of sites as you would on a search engine results page.

To begin using the tool, sign up for an account at www.stumbleupon .com, select topic categories you're interested in (for example "tech gadgets" and "computer hardware"), and download the StumbleUpon toolbar that's installed in your browser (you need a Mozilla-based browser to do this). From here you can click the thumbs-up or thumbs-down buttons on the toolbar to vote for or against websites as you browse. Clicking the "Stumble!" button takes you to the popular Web pages that others have voted for within the category preferences you've selected. If you have a website or blog, having a page from either that's popular on StumbleUpon can be an excellent source of traffic that is also *qualified*, since the people clicking through to your site have specified that they're interested in your content. Although StumbleUpon tends to deliver lower overall traffic than if your page reaches the first page of other social bookmarking sites like Digg or Delicious, the traffic is steadier and more consistent, which over time makes it an equally effective way of increasing your site's exposure. The social networking part of StumbleUpon is also a useful way of matching you up with people of similar interests, which can be a good way of connecting with others in your industry.

To begin receiving traffic from StumbleUpon to your site, you need to have at least one of your pages submitted. You can either have someone else do this for you or do it yourself (though don't do this too often) by selecting the thumbs-up button on the toolbar when one of your site pages is loaded into your browser.

TIP 170 Connect directly with other users

Besides finding new content on a particular subject, StumbleUpon contains an active social community that provides an excellent way of making contact with other people in your industry. There are two ways you can connect directly with someone on StumbleUpon:

1. Friends. In this context friends are considered to be people you know directly; StumbleUpon searches your existing Web-based e-mail accounts like Gmail and Yahoo! Mail to find contacts of yours that are already on the site. To start adding friends, click the "Stumble" menu item from the home page of your StumbleUpon account and then click the "Find Friends" button to the right of the page. You'll then be prompted to add in your e-mail address and password, after which StumbleUpon will find friends of yours who are existing members. Once you're friends with someone, you can share content directly with each other and can see other friends' reviews. Friends' content will be shared with you only when it matches your interests.

2. Subscribers. Subscribers are "stumblers" you may not personally know but whose content you're interested in. For example, you could subscribe to an influential blogger in your industry who will let you keep track of his or her favorites and stumbles in the "Recent Activity" section of your account. Subscribing to people can be useful for keeping track of news and trends in your industry, as well as finding inspiration for creating new blog content. In turn, someone who likes your content can subscribe to you. If you subscribe to someone and that person subscribes to you (known as *mutual subscribers*), you can choose to Direct Share, which allows you to share sites with each other from your toolbar. In this way you both gain the benefit of new content that you're both likely to be interested in. The best way to build subscribers to your account is to stumble often. By being active on the site, you increase your chances of being noticed, and you're seen to add value in terms of providing new and useful content to other StumbleUpon users.

Find new stumblers

The main advantages of subscribing to other users on StumbleUpon are to interface with others in your industry and to be exposed to new content you're interested in. The best way to connect with someone you don't personally know is to subscribe to the person. There are several different ways to find new subscribers:

- **Browse profiles:** Click the "Visitors" link in the top right navigation menu of your home page and then click on the "Meet a stumbler" button on the "Stumblers" tab. From here you can view that person's profile and decide whether you want to subscribe to him or her. If you do, click the green "Subscribe" button to the right of the person's page. To find more stumblers, click the link underneath that button that says "Meet another stumbler."

- **Read reviews:** StumbleUpon lets users write reviews about sites they like, which you can view by clicking the "Info" button on the toolbar when you're on a site you like. If you click this link, you can read the reviews, navigate to users' profile pages, and then subscribe to them. Writing reviews of sites is therefore a good way of increasing your exposure and in turn your subscriber base. Note that a site has to exist in the StumbleUpon directory for it to have a review page.

- **Browse your favorite topics:** When you create your StumbleUpon account, you'll be asked to select topics that interest you, which are then added as tags to your account. To see which users are interested in the same tags, click the "tags" menu item from the "Favorites" tab. From here, select one of your tags from the dropdown menu; on the page that follows, click the link that says "See more pages liked by other stumblers." From here you can click on each user name to subscribe to that user from his or her profile page.

- **Join groups:** Joining a group on a particular subject is a good way to identify subscribers with common interests. For example, if you're a copywriter, you may join the group "Writer/Writers," where you can discuss writing as a subject and connect with fellow stumblers who are interested in the same subject. To browse groups, click the "Groups" link under the "Community" section in the footer of the home page and then click the category that relates most to your website, such as "Media."

Make your page "stumble-worthy"

To drive traffic to your site from StumbleUpon, you need to make sure the content on the page you're submitting will appeal to stumblers who will view it. In general, content that does well on sites like Digg and Delicious tends to be news related, while StumbleUpon sees more success with content that isn't necessarily about current affairs but is unusual or unique in a particular subject area. Successful content on StumbleUpon also tends to contain a variety of media, such as videos, pictures, or other images, within the page. StumbleUpon content that does well is also largely noncommercial, so steer clear of any blog posts or articles that contain a heavy promotion of your business or even that contain a lot of on-page advertising. Instead, focus on providing content that is genuinely useful to StumbleUpon users while containing an original angle.

Site design also has a lot to do with how stumblers will favor your content. A stumbler behaves differently from a regular blog reader or someone who has searched for your company name on a search engine and landed on your website. There's a good chance that StumbleUpon users who have landed on your page have no idea who you are and have no previous exposure to your brand. Bearing this in mind, make sure that content you submit to the site is clear and unambiguous and doesn't require context to be understood. Design also matters: the page should be uncluttered, and the most interesting and important content (such as a catchy title and intro paragraph) should be above the fold. Overall, readers landing on your page should not have to struggle to learn what the page is about.

The best way to find out what content performs well on StumbleUpon in your specific industry is to look at content that has already worked on the site. Find pages that have a lot of positive votes within your subject area. What did stumblers like about this page's content? Was it a unique idea, or was it that the article was written in a unique way? If you can create content that emulates whatever was popular, you're on your way to building content that has traction with a large number of StumbleUpon users.

Increase your content's popularity

Although it's acceptable to add and vote for your own content on Stumble-Upon, you should keep moderation in mind. Strive for a ratio that favors submissions from external sources so you build a reputation of providing useful content first and marketing your own blog or website second. There are several things you can do to increase the popularity of your content:

- **Submit your content:** In this first step, make sure your page contains something that is unique or interesting in some way. For more tips on how to make your content "stumble-worthy," see Tip 172.

- **Ensure that your content is submitted within the right category:** Your blog post or article should be related thematically to its category to ensure that the right target market sees it and is likely to be interested in it.

- **Use multiple tags:** By categorizing your page in several areas, you broaden the exposure of the article to more people on the site. If you do use multiple tags, make sure each one is related to the content of the post or article.

- **Send the page to your friends or mutual subscribers:** Once you've submitted your page to StumbleUpon, ask your friends, partners, and other business contacts to vote for it. You can also share the link with mutual subscribers on the site. As with submitting content to the site, make sure you don't share your own content with mutual subscribers too often.

- **Give positive ratings to sites that link to your page:** StumbleUpon rewards people who are active on the site. If you take the time to rate and review websites other than your own, those site owners will be more likely to give a thumbs up to your own pages when you submit them.

- **Build up your subscriber base:** The more subscribers you have, the more people will see your new Web pages, which will in turn increase the number of thumbs up you get and the amount of traffic you generate to those pages.

TIP 174 Retain your StumbleUpon traffic

As explained in Tip 172, StumbleUpon visitors are different from regular visitors to your website in that there's a good chance they won't have had any previous exposure to your brand when they land on your site. As opposed to people who searched for you on Google, or who found your blog by reading a product on your site, people who arrive at your site from StumbleUpon are less invested in your content and the potential that your business has to offer. This means there's a greater chance that they'll leave as soon as they've arrived if what they see doesn't immediately capture their attention. Any page you submit to StumbleUpon should therefore be as compelling as possible to entice a visitor to stay. There are several ways to do this:

- **Make the page interesting throughout:** Even if you have a catchy title and opening paragraph, the page has to make the person want to read on beyond just scanning the two first sentences. An ideal page on Stumble-Upon has a compelling opening paragraph that encourages someone to read further and stay on the site longer.

- **Create a call to action:** If someone does make it to the end of your blog post or article, is there a call to action to engage further on the site? You could provide links to related blog posts, ask visitors to give feedback on your content, or point them to content elsewhere on the site that they may be interested in.

- **Make it easy to subscribe:** Make sure you have an e-mail subscription form and an RSS subscription button above the fold, so that anyone who is interested in your content can easily receive more of it. Even if they leave after clicking the button, you'll have converted onetime visitors into subscribers who are likely to visit your blog or site again.

- **Make your contact details visible:** Make sure your contact details are clearly visible on the page to make it easy for someone to e-mail you or find out more about the product or services you offer. Make sure too that your navigation items are clear and easy to understand to enable easy browsing throughout your site.

TIP 175   Submit other useful content

Although it's acceptable to submit your own content on StumbleUpon, you shouldn't do this for the majority of your stumbles. However, even submitting content that's not yours can affect your reputation positively or negatively on the site. Consequently, it's wise to follow these submission guidelines:

- **Stay away from spam:** Always submit content that is genuinely useful. Stay away from pages that push a product or service too hard or that contain too much advertising.

- **Be original:** Submit articles and blog posts that cut through the noise in some way. Finding content that is truly unique and original may take an investment of time to find, but it's worth it because this type of page is likely to be more successful on the site. It's also worth taking the time to stumble upon articles within your preferred category so you can see which content not to repeat that's already been submitted previously.

- **Stick to what you know:** The more invested or interested you are in a topic, the more likely it is that you'll submit interesting content that will perform well on the site. This is because you know more about the subject, and so you're more likely to know what others will be interested in. Also, by staying focused, you build up your StumbleUpon "brand" in a certain category, which relates to your business and allows you to become known as an expert in a particular topic.

- **Stumble often:** The more active you are on the site, the more useful you'll become to others as a fellow stumbler and the more subscriptions you'll gain. Then, when the time does come to submit your own stuff, people will be more willing to view your content. Stumbling often also means that you can submit your own content more often. For example, if you're maintaining a ten-to-one ratio of other sites versus your own, and you're submitting eleven articles every day, you'll be able to submit your own content once a day.

- **Tag properly:** When you submit content, make sure you put it in the correct category. Also, use more than one tag—this will get the submission in front of more people, which helps you build your reputation as an active user more quickly. Any tags that you assign to content should always be related to the subject of the Web page, blog post, or article.

TIP 176 Pay for sponsored stumbles

An alternative to submitting your own content to StumbleUpon is to pay for stumbles to be delivered to a specified target audience. Sponsored stumbles are similar to normal stumbles, although the page will be clearly marked that the advertiser has paid for it. The payment model is based on cost per visitor, with a minimum of 5 cents per visitor and a maximum of two thousand visitors a day. Set up your campaign as follows:

1. Click on the "StumbleUpon Ads" link under the "Tool and Services" section of the footer.

2. Click on the "Create a campaign now" button.

3. Select a URL to which you want to send visitors. Just as you would do when submitting a normal StumbleUpon page, think about useful and informative content to which to send your visitors, rather than a heavily advertised page that markets your product or service. Pages that have other media such as videos or photos also work well here.

4. Select the interest groups you want to target. This will determine the audience who will see your listing. Make sure the content of your URL is closely matched to the groups you select here. Under each category you'll see the number of users who are subscribed, which will give you an idea of the type of visitor numbers you can expect.

5. On the right side of the page, choose how many visitors you want to see your page, which will determine the amount you spend. Start with a lower number initially while you test. You can also decide on the maximum expenditure per day—after this limit is reached, you'll get no more traffic for that day.

6. Click the "Advanced Options" link to choose a geographic location, gender, and age group that you want to target.

7. Enter an e-mail and password to create an administrator account. When this is done, click the "Create Campaign Now" button.

8. On the next page you'll process payment using prepaid PayPal with a minimum starting amount of $25. You'll be e-mailed when you run out of funds, and you can top up by logging in to your account.

9. Once you've added funds, your ad will be submitted for editorial review and should start showing within a day.

TIP 177 Track and improve your sponsored stumbles

Once your sponsored pages have been approved, your pages will start appearing to other StumbleUpon users within the category you select for your content. StumbleUpon gives you a useful reporting interface that you can use to view several key statistics about your pages:

- **Total visitors:** This shows you how many visitors arrived at your site from the link and how much of your budget you're spending as a result. You can use the number of total visitors to work out how successful different pages are that you've submitted in the sponsored program.

- **Thumbs up/thumbs down:** This shows you an aggregate of StumbleUpon users who liked your pages and those who didn't. This is a fantastic way to connect directly with your target market to see which links work better than others. Based on this feedback, you can change the links you submit to be more in line with the kind of content stumblers are voting for.

- **Comments:** This shows you the comments that users wrote about your page, which is another great form of direct feedback about the content you're submitting. You can use this as a direct insight into which pages are working and which ones aren't and then make changes accordingly.

Once you've analyzed these key stats, you can do testing to make your campaign even more effective in delivering quality traffic to your site. The key idea here is to isolate variables to see which are more effective in terms of click-through. For example, you could create multiple campaigns using the same URLs or different URLs sent to the same audience targeted to different audiences. You could also send the same URL to different categories. Note that whichever category you select for your content, it should always be related to the content you're submitting. For example, if you're a photography company and your content is a blog post that compares digital photo editing software, you could create two separate campaigns to submit the link to both the photography and multimedia categories. From here you can compare categories to see which one is more effective in delivering visitors to your site.

Google Reader

TIP 178 Understand Google Reader

Although Google Reader was initially a basic RSS feeder that allowed you to subscribe to news feeds (for more on RSS, see Tip 11), Google has in recent years added social functionality so that it has essentially become a social bookmarking tool as well. In addition to allowing you to subscribe to your own feeds, Google Reader lets you subscribe to other people's feeds so you can see what they're reading too. You can share different parts of your feed with different people by creating a custom friends list, and when you share an article you can append it with a comment or indicate that you think it's useful by "liking" it. These two actions let you add value and insight for people who are following what you're reading. Google also lets you choose how private you want your feed to be: if you make it public, it will be available for others to access from your Google user profile page via the "What I'm Reading" link. With Google Reader's ability to connect and share information with others in these ways, the tool is valuable for keeping up to date with others in your industry and with what's said about your company, as well as to network with others in your industry, including bloggers, partners, and prospective customers.

To access Google Reader, go to www.google.com/reader and sign in with your Google account (if you don't already have one, you'll be prompted to create one). Once you've logged in, you can begin setting up your feeds. Click the "Add a subscription" button at the top left of the screen and search for feeds that interest you. Once the feed has been added, you can use labeling tools to organize them into subject categories to make them easier to read and sort through on a regular basis. For example, you could keep all feeds relating to your business and industry separate from personal feeds you've created.

Once your feeds are set up, you can share articles from them with others. To do this, click the "Share" button under an article you want your followers to see. Note that anything you share will be viewable in your public feed URL. To get even more exposure to it, you can link your feed URL from your Google profile as well. If you don't have one already, set one up by going to www.google.com/profiles.

Subscribe to other feeds and people

Google Reader lets you follow the feeds of others as well as your own by subscribing to their public feeds. Feed subscriptions are a useful way of keeping track of news and conversations in your industry and identifying new trends in your particular space. You can also use it as a source of regular content from which to write new blog posts if you have a business blog. The main difference between social bookmarking tools like Google Reader and social networking tools like Facebook and Twitter is that with social bookmarking tools, you're sharing resources rather than personal updates.

Subscribing to feeds on Google Reader used to be a difficult task, since you could subscribe only to people who were already in your friends list or whose shared feed URL you knew. With the recent addition of a search function, however, you can now find feeds that you want to subscribe to by searching on people, topics, or locations. This means you don't need to be personally connected with someone or know the person's feed URL to subscribe, which means you can follow people like influential industry bloggers rather than just your close business contacts or friends.

To begin searching for feeds, log in to your Google Reader account and click the "Browse for stuff" link on the left menu of the home page. From here Google gives you several ways to find a feed: you can search by general topic or by a person's name or geographic location. For example, if you own a landscape gardening business, you can enter the keyword *gardening* in the top search field to find feeds related to your industry. Or, if you know the name of a top gardening blogger, enter that in the second people search field below it. In the feeds that are returned, click "Subscribe" below the feeds you're interested in following. All feeds that you subscribe to in this way will appear in a list on your account.

TIP 180 Select those to share items with

Like most social bookmarking tools, Google Reader lets you share articles from your subscribed feeds with people you choose. To do this, log in to your account and click the "Share" button underneath the particular article you want to share. By default, these articles will be shared with everyone who is following you and will be visible in your public feed. (To see what you're sharing, click the "Shared Items" link under "Your Stuff" in the left menu of the Google Reader). Although this capability can be useful, you may have people you're following with whom you want to share different information. For example, you may want to share an article about a competitor only with your colleagues, while you may want to share a more general article that gives insights into your industry with everyone you're professionally connected with.

As a solution, Google Reader lets you separate your feed followers into custom friends lists. You can separate your friends into groupings such as "colleagues," "friends," or "customers." To begin organizing this, click on the "Sharing settings" link from the left menu of your home page. From here, click the first dropdown box that asks you whom you want to share your items with. Choose the option that says "Protected (Share with selected groups)." From here, click "Create, edit and bulk manage your groups using Google Contacts," which will take you to your list of Google contacts, in which you can make your own groups. Once this is done, you can check the boxes of people with whom you want to share the item. Note that only your Google Contacts can make comments on the items you've shared publicly, even though everyone may be able to see the article.

You can also add a comment on any article that you share. To do this, click the "Share with Note" button, which lets you enter in your own thoughts alongside the article you're sharing. By adding a comment, you can show your expertise and why you're choosing to share an article with someone and provide your own insights. This lets your network know why the article is relevant to them and so helps you build your reputation among your followers as a useful knowledge resource.

TIP 181 Build your readership

Building up a solid follower base on Google Reader is the best way to leverage its power in establishing a reputation within your industry. There are several ways you can increase the number of people who subscribe to your feed:

- **E-mail your feed:** Once you've shared items publicly, you can e-mail people to tell them about the articles you've shared. Doing this lets you be proactive about sharing useful information with other people, rather than waiting for them to log in to Google Reader to see the content you've shared. To e-mail an article to others, click "Sharing Settings" from the left menu and then scroll to the bottom of the page. From here, click the "e-mail" link, which will let you add specific people you want to e-mail and also gives you the option to include a note along with your e-mail.

- **Add a clip to your blog:** A good way to encourage people to subscribe to your feed is to publicize it on external places such as your blog, website, or Facebook page. You can do this by adding a Google Reader clip, which is a widget containing the latest headlines from your Google Reader account. You can choose which information is displayed, such as only articles tagged with a particular keyword phrase. To add a clip to your website, click the "Settings" link in the top right menu of your Google Reader account and then the "Folders and Tags" tab. Click the "Put a clip on your website" link, which will open a new window containing a snippet of code to paste into your website.

- **"Like" your post:** In addition to sharing an article with other contacts or adding a comment to it, you can also "like" a post by clicking the "Like" button underneath that article. "Liking" an article is quicker and simpler than adding a comment and still means that everyone who reads the item will see your name linked underneath it. Your name will be hyperlinked to your profile, which means you can use the "Like" functionality to increase traffic to your profile page quickly and easily. Note that "liking" is a public action that displays on your public feed.

TIP 182 Share posts in other services

Once you've started posting regularly to Google Reader, it's a good idea to publicize it to other places where you already have a captive audience. Doing so has two main advantages: it lets you add more value in terms of information you're sharing with them, and it helps you build up your follower base within Google Reader.

The first way you can publicize your account is by adding a Google Reader clip to your website. This is a widget that contains recent headlines you've tagged or shared in your Google Reader account (for more on the clip and how to install it, see Tip 181). The other way you can publicize the content in your Google Reader account is to share articles on other social media sites like Twitter and Facebook. Besides helping to increase the amount of people who subscribe to you, doing this is a convenient way of ensuring you have fresh and regular content on these sites to make sure your audience on each site returns regularly.

Google Reader contains built-in functionality in the form of a "Send to" menu under each article that lets you select the social media site on which you want to share the article—all without your needing to leave the Google Reader interface. To enable this functionality, you first need to select the service to which you want to be able to send articles. First, log in to Google Reader and click the "Manage Subscriptions" link from the left navigation menu, followed by the "Send to" tab. In this page, check the boxes of the services you want to send the article to, such as Facebook, Blogger, Twitter, and so on. Now, when you want to share an individual article from within Google Reader, click the "Send to" dropdown menu underneath the article and select the service to which you want to send it. You'll be prompted to add the details for those specific services—for example, adding a title and description if you're sending it as a bookmark to Delicious. Repeat this process by selecting a different service under the "Send to" menu for each service to which you want to cross-post the article.

Reddit

TIP 183 | Understand Reddit

One of the simplest and most popular social bookmarking sites around, Reddit lets you find and make a note of, or bookmark, content that you can share with other people or refer back to later. Because of Reddit's large user base, links that appear on its front page or subpages gain wide exposure, which means that if a link to content on your blog or website appears on these pages, you'll increase your brand's exposure and site traffic. Reddit is a good way of connecting with other people in your industry and keeping up to date with news and trends related to your business, as well as sourcing content for blog posts if you have a business blog.

Reddit consists of a general home page containing the most popular links overall and subsections, known as *subreddits*, which contain links that are topic-specific (such as world news, science, or environment). Leveraging its social community, Reddit orders links via a voting system rather than an editorial one: as a Reddit user, you can vote for or against a link, which influences how high up on the page it appears. The more positive votes a link receives, the higher up it will be on the page until it will eventually appear on the first page of a subreddit or on the home page. Conversely, the more negative votes a link receives, the lower down on the page it will move. You can see the submission score alongside each link, which is the net number of votes for and against it. Although it can be risky if your link isn't popular in that it will quickly develop a negative buzz, a useful link is rewarded by steadily increasing visibility as it moves up to page 1.

It is acceptable to post your own links on Reddit, but as with most other social bookmarking tools it's important to add value as a member by submitting other content and commenting and voting on other submissions. By adding genuine value to other Reddit users, you become a valued member of the community, which can help you gain an audience when you do submit your own content. Besides enabling you to vote for or against a link, Reddit allows you to comment on your own links or others that have been posted. Reddit users can vote for or against not just links but also comments, depending on whether they find them useful.

To sign up on Reddit, go to www.reddit.com, choose a user name and password, and click "Register" at the top right of the page. Once you've registered, click "Preferences" to change the way articles and comments are displayed in your account, as well as to designate who can publicly see your votes.

Once you've logged in to your account, you'll see the twenty-five most popular content links on the site on the home page. Along the top navigation menu, you'll see links to Reddit's category pages (known as *subreddits*). Clicking on each of these links will take you to a page of submissions that are specific to that particular topic. Subreddits make it easier to find content in a specific subject area, and submitting content to these means you have a more targeted audience viewing it. Below the subreddit menu at the top of the home page, you'll see links organized into various tabs—"newest" for the newest links, "hottest" for links gaining popularity fastest, "controversial" for the links generating the most conversation, "top" for the most popular links of all time, and "saved" for the links you've bookmarked.

Reddit allows you to do three main things on the site: vote for links, submit content (for more on this, see Tip 185), and comment on links that you or others have submitted. When you're new to Reddit, it's a good idea to spend some time becoming familiar with the site and reading the content that is already submitted and voting for it before you start submitting your own. This will help you see what kind of content does well and what doesn't in your particular industry. To vote for a link submitted by someone else, first click on the link to read it. Then, to vote, click the back button and click the up or down arrow next to the link to vote for or against it. Each time you click a link, your vote counts for one point that is added or taken away from its overall score, which you can see to the left of each link displayed on the site. For comments, you can add these either to a link you've submitted or to someone else's. As with links, the community can vote for or against your comment, which will count toward or against your karma score (for more on karma, see Tip 186).

TIP 185 Submit content

Before you start submitting your own content to Reddit, spend some time submitting content that's not your own. This will help you build up link karma and establish your reputation as a value-added Reddit user. The types of links that do well on Reddit tend to be "newsy" articles on hot topics of the moment or current affairs, so try to find content that is newsworthy to submit. These links should also be related to your industry—this will allow you to build up your brand on the site as an expert in your specific industry.

Submitting a link to Reddit requires the URL of the page and a title for the link. If you're submitting the link from within Reddit, click the "submit a link" button at the right of the home page or the subreddit you're on (for more on submitting to subreddits, see Tip 187). You'll be prompted to paste in the URL and fill in a title for the link. Unlike other bookmarking sites like Digg or StumbleUpon, Reddit doesn't provide users with a summary of the link, so the link title is even more important in encouraging click-through and votes. You can also click "suggest title" for Reddit to provide a default title. Next, you can select a subcategory (this will be auto-filled if you've navigated to a subreddit from within the site). Once you've submitted the link, it will appear in the new-submissions page of the site, where it will begin to gather votes for or against it.

The other way to submit content to Reddit is from within your browser via the Reddit bookmarklet. To install this, click "bookmarklet" under the tools section of the Reddit.com footer or go to www.reddit.com/bookmark let. Select your browser and then click and drag the three links onto the bookmark bar. Then, when you're on a page in your browser that you want to bookmark, click the "Submit" button. You'll be taken to a page where the URL will be auto-filled. Choose a title and subcategory if you're submitting to a subreddit, and then click "Submit." From here, your URL is ready to accumulate votes.

TIP 186 Build up karma

Within your Reddit account, you'll see a number next to your user name on the home page in parentheses. This is known as your Reddit "karma," which is a reflection of the amount of quality content you've provided the Reddit community. Reddit karma is split into two subcategories: **link karma**, which is accumulated by submitting links that are useful to others, and **comment karma**, which is accumulated by gathering positive votes on comments you make on links submitted. When someone votes in favor of a link that you submitted or a comment you made, your link karma and comment karma rises by one. Conversely, when people vote against a link or a comment you made, one point is subtracted from your link or comment karma score. The higher your score, the more influence you have on the site in terms of followers and visibility.

As your karma builds, people will be more likely to vote your links "up" and become your followers since they'll see you as a genuinely useful resource. You'll therefore have an increased number of people seeing links to your own content that you submit. High karma also affects your links' longevity on the site: if you have very high karma, chances are your link will show up for longer in the "New" tab, which means it will be exposed to more people who can vote positively for it. As far as personal branding on the site goes, having high karma means you have high credibility on the site, which positively affects your business's reputation with the Reddit user base. Reddit's karma system is therefore a democratic one in that everyone has an equal say in the degree of influence that every other user has on the site.

Note that karma rewards high-*quality* content rather than a high *quantity* of content: your score is raised not just by submitting a link or a comment but rather by the number of positive votes those submissions receive. However, the more links you submit, the more chance you have to gain more positive votes (provided you're discerning about what content you provide). Ultimately, then, the best way of building up karma is to submit quality content on a regular basis. Taking part in the general community such as networking, making friends, submitting links, and making comments will also help to improve your karma score.

Post to subreddits

As mentioned in Tip 183, Reddit consists of a main front page and several subcategories or subreddits. Links on the front page are uncategorized and are the most popular links on the site overall, while links on subreddits are related to a specific subject, such as science, technology, design, and world news. Links on the Reddit front page are exposed to more people than links on individual subreddits, and so a front-page link will result in more site traffic than a link appearing on a subreddit. Link content also differs slightly between the two sections: articles on the front page tend to be more "breaking news" in nature, while links on subreddits are subject-specific and don't necessarily date as quickly. Therefore, if you submit a link within a particular subreddit, you may not have as many people viewing the link as you would if you submitted the link to the front page. However, there are two advantages to submitting to subreddits that outweigh this factor:

1. Fewer stories compete for page real estate on subreddits, so your link has more chance of rising to the top of its category and being seen by more people.

2. When submitting to a subreddit, your audience is more targeted and therefore more likely to be interested in your content. This means a higher click-through rate on the link and a higher retention rate for these visitors when they arrive at your site.

Submitting content to subreddits can therefore be a good strategy for achieving targeted visibility on the site. The prerequisite for success is that you submit content that fits well within the specific subject matter of that subreddit. If you submit content that doesn't fit in with the topic, your link will be voted down, and you may be seen as a spammer, which will harm your reputation on the site.

To submit an article to a specific subreddit, select the category when you're entering the URL and title of a link. If you submit the article from within a subreddit on the site itself, this field will be auto-filled with that category name; if you're submitting from within your browser using the bookmarklet, you'll need to fill it in. You can see category names across the top of the Reddit home page—note that some categories are one word, such as *worldnews* for "world news."

TIP 188   Get your content noticed

Although it's easy enough to submit content on Reddit, competing with other content and getting enough votes for it to rise to the front pages can be more difficult. There are certain best practices you can follow to make sure your content has the best chance of receiving the most votes possible so that it rises to the most visible pages on the site:

■ **Submit good content:** Any content you submit should be of a good quality and should appeal to the average Reddit user. For more on submitting good Reddit content, see Tip 191.

■ **Stick to the source:** Reddit favors content that is the original source of a story. For example, rather than submitting a blog post that quotes an original source elsewhere, try to track the original source article and submit that instead.

■ **Submit at the right time:** Since the United States has the largest number of Reddit users, it's a good idea to submit content during U.S. daytime, when most Americans are online and your article will get the most exposure. Aim for midmorning Eastern Standard Time as a rough time window.

■ **Build up your link karma:** When you build up your link and comment karma (see Tip 186 for how to do this), you build up a better reputation among other Reddit users. This makes them more likely to vote your story up and become one of your followers.

■ **Link to permanent pages on your site:** Reddit prefers a permanent, specific URL as the location for content you submit. This applies specifically if you're submitting a blog post—submit the blog's permalink URL rather than the home page of your blog. In general, always submit a specific article or other piece of content rather than the overall site URL.

■ **Don't submit only your own content:** If you join Reddit and submit only your own content, you'll quickly be identified as someone who's not on the site to add real value. Above all, view the site as a place to share useful information with your community rather than as a way to push your business. A good ratio is to submit one piece of your own content for every ten pieces of someone else's that you submit. You can still build your brand by submitting others' content: by submitting content related to your business and industry, you provide a useful resource to others, which positively impacts your brand image on the site.

TIP 189 **Encourage others to post your content**

Although it's acceptable to submit your own content on Reddit, it can be more effective if someone else submits it instead of you, as you then remain objective while still benefiting from the increased visibility your content will achieve. A good way of allowing others to quickly and easily submit your content is by including Reddit buttons on your blog or website. To do this, log in to your Reddit account and click the "Buttons" link under the tools section in the footer. On this page, you'll be given various options for the button's appearance, such as having links only or including graphics as well. Once you've decided on the type of button you want, click the "View code" link, which will generate a snippet of code that you'll need to paste into the source code of your blog or website where you want the button to appear. Be sure to place the buttons in a clear place where your readers will see them, either at the beginning or at the end of the article.

In addition to including buttons, you can install a Reddit widget that pulls through a feed of articles you've submitted on the site and lets your readers vote for or against them. Chances are your blog readers are more likely to vote in favor of your content than against it, which means that widgets are an excellent way of building up positive votes and increasing visibility. Although some people feel that including a Reddit widget on your site encourages your users to click away and leave your site, it can also be argued that you're providing your visitors with additional useful resources on the subject they're reading about.

To add a widget to your blog or site, click the "Widget" link under the "Reddit tools" section of the footer. From here you can choose various settings such as filtering the list of links that have been submitted by a specific user name (e.g., only by you). After you've selected other options, such as the number of links you want to display, the content date range, and the color scheme, the code will be generated for you to paste into the source code of your blog or website as you did with Reddit buttons.

TIP 190   Make friends

In addition to submitting content, voting for other content, and leaving comments, being active in the Reddit community means networking with other Reddit users. Building relationships with others on the site who are interested in similar topics related to your industry means they're more likely to vote favorably when you submit your own content, since they're more likely to find it useful. More positive votes for your link increase its exposure as it moves up the front pages of the site. In addition to helping your own content increase its visibility, Reddit friends are a good way of staying up to date with news and trends related to your business and recognizing new potential customers or business opportunities. Following friends' submissions is also a useful way of finding new content to blog about and a way of staying informed about what others are saying about your brand.

To add someone as a friend on Reddit, visit the person's profile page and click the green "+ friends" button in the right column of the page. Once you've added them, you can view all the content submissions they've made by visiting http://friends.reddit.com. You can also interact with them via private messages, which are similar to e-mails in that you can interact directly with them in private, one-on-one conversations. Because you already have a relationship with these users, they're more likely to vote favorably for content you submit. So, once you've submitted your content, send them a private message telling them about it and asking them to vote for it. Be careful not to do this too often so as to annoy them. A good way to ensure that you don't overdo it is to split your friends into different groups according to your relationship with them or the content they're interested in. Then, when you submit a piece of content, you'll be e-mailing only a subset of friends each time.

If you want to remove someone as a friend, click the "Remove from friends" link in the same place on their profile page.

TIP 191 Post good content

Whether you're submitting your own content (and you shouldn't do this too often) or other links you've found, being part of the Reddit community means adding value to others on the site. This is best achieved by submitting good content. The karma scheme, where other users can add or take away points depending on how useful they think your content is, means that the more useful your content, the more influence you'll have on the site by way of a high karma score (for more on karma, see Tip 186).

So what constitutes good content to submit on Reddit? The first step in answering this question is to find out which links are already popular within your industry. Spend time reading the top links within the subreddits related to your industry so that you get a feel for what's successful on the site in terms of user votes. In general, articles that tend to perform well on social bookmarking sites are breaking news and current affairs pieces or content that contains lists, humor, or a compilation of useful resources (for more on writing useful blog content, see Tips 15–22). Remember that Reddit favors articles that are the original source of a particular story, so if you are breaking a story, make sure you submit the article that is the original source. Although breaking news stories almost always do well on the site, it can be a difficult task to submit such stories before any other Reddit user. Even if you aren't the first to break a piece of news, you can write an article or find a piece of content that takes a unique angle or gives an original insight on the topic. In this way you're able to piggyback on the momentum of the base story as a way to increase the visibility of your Reddit profile (and your blog or website if you wrote the piece).

When you submit your own content, don't submit every blog post you write. Be discerning by submitting only the highest-quality posts, such as the results of research you've conducted, or a link to a white paper you've written. Being picky about the content you submit may mean that you submit only one out of every five or ten blog posts you write.

TIP 192 Leverage your existing network

A piece of content submitted to Reddit needs a fairly high number of votes within a short span of time for it to move from the new-submissions page to the top page of a particular subreddit (for more on submitting to these, see Tip 187), and even more votes to appear at the top of the general front page.

The first way to get lots of votes for your content is by being active on the site and networking with other Reddit users. You can also increase the visibility of your submissions by leveraging your existing network of contacts. In other words, aim to get your friends, family, and business contacts involved in voting for an article you submit, which increases its chances of rising to the top of the front page or of a subreddit. When you post a link to your content on the site, e-mail your contacts and ask them to vote for it. Be careful not to do this too often, though. In addition, capitalize on your existing blog or website readership by including submission buttons and widgets on your site so that your readers can easily post and vote for content while on your site (for more on how to do this, see Tip 189).

Another method of increasing votes for your content is to build a network of business partners, colleagues, or other industry bloggers who are also Reddit users and then make an agreement to e-mail each other when you submit content so that the rest of the group can vote it up. This method lets you build up a powerful business network where every time you submit a piece of content you'll get several positive votes for it in return for doing the same for someone else. Be sure that the people in your network are also regular contributors to Reddit in their own right in terms of submitting links, voting, and leaving comments. If someone joins the site simply to vote once for one piece of content, there's a good chance that other Reddit users will see that that person is not adding value, which will lower his or her karma on the site (for more on karma, see Tip 186). Those with low karma will have less visibility when they submit or comment on content, and thus less influence, and are likely to be connected with fewer people on the site, so they won't be the most effective people with whom to network.

6

Multimedia

OVER RECENT years the widespread availability of high-speed Internet in the United States and elsewhere has permanently changed the online advertising landscape. Before, spreading the word about your brand online meant you were limited largely to using text or static images (whether in the form of websites, text ads, or banner ads) that couldn't allow direct interaction between you and your target market. These days, however, you can engage with prospective customers online with rich media such as video and audio, and you can achieve much more interaction between customer and business through blogging platforms and social media platforms like Facebook and Twitter. With today's online marketing capabilities businesses have moved away from one-sided "push marketing" toward a more social, two-way conversation in which the potential customer can fully engage with the brand, which makes them more likely to become loyal customers. As an example, businesses are increasingly interacting with their audience through user-generated video and audio that fans can upload to their Facebook or MySpace page or to sites like YouTube and Flickr. Businesses are using these multimedia platforms to provide resources to their audiences, from how-to videos and podcasts to photo albums and audio files.

Using multimedia as part of your social media strategy, such as by uploading resources on sites like YouTube and Flickr, is a great way to position your brand as adding value to your audience. When this is established, your target market is more likely to continue to engage with you, which enables you to continue the conversation with them. The richer this relationship becomes, the easier it is to convert them from readers to customers.

Flickr

TIP 193 | Understand Flickr

Yahoo!-owned Flickr is a social photography site where you can upload and share photos with the Flickr community, your own network, and people searching for related images on search engines. Since its origins in 2004, Flickr has grown into one of the most active photography communities on the Internet and as of April 2010 hosted more than four and a half billion photos. Flickr can be used in a variety of ways: amateur and professional photographers use the site to get feedback on their photos and participate in photographic communities, while many bloggers use the site to host their images. More recently, marketers have realized that Flickr's social sharing abilities make it a powerful brand-building tool. With the right strategy, you can use the site to share photos related to your business with the site's large and active user base, which helps to increase your brand awareness on the site and, ultimately, your customer base.

A Flickr account is free; all you need is a Yahoo! ID to sign up (if you don't have one, create one at www.yahoo.com). Once you've signed in, you can start uploading photos to your account, which you can organize into albums or "sets." You can change privacy settings for images, such as "Public," "Visible to friends," and "Public." Everything you've ever uploaded to Flickr is displayed in a "photostream," which will also differ according to your privacy settings and who the viewer is. This allows you to, for example, allow family to see certain images in your photostream, but not business contacts.

The main way to get your photos seen by others is to join Flickr groups. These are themed around a particular topic, and as a member you can post photos related to that topic and participate in relevant discussions. For example, if you're a hotel owner in Sydney, Australia, you can post photos of scenic areas around the city in a group about Sydney tourism.

If you use Flickr as a marketing tool, tread carefully, since the site forbids posting photos just to advertise or market your product or service. However, being a genuinely active and useful Flickr user and participating in groups related to your business still means you can achieve brand reach without violating the site's terms of service. In the preceding example, posting photos to a group about Sydney tourism as a hotel owner provides genuinely useful content to people researching a trip to the city. In providing this information, you expose your brand to Flickr users, which could mean that people viewing your photos end up choosing your hotel when they research travel options.

TIP 194   **Write your profile**

When signing up for a new Flickr account, you'll need to choose a screen name. Whenever you participate on Flickr, such as when you upload or comment on a photo, your user name will be displayed, which makes it an important element of your branding on the site. For this reason, think of a user name related to your business in some way, such as your brand name, your website URL, or the user name you use on other social media sites such as Facebook and Twitter.

Once you have your user name, you can personalize your account by going to www.flickr.com/configurator. There are three steps to this process:

1. Select a buddy icon. This is an image that will accompany your profile and user name when you leave a comment or post a photo—you can use any image you wish here, such as a personal photo or your company logo. Whatever you choose, the image should be attention grabbing, since it is fairly small when displayed (48 by 48 pixels).

2. Create a custom URL. You'll be given the option to create a custom Flickr URL in the format www.flickr.com/photos/[your-selected-name]. For the sake of brand consistency, keep this URL in line with your Flickr user name, which will most likely be related to your business's name. Having a URL that contains your business name is also useful for branding purposes when sharing the URL with others and can also help your Flickr account to appear in top search engine results for related searches to your business.

3. Personalize your profile. An informative and interesting Flickr profile is your main way of communicating your brand message to other Flickr users. In addition to details like your name and geographical information, describe your business and the services you have to offer in the "Describe Yourself" section. Keep the tone light and informal and write it specifically with Flickr users in mind; that is, make it about the photographs rather than about your business. Within this section you can also link back to your company URL as a way to let readers find out more about your business if they're interested.

TIP 195 Upload photos

Once your account has been set up, you can start uploading photos. If you're using Flickr to market your business, your photos should relate to your business in some way. Here are some examples:

- **Tour operators:** upload photos of the city or region in which you conduct your tours.

- **Nursery owners:** upload photos of the plants that you sell or of your nursery locations.

- **Restaurant owners:** upload photos of your premises, the food you sell, and your menu.

It's important to note that even though Flickr can be used as a marketing tool, it is first and foremost a site for sharing high-quality photography with a discerning audience. Always make sure, therefore, that the photos you'll be uploading are of high quality; this doesn't mean you must have your photos taken by a professional, but it does mean selecting only your best images to upload to your account.

You can either upload the photos directly from the Flickr website or use uploading tools such as Flickr Uploadr. These desktop tools are downloaded onto your desktop for faster uploading, which is a good idea if you're uploading lots of photos regularly. Once you've uploaded a photo, you can add three important pieces of information to it:

1. Photo title. A descriptive title will encourage people to click through to the photo from your sets and is useful for visibility in Flickr's internal search and on external search engine results.

2. Description. This explains the context of the photo. Remember that you generate interest for your business on Flickr as a result of interesting photos, so your description should be of the photo rather than of your business. Captions also allow you to link out, so if you're talking about a particular subject that you refer to in your blog post, you can add the link in here to drive more traffic to your blog.

3. Tags. These are keywords that categorize your photos into subject themes. For example, if you were uploading photos of food in your New York restaurant, you could use the words *New York*, *food*, and *restaurant* to categorize the picture under these three subjects. Tagging is also an important way for your pictures to come up on internal searches in addition to search engine visibility. (For more on tags, see Tip 30.)

Promote your account

While uploading photos is the first step to take after you've created your Flickr account, your success with the site as a marketing tool depends largely on the exposure you can get to these photos since this will affect how many Flickr users click through to your website. Besides being active within the Flickr community by doing things like joining groups and commenting, you should try to promote your Flickr account externally. Some ways to do this:

- **Use social websites:** A good way to promote a specific photo or album is to upload the album URL to social bookmarking sites such as Stumble-Upon, Digg, and Delicious. If you do go this route, your pictures should be unusual or interesting in some way to warrant the bookmark. Generally, content that is current and topical performs well on social bookmarking sites, so if you do bookmark one of your albums, try to select photos that are newsworthy in some way.

- **Use your own websites:** Capitalize on the users who are already on your blog, website, or other social media profiles you may have such as Facebook and Twitter, by linking back to your Flickr account from these locations. You can also install a Flickr badge on your site (see Tip 200), which pulls through images on to your website or blog interface.

- **Flickr Explore:** If your photo is considered interesting enough, it could be included on Flickr Explore, which is a compilation of the five hundred most interesting photos on Flickr. Flickr decides on this list based on click-throughs, comments, how many times it's been favorited by others, and the value of the site from which the click-throughs originate.

- **Send sets manually:** Flickr lets you create albums (known as *sets*) that you can organize into themes. For example, if you're a bar owner, you could have sets for your staff, for events you have at the bar, for drinks you serve, and for regular customers. Then you can send a specific set to a particular group of people—such as sending your set of cocktail images to customers who are subscribed to receive new cocktail recipes each month.

TIP 197   Join groups

Flickr groups are one of the most valuable ways to network on the site. Groups allow people with similar interests to share photos and participate in discussions with other members. Participating in Flickr groups is an excellent way of developing your reputation as a resource on a particular subject area related to your industry. When you participate in a group, every discussion or comment you make and every photo you upload is accompanied by your user name, which is linked to your profile page, which contains all your albums and photos. Therefore, the more active you are in groups, the more your Flickr profile will be exposed to other users. Being active in Flickr groups also helps you connect with other influential Flickr users, who can be important to build your business—whether they eventually become customers, partners, or employees.

Flickr groups organized around a particular topic can have three levels of visibility: public (anyone can join), invite only (where you can view the page but need to be invited to join), and private (where only certain people can see the group and join it when invited). To start looking for existing groups in your industry, select "Search for a group" under the "Groups" dropdown. You can search on keywords relating to your industry or to the location you're in. For example, if you're a tour operator in San Francisco, you may enter *photography San Francisco* to find photography groups in your area. From here you'll see the group description and statistics such as the number of users, discussions, and photos. Groups that are active are more useful to network in, so take note of the last discussion post as well as the date that the last image was uploaded. If you want to join the group after viewing this, click the "Join" link.

When participating in a group, aim to add value: rather than just upload photos, interact with other users and comment on photos and on discussions. Always keep your comments and input related to the photo or subject being discussed, rather than using your interaction as a way to promote your business.

Create your own group

As mentioned in Tip 197, Flickr groups are one of the most valuable ways to build connections and interact with other Flickr users. However, if you find that no existing groups match your specific business slant or topic, you may want to create a new group. As with joining an existing group, creating a group is a good way of generating discussions in your industry and leveraging yourself as an expert in a particular area, especially if you're the creator of the group. Besides connecting with others, creating a group allows you to provide useful resources to your customers and to monitor the conversation happening about your brand. Flickr groups can also be a good source of traffic to your blog or website as people become familiar with your brand and business through group interaction.

Before you create a group on Flickr, check that no groups exist on your particular topics. Once you've made sure this is the case, select the "Create a Group" link from the "Groups" dropdown menu. You'll first be asked to select the group type:

- Choose **public: anyone can join** if you want anyone to see the group and be able to join it.

- Choose **public: invitation only** if you want anyone to see the group but want control over members and so have to invite them by e-mail.

- Choose **private** if you want the group to be seen and joined only by specific people, such as your colleagues.

Generally, if you're looking to market your business through Flickr, you should choose one of the first two options, which means your group will show up in search results and anyone can see the group page. Next, you'll need to select a name for your group. Be sure to make this descriptive of the general purpose of your group; for example, "Architects in Los Angeles." Underneath, in the description field, write a bit about what your group is about. Both of these include keywords that relate to your group—these are the ones people are likely to be searching with to find your group.

TIP 199 Promote your group

Once you've created your group (for more on this, see Tip 198), you can promote it. The more users you have who have joined your group, the more successfully you'll be able to spread your brand's message to more Flickr users, and the more traffic will be driven to your blog or website from your Flickr account. There are several ways you can publicize your group, both within the Flickr site and externally:

- **Think about your group settings:** Flickr allows you to choose three types of groups: public, meaning anyone can see it and join the group; invite only, meaning anyone can see the group page but have to be invited to join; and private, where only selected people can view the group page or join it. To market your group as widely as possible, select the "public" or "invite only" option for your group.

- **Encourage interaction:** When you create the group, encourage interaction by starting off discussions and asking for input. When you upload your first set of photos, encourage group members to do the same.

- **Find related groups:** Use Flickr's search function to find other related groups, which you can then join and participate in their discussions in which you can link back to your group. If you do this, be sure to provide useful input in a group discussion or comment rather than simply linking back to your own group page.

- **Recommend a tag:** Once you've created a group, you can decide on a tag that is related to the group and ask people to tag photos they upload with this one tag that contains keywords related to your group. This means that if people are searching for related content either on Flickr or on search engines, a greater number of photos will appear in the results.

- **Invite people individually:** You may know photographers who have done work on your specific topic who would be valuable additions to your group. Consider contacting them directly and asking them to post photos in your group.

- **Cross-promote your group:** As with promoting your Flickr account, provide a link to your group on other sites that you own, such as your website, blog, or Facebook page. This is a great way to enrich your existing sites and to drive people from your existing sites to your Flickr page.

Add a Flickr badge

Although being an active Flickr user will help you promote your brand within the site, marketing your account externally is important to drive traffic to it and increase its visibility to a targeted audience. One of the most effective ways of promoting your Flickr account is to install the Flickr badge, which allows you to embed photos from selected Flickr sets directly into your blog or website. By linking to your Flickr account from your badge, you're creating an extra resource for your readers, while capitalizing on the existing audience you have to drive traffic to your Flickr account.

If you have a blog with major blogging platforms like Blogger or Word-Press, the badge is easy to install:

1. To start, go to www.flickr.com/badge.gne. You can choose two types of badges, depending on the format you'd like: HTML or Flash, which contains moving animation within the badge.

2. Once you've selected the option you'd like, click the "Choose content" button. On this page, you can choose what content you'd like displayed within the badge. You can display either all your albums or specific albums tagged with certain keywords. This is a good option if your Flickr account contains sets on many different subjects and you want only photos related to your business to display. You can also choose to display only content from a certain group pertaining to your business. This is a good option to choose if you've created a new group and are trying to drive traffic to it.

3. When you're finished selecting the content, click the "Layout" button, which will let you select your preferred layout, including the badge's size, how many photos you want displayed, and whether you want your most recent photos or all photos displayed.

4. Under "Colors," choose the look and feel of the badge, which should be in line with the look and feel of your site.

5. Finally, Flickr gives you a preview of what the badge will look like and provides you with custom-generated code. Copy and paste this code into the HTML of the page on which you want the badge to appear (such as the main page of your blog or the "Photos" page of your website). Then republish the page to see the badge included.

TIP 201 Decide between a free and a pro account

Whether you opt for a free or pro Flickr account depends on several factors: how big your business is, how active you'll be on Flickr, and how central the site will be to your online marketing strategy. A free account on Flickr gives you 100 MB of bandwidth per month (with a limit of 10 MB per photo), and you can upload two videos per month. You can upload photos to up to ten groups, and only your smaller file sizes are accessible once you've uploaded your photos. Finally, people viewing your account can see only your two hundred most recent images. If you're using Flickr for a blog that is still small and hasn't yet built up significant traffic numbers, these limitations shouldn't have too much impact on your activity on the site, so a free account should be sufficient. If you have a larger blog or website and want to use Flickr to host all your images, a pro account gives you unlimited bandwidth and storage, and it costs $24.95 a year. A pro account also has these advantages:

- You can upload unlimited numbers of photos and videos (at a limit of 20 MB per photo and 500 MB per video).

- You have unlimited storage and bandwidth.

- You have access to HD playback when you upload videos to your account.

- No ads are displayed on your account.

- You can replace photos and access your original high-resolution images.

- You can view statistics related to photo views and activity on your account.

- You can post in up to sixty Flickr groups, as opposed to only ten if you have a free account.

If you're marketing your business on Flickr, a pro account automatically makes you look more credible and respected within the Flickr community when you're doing things like commenting on photos or participating in group discussions. Also, having a pro account means that a "pro" icon will be displayed alongside your user name, which further adds to your credibility. This can be especially useful if you're creating your own Flickr group.

If you're new to Flickr, it's a good idea to start out with a free account while you build your activity and photo sets on the site. Then, if your traffic builds to a certain level, consider upgrading to a pro account at www.flickr.com/upgrade.

Use Flickr images for your blog content

You can use a Flickr account not only as a way to promote your own business but also as a way to source image content to include in your blog. The first step in doing this is to find the images on Flickr that you want to include by using Flickr's search function on the home page. Flickr has three main ways you can search: on groups, on people, or on tags. While searching on groups and people is the best way of finding other Flickr users with whom to network, if you're looking for images on a certain subject, it's best to search on tags. You can also choose how narrow you want your tag search to be, such as by searching photos only within your contacts or within all Flickr user accounts.

If you find a photo you like, Flickr includes functionality for you to send it directly to your blog or Twitter account from within the Flickr interface. To do this, you first need to configure your blog to your Flickr account. To start this process, visit www.flickr.com/blogs.gne, where you'll be guided through the steps. After providing your blog URL, user name, and password, you'll be able to select the type of layout you'd like when you send a Flickr image to your blog. Flickr supports all major blogging platforms, including Blogger, TypePad, WordPress, and Movable Type, as well as Twitter. Once you've selected the type of blog you have, you'll need to validate it through the specific blogging platform that you're allowing Flickr to interface with.

Once you've configured your blog (or your Twitter account), you're ready to send Flickr images to it. To do this, click on the photo from within the set. Then click on the "Share this" link at the top right of the photo page. A dropdown box will appear; from here, select the "blog this" link. From here you'll be able to select a title and description for the post in which the image will appear, and you'll be given a link to the post so you can check what it will look like before you publish it. If you've configured your Flickr account to interface with your Twitter account, when you click the "blog it" link you'll be prompted to write a tweet and provided with a link to the video or photo.

TIP 203   Analyze your stats

As with any other type of marketing, you should measure the efforts you're putting into promoting your business through Flickr so that you can compare what works and what doesn't in terms of people viewing your photos and interacting with you on the site. A key way to measure the reach you're getting is to enable statistics for your Flickr account. Note that you have to have a pro account for this. To upgrade, visit www.flickr.com/upgrade. Once your statistics are enabled, you'll see them by adding */stats/* to the end of your Flickr URL. For more on pro versus free Flickr accounts, see Tip 201.

Within the statistics interface, you'll be able to see several different measurements related to your account:

- **Overall views:** This tells you how many people have viewed your Flickr account and how this number increased or decreased over time. Overall views are a good way to see how effective your efforts are at marketing your Flickr account in external locations.

- **Individual views:** This lets you compare statistics for individual photos so that you can see which images are the most popular in your account and which have the most search engine visibility. You can also see which are your most popular photos over time—this week, last week, or over a certain period. This is especially helpful if, for example, you have images of products that are seasonal.

- **Referrals:** This tells you where your traffic is coming from. For example, you can measure the impact of installing a Flickr badge on your blog in terms of how much extra traffic you get to the site as a result. You can also see this statistic per set, so that you can identify which types of photos do better in your account. Within referrals, Flickr also tells you what search engines your visitors are coming from and what keywords they typed in to find your image. From here you can see on which search engine your site has the most visibility and also how well your tags, titles, and descriptions are doing in terms of matching up relevant content to related searches.

TIP 204 Don't spam

Although Flickr can be a powerful tool for marketing your business, it's essential to think of your membership on the site as being part of a discerning photography community. This means that as a community member your ultimate priority should be to add value in the form of quality photos and videos, rather than to use it as a platform to promote your business. Instead, use quality content that you upload and input you provide to others as a way to improve your business's reputation and brand reach on the site. Then, as long as you have adequate linking to your blog or website from within your Flickr profile, people will be able to click through to your other properties to find out more about you.

Overall, then, the hard-sell method does not work. In addition, Flickr's community guidelines state that the site is for personal use only, and your account will be terminated if you use it to sell products, services, or yourself through your photostream. Even if you use Flickr purely for commercial purposes and you're not caught, your reputation will be compromised among existing Flickr users, and you're unlikely to build a following for your account. Therefore:

- Do not stuff keywords into your tags, titles, or descriptions.

- Do not include your URL in every single photo you upload.

- Do not post product promotions in comments or when you participate in groups.

Success on Flickr is generally built slowly over time, where you prove your reputation by providing as much value as possible. Then, once you are a respected Flickr member, you will have built up credibility and connections, so that when you perform an activity on the site such as posting an image, commenting on someone else's photo, or participating in group discussions, people will be more likely to click on your user name, read your profile, and click through to your website if they want to engage with you further.

Share quality photos

To use Flickr successfully as a marketing tool for your business, it's crucial that you have good photos to share with other users. Above everything else, Flickr is a site where photography enthusiasts gather, so anything you upload should be worthwhile and of good quality. This is even more important than if you have a personal Flickr account, since the quality of the photos you upload to your Flickr account will subconsciously influence how people see the quality of your business. And, if you have good photos, they're more likely to be spread among other Flickr users, as well as farther afield. Here are some ways to ensure that your account contains images that people will like:

- **Learn from the pros:** Before you upload photos, spend time browsing through the Flickr site to see the kinds of images that are most popular. You can also browse parts of the site like Flickr Explore to see what Flickr thinks the most interesting photos are and then try to emulate the same kinds of photos for your particular industry.

- **Upload a lot of photos:** The more photos you have to share, the more you'll be seen as a value-added Flickr user—and the more chance you have of others seeing them and liking one or more of them. It also makes you more of an active Flickr user since it gives you a broader platform from which to engage with others.

- **Keep them authentic:** Although you should upload quality photos, preferably with a good camera, you don't have to use a professional photographer—in fact, uploading only professionally shot photos may make your sets less authentic. If you can, though, be selective and choose only the best images you have: favor uploading fewer high-quality images over uploading many average ones.

- **Keep them noncommercial:** Although your photos can market your business in a way, such as by being related to your business, they should primarily be about the photos themselves rather than the actual marketing. For this reason, stick to photos of real things and people and places, rather than promotional photos.

Think about search engines

One of the main advantages of marketing your business on Flickr is that the site has a huge amount of credibility (and therefore visibility) on major search engines like Google. What this means is that especially if you're a small business, or one that's new and still being established, it can be extremely useful to be a part of a site like Flickr, where you can achieve search engine visibility by being part of the site while you wait for your own website to build up credibility and improve its search engine rankings. There are two main areas in which you can influence how well your Flickr account performs on search engine result pages:

1. Linking. The number of links pointing into your site affects how credible it seems to a search engine. For this reason, linking back to your Flickr account is important to drive traffic but is also important for search engine visibility. To increase the number of inbound links to your Flickr account, leverage your other areas of online real estate that you have by linking to your Flickr account from your blog, website, and other sites like Twitter and Facebook. While you can link back to your overall Flickr URL, it's also a good idea to link back to specific pages of your collections, sets, or individual images, which will give your individual photos increased visibility as well. When you link back to them, include keyword-rich anchor text in your URL so that Google will have thematic context for the destination of the link. This, in turn, will help the page rank for that specific keyword search.

2. Keywords. In addition to the links pointing to your Flickr account, the content that is visible on the page is important for search engines to discern what the main subject of that page is about, which in turn affects how it ranks for certain keyword searches. For this reason, include keywords that you think others may be searching to find your content within the body of your Flickr page. This can mean including keywords in elements such as your individual photo or photo set titles. As a default, Flickr gives you the camera-generated titles, so be sure to change these to keyword-rich titles. Then you can include keywords in the descriptions you attach to an image or a photo set. Be sure to keep this natural and readable, though, rather than "stuffing" their contents with too many keywords. Finally, include relevant keywords as tags that you associate with each image.

TIP 207 Control how your photos are shared

While Flickr's social sharing nature makes it an excellent tool to spread the word about your brand, you'll typically want to retain a degree of control over who uses your images and how they are reproduced. Conversely, if you're using other people's images, you should ensure that you have the proper permission to use them. By default, your Flickr images are "All rights reserved," meaning that no one else has permission to reproduce them. However, if you don't allow anyone to republish your pictures, you're preventing brand exposure through sharing of your photos with other Flickr users' network of contacts. As a solution, Flickr lets you apply Creative Commons licensing to your photos. The Creative Commons wiki explains: "Creative Commons licenses give you the ability to dictate how others may exercise your copyright rights—such as the right of others to copy your work, make derivative works or adaptations of your work, to distribute your work and/or make money from your work."[1] In essence, a Creative Commons license allows your images to be shared while ensuring that you retain some degree of control over them.

You can apply several different types of Creative Commons licenses, each of which imposes different limitations on how your images can be used. For example, an "Attribution Non-commercial No derivatives" license lets others share your images as long as they're in their original form and you're named as the source and linked to from where the image is used. With this license, however, people can't use your images for commercial gains. In contrast, the "Attribution No Derivatives" license means others can reproduce your images (as long as they're credited) for both commercial and noncommercial purposes. Which license you choose depends largely on the nature of your business. If you're a photographer who sells your images, for example, you'll want your photos to get exposure but won't want others to make money from them. You may therefore choose the most restrictive, "Attribution Non-commercial No derivatives" license.

Flickr lets you apply Creative Commons licensing to your photostream. To read more about this and to set your preferences, visit www.flickr.com/account/prefs/license.

SmugMug

TIP 208 | Understand SmugMug

Like Flickr, SmugMug is a photo-sharing site where you can upload photos online, organize them into galleries, and share them with both your personal contacts and the general SmugMug community. There are several key differences between the two sites, however, which makes each more or less suitable depending on your business goals. Firstly, unlike Flickr, SmugMug doesn't offer a free membership option. Instead, you can choose among three types of paid accounts: a "standard" account for $39.95 a year, a "power" account for $59.95 a year, or a "pro" account for $149.95 a year. As with Flickr's pro account option, there is no limit to the number of uploads or storage space you can have, and you can also upload video. However, SmugMug offers three key differentiating features:

1. The two upper membership levels let you customize your SmugMug page's look and feel, and you can map it to your own domain name. With these two functions, your SmugMug account can appear completely integrated into your own website.

2. A SmugMug pro account lets you sell prints directly from your SmugMug page.

3. You have a large degree of control over who can see your images and how they're accessed—for example, you can add watermarks to your photos or block access to images over a certain size.

On the other hand, the SmugMug community is smaller than Flickr's, and so the amount of exposure you'll get for your photos online is more limited. However, individuals viewing photos on SmugMug can have a more active role than they do on Flickr. Through a system called PhotoRank (which you can deactivate on your account if you wish), people viewing your photos can vote for their favorite images, which are then shown as popular photos on your home page. If photos reach a certain level of popularity, they can appear within the site's most popular images in a certain category that can be accessed from SmugMug's overall "Browse" page.

In summary, you might choose SmugMug over Flickr if your images or photos form a key part of your business and you want to share or sell them directly from your website, such as if you're a professional photographer or graphic designer. You may choose Flickr instead if it's more important to you to gain high levels of exposure for your photos among a larger photo-viewing community.

TIP 209   Sign up and customize

Sign up for an account at www.smugmug.com by clicking the "Try Us Free" button. You'll be prompted to enter your details, including your e-mail address, a password, and a user name, and to select one of three account types: standard, power, or pro. The main differences among the three accounts are:

Standard Account	Power Account	Pro Account
$39.95 per year	$59.95 per year; all functionality of a standard account, plus:	$149.95 per year; all functionality of a power account, plus:
Select from predesigned themes at www.themes.smugmug.com	Can customize with your own themes	Can sell your prints via your SmugMug account
Domain name mapped to Smug-Mug domain (e.g., http://joes photography.smugmug.com)	Can map your own domain name to SmugMug account (e.g., http://gallery.joesphotography.com)	Can upload high-definition video
Can order prints	Can upload video	Image protection, including watermarking
Unlimited storage and photo uploads		

Generally, if your photos are central to your business offering—for example, you're a professional photographer—a pro account gives you the most flexibility and commercial applications for your photos. If you want your photo galleries to integrate into your blog or website but don't need to sell your prints online, a power account may be the better option. In all cases, SmugMug starts you off with a fourteen-day free trial, so you can try different account types during that period.

After selecting your account type, you can start uploading photos (see Tip 210 for how to do this), or you can come back and do it later. Customize your profile by clicking "Go to Control Panel" from the "Tools" button on your home page and then the "Customize" tab. Start by adding a biography about yourself—this is important to fill out since it is the primary way you'll drive Smug-Mug traffic to your own website or blog. You can use HTML tags within your biography, so include a link to your blog or website to convert your SmugMug traffic into your own website traffic. Finally, choose a theme for your account to customize it. If you have a power or pro account, click "Advanced site-wide customization" to add your own custom theme. To customize without having knowledge of CSS or HTML, use the "Easy Customizer" link.

TIP 210 Upload photos

To add a new gallery to your SmugMug account, click the "Add Photos" button on your home page and then "New Gallery." When naming your gallery, use general keywords that relate to your subject in the title, such as *Wooden Kids' Toys* if your gallery contains images of wooden children's toys. Including related keywords in this way helps to make your gallery visible for SmugMug users searching for related content on the site, as well as to people searching for related images on search engines (for more about this, see Tip 211). After you've written a title, select an appropriate category for your photos, a theme for its look and feel, how you want your thumbnails to appear, and the privacy settings you prefer—select "public" if you want anyone to find it, "unlisted" if you want only certain people to view it by e-mailing them the URL, and "lock it down" if you want it to be password-protected and not indexed by search engines. When you're finished, click the "Save" button at the bottom of the page.

Once you've created your gallery, start uploading photos from within your browser or via several uploader tools that you can use depending on your computer operating system. When you've finished, click "Done" to return to your gallery. Click the "add description" link to write a sentence describing your gallery subject. Just as with your gallery title, include general keywords that people may be searching for within this description. You should also add more specific keywords that describe particular images within your gallery in the photo captions and keywords fields for each image (click the "Add caption" and "keywords" links underneath each photo to do this).

Once you've created your gallery, change your settings by clicking the "Gallery Settings" item in the dropdown menu under the "Tools" button. To get the most potential visibility for your photos, enable PhotoRank so people viewing an image can give it a "thumbs up" or "thumbs down" vote. Images with the most votes will then appear in the popular photos section of your home page. If they are popular enough, they could appear on the "most popular" page for a particular category, which anyone can access from the SmugMug "Browse" page or general search results.

TIP 211 | Optimize your photos

Along with making it easier for your photos to be found within SmugMug, optimizing them means that you'll have good visibility on external search engine results pages. How well you rank on search engine results depends on two main factors: the links pointing to a page and the relevance of the page content to people searching similar keywords. Within your SmugMug galleries, create on-page thematic relevance by including keywords in the following places:

■ **Bio:** Your biography appears on your home page, which has the best chance of ranking for general phrases related to your business. To access your bio, click the "Tools" button from your home page and then select "Go to Control Panel." From here, click the "Your Bio" link to edit.

■ **Keywords:** Also known as *tags* (for more about these in a blogging context, see Tip 30), keywords on SmugMug are hyperlinked to pages that pull through all images containing that tag. For gallery keywords, include general keywords that relate to the overall theme (for example *San Francisco* or *SF* for a gallery about San Francisco). For specific photos, include keywords that relate to that specific image (for example, *Golden Gate Bridge* or *Chinatown*).

■ **Categories and subcategories:** These let you aggregate galleries within a particular theme, which gives you another opportunity to create thematic groups of images relating to specific keywords. To change your home page so that it displays categories instead of galleries, click the "Home page Layout" button and then, under "Gallery Categories," select to display categories from the right link.

■ **Titles:** This is one of the most important places on a page that search engines look at to help them work out what the page is about, so include your most important keyword phrase in the title of your gallery.

■ **Custom URL:** Keyword-rich URLs are an important ranking factor. SmugMug automatically generates these (which they call a "NiceName" URL) based on your gallery and category names, but you can enter your own keywords to form part of the URL (these can be alphanumeric characters or dashes, with the overall length up to thirty characters).

TIP 212 | Share your photos

There are several ways you can share photos on SmugMug with your broader network:

- **Social media platforms:** SmugMug lets you post photos to Twitter, Facebook, FriendFeed, and Tumblr from within your account. When you're on a gallery page, click the "Share" button and then "Be Social"—you'll see four links to each of the four services. You'll need to log in to each account separately for SmugMug to interface with it. To share a gallery on Twitter, for example, click "Connect with Twitter." You'll then be prompted to enter your Twitter log-in details and then click "Share," which will post your gallery URL as a Twitter update.

- **Social bookmarking:** You can post links to your galleries across eight social bookmaking sites, including Digg, Delicious, StumbleUpon, and Reddit. To post to these, select one of the services from the "Social bookmarking" menu item under the "Share" menu. Clicking on a service will take you to that site, where you can add the link as a bookmark.

- **E-mail:** SmugMug gives you a custom URL for each gallery, which makes it easy to share with your network. To access this URL, click the "get a link" item from the "Share" menu when you're in the gallery. You can either e-mail the link manually or select "Send an e-mail" to send it from within your SmugMug account. Sharegroups allow you to share multiple galleries with a group of people via a single URL; to create a new Sharegroup, click the "Settings" tab on the "Tools" menu and then click the "Sharegroups" link.

- **Badges:** SmugMug lets you embed a badge on your blog or website that features photos from your SmugMug account. By publicizing photos on other channels, you can encourage audiences you've built up on other sites to visit your SmugMug page. To include a badge on your site, first navigate to the gallery you want to share and then select "Show Off" from the drop-down menu of the "Share" button. Click on the "Badge" tab. From here, click "Configure Options" to change the look and feel and size of the badge and then click the "Update badge" button. Once this is done, click "Copy embed code" and paste this within the HTML of the page on your blog or website where you want the badge to appear.

TIP 213 Join communities

SmugMug communities are a good way to network with other members of your industry and to connect with potential partners or new customers for your business. Connecting with people in a two-way conversation is a much more effective way of engaging people with your brand than the more traditional one-directional marketing methods such as press releases or print advertising. Communities can also be a good source of images to link to and write about if you have a business. Besides joining an existing SmugMug community, you can create your own as a way for people within your own network, such as your employees or blog readers, to share and comment on photos. Just like your own SmugMug home page, communities can be customized with an individual look and feel to be integrated seamlessly within other external websites.

To join a community, click "Communities" in the footer of your home page when you're logged in. You can search on a community by name, or you can browse by the first letter of the community or those that are the most popular. From the search results you can either click the "Join" link of a community you're interested in or click through to browse that community's page. From there you can join by clicking the "join community" link. After confirming that you want to join, click "submit." Note that if the community is invitation only, you'll need to contact the owner to be invited. Once you've joined a community, you can, along with your fellow community members, associate your photo galleries with it. In this way users with similar interests and within the same industry can view one another's photos in one central location.

If you want to create a new community, click the "create your own" link from the main communities page. After naming it and deciding on your permission preferences for people to join (for example, allowing anyone to join or requiring that you authorize a member first), click the "submit" button. Once you've created your community, start by associating your own galleries with it and then inviting others to join.

Video-Sharing Sites

TIP 214 | Understand the video landscape

Video marketing has become popular in recent years not least due to the widespread adoption of high-speed Internet. As opposed to text or plain images, video uses sight, sound, and movement together, which can make your messaging more appealing to your target audience. Uploading this engaging content to video-sharing sites like YouTube provides another channel to drive traffic to your own website, while including video in your own blog or website increases the likelihood that your visitors will stay on your site longer. This, in turn, makes it more likely that they'll fulfill a desired action while they're there, such as downloading resources, subscribing as blog readers, or inquiring about a product or service.

When it comes to the video-sharing landscape, YouTube is the undisputed leader in terms of market share, audience reach, and volume of video content uploaded to the site. If you're starting out with video and want the largest possible reach for your content, YouTube is a good place to start (for more on YouTube, see Tips 223–236). Ironically, YouTube's main weakness comes as a result of its greatest strength: the huge number of people uploading and watching videos on the site means your content is exposed to a large audience, but it also means that it can be hard to stand out above many other competitors in your industry who are also on the site. Additionally, the fact that anyone can post a video on any subject means that the audience is large and disparate and, despite the internal search function, can be hard to target. In response to this drawback, several other players in the video space have emerged: Metacafe, for example, has a user review system that determines how much visibility a video will get depending on its quality, while Vimeo is a niche site that emphasizes the quality of its video content rather than the size of its audience. With this in mind, it's worth starting with YouTube and then expanding your reach by uploading content to other video-sharing sites as well. Which sites you choose will depend on the nature of your business, the content you're uploading, and the intention of the video—whether it's to teach, to entertain, or to establish yourself as an expert in your particular industry.

TIP 215   It's all about the content

Before you can start thinking about uploading content to video-sharing sites, you need to create a good video. Above all, your video should be interesting enough for people to watch it and preferably share it, whether that means that it's educational, entertaining, or unusual. You should also make sure its content is closely related to your area of knowledge so that it ties back to your business offering in some way. For example, if you sell golf equipment, you could create a set of how-to videos on selecting the right set of golf clubs. If you sell Caribbean cruises, your videos could showcase the beach destinations you visit and insights into local culture. Other ideas for content creation include:

- **Product how-tos:** If you sell tech gadgets or other complex products, create videos as user manuals that explain how products work and how best to use them.

- **Presentations:** Create summary videos of you giving presentations at conferences and other events.

- **Answers to questions:** Answer common questions asked by your customers and then use videos to illustrate the answers.

- **Customer testimonials:** Instead of having plain text testimonials on your site, encourage customers to upload videos of them talking about your business's products or services.

- **Personal messages:** Create video new-product updates or news about your company that will interest your customers.

- **Projects:** Create "fly on the wall" videos that document projects that your company is involved with, such as the construction of a new boat if you're a yachting company or the anatomy of a photographic shoot if you're a modeling agency.

- **Comedy sketches:** Humorous videos tend to become "viral" and spread more easily than any other type of video. If you have the necessary comedic ability, create a comedy sketch or humorous take on aspects of your business.

- **Excerpts:** If your product is in video format, such as a workout or Pilates DVD, you can create a short excerpt of it as a way to advertise its content to prospective customers.

TIP 216 Keep best practices in mind

To make sure your video is as effective as possible in persuading your audience to fulfill a particular call to action, whether it's to teach, entertain, or sell, bear these best practices in mind:

- **Know what your audience wants:** No matter what industry you're in, your content should appeal to your target audience. To know what this is, you need to be familiar with your potential customer. Are they an academic audience interested in research videos, or are they looking for practical tips that are illustrated simply and clearly? How old your target audience is will also affect the type of video you create, especially if, for example, you're creating a funny video that you want to spread virally.

- **Shoot a good-quality video:** When you create your video, create it as professionally as you can, as a well-made video can positively influence the perceptions people will have of your business and brand. This doesn't mean you should get a professional to shoot it, but you should consider using simple tools like a tripod so that your video is smoother and easier to watch and editing it properly so that you keep your audience's attention.

- **Don't make it too long:** It's important not to make your video too long so that you can maintain your viewers' attention throughout; a good guideline is to keep your video between three and five minutes long. This also helps you stay within the file limits that most video-sharing sites impose. If you have a lot of content, consider breaking it up into multiple video segments rather than risking losing your audience halfway through a video that's too long. At the end of each segmented video, provide a teaser for the next one to encourage further viewing.

- **Include a call to action:** Think about what the purpose of your video is and emphasize this call to action. Most video creators want their audience to engage with their brand further even after the video has finished, so find a way to include this in your video strategy. Examples include asking people to visit your website within your video, including links to your website at the end of the clip, and prompting people to watch the next video if yours is a video series.

TIP 217 | Share your videos

Once you've created your video, encourage people to share it within their own network to expose your brand to a larger audience. You can do this in several ways:

1. Upload to your website and blog. Provide a central location for your video on your own website or blog so that you can also capitalize on your existing audience watching it as well as users on video-sharing sites. Most of these sites let you easily embed the video on your own site while they host it, which saves you bandwidth but increases your video's exposure.

2. Allow people to share it. Make sure that wherever your video resides, people can easily share it themselves, such as by e-mailing it, linking to it, or embedding it in their own site. Most video-sharing sites do this for you but extend this functionality to your own website and blog too.

3. Ask people to share it. If you've created a video, e-mail the link to your partners, suppliers, or employees to encourage them to share it with their own contacts. You can also ask existing contacts to mention the video in their newsletters or include it as a resource in their blog.

4. Encourage comments. Comments on your video are a good way of encouraging feedback and continuing the two-way conversation between you and your target audience. Whether you're posting your video on a video-sharing site or on your own site, allow them to comment. Don't be afraid of negative feedback—if you do get negative responses to your video, address the issue quickly and openly.

5. Upload to other social media sites. Post a link to your video on other social sites such as Twitter or Facebook and bookmark it to sites like Digg or Delicious. You can also upload your video to other social networking sites that support video, such as MySpace or Facebook.

Although YouTube is the market leader in video sharing, Metacafe (www
.metacafe.com) is older, having been launched in July 2002. Especially since
the purchase of YouTube by Google in 2006, Metacafe is today one of the
largest independent video sites around, with more than forty-five million
unique visitors to the site per month.[1] The site places its focus squarely on
original, user-generated content rather than secondhand content such as
recordings of television shows or movie clips, which is especially suitable
if you're creating unique and original video that you want to be uploaded
and shared among a wider community. Metacafe specializes in "short-form
content" rather than longer content found in episodic television shows or
educational DVDs. Much of the content on Metacafe is meant for entertainment, so although you can upload short-form how-to videos, for example, if
you have funny or entertaining content, it's likely to perform much better.

Metacafe differentiates itself from other video-sharing sites in the following ways:

- It empowers its user community to have an active say in which videos
become visible on the site based on user reviews and rankings. Using this
democratic voting system, Metacafe empowers its users to choose which
videos become the most visible on the site. In doing so, the community
ensures that only the most entertaining and high-quality videos get the
most exposure on the site.

- It features a system where community members review videos as they
are submitted to keep the site free of spam, duplicates, and inappropriate
content. The site has a fairly strict submissions policy, and users need to
flag the content with appropriate content filters for explicit violence, language, or images.

- Metacafe's "Wikicafe" system allows community members to edit titles,
descriptions, and tags on videos so that they can be found more easily on
internal and external search engines.

To start submitting videos, you need to register as a user by signing up
for an account at www.metacafe.com.

TIP 219 Use Yahoo! Video

Just as Google pulls related videos from YouTube into its regular search results for certain queries, Yahoo! populates its search results with video content that it sources from Yahoo! Video. This means that if you submit your video to Yahoo! Video, you're exposing it not only to Yahoo! Video's audience but also to people searching on Yahoo!'s regular search engine for related content. More recently, Yahoo! has added functionality that allows videos to be watched from within the search results interface. This, together with the fact that the most popular content on Yahoo! Video periodically features in Yahoo!'s home page, means that you drive significant external traffic to your video by uploading it on Yahoo! Video.

Like most other video-sharing sites, Yahoo! Video has an active community that you can engage with by sharing, reviewing, and rating videos. You can also share your videos via other Yahoo! properties, including Yahoo! Messenger and Yahoo! Mail, and you can easily embed your video into your own blog or website. Sharing video in this way is a good way of sharing your content on other properties where your target market is likely to be.

To upload videos, sign up for an account at http://video.yahoo.com using your Yahoo! log-in (if you don't already have one, you'll be prompted to create one) and then click "Upload" in the top right menu of the home page. Although the site limits you to videos of 150 MB and fifteen minutes or less, there is no limit on bandwidth or storage. When you submit a video, you'll be prompted to add a title, description, and at least one tag. Within these three fields, add keyword phrases (also known as *tags*) that relate to your video so that you increase your visibility on search results for related searches. Then select a predefined category into which your video fits (for example, "Food," "Health & Beauty," or "Travel"), the language your video is in, and then click the "Upload it!" button. Within a few minutes you should be able to see all videos you've uploaded by clicking the "My Videos" main menu option.

TIP 220   Use Viddler

Viddler is a video-sharing site that lends itself well to how-to and instructional videos. There are several types of Viddler accounts to choose from:

- **Personal account:** For noncommercial use only, a free account limits you to 500 MB of video per month, a 2 GB limit on bandwidth and storage, and ads are shown while the videos play.

- **Business account:** Business accounts are broken into three tiers, starting with a startup account that gives you 50 GB of uploads and storage a month. Most notably, a business account allows you to customize the player's color scheme, logo insertion, and permalink, which means you can link a video directly to your website.

- **Partner account:** If your videos are popular enough and Viddler deems them to be of a high-enough quality, you can monetize views through a revenue-sharing agreement by allowing ads to show on your video either as overlays, before, or after your video. You also get access to detailed analytics, including comments, total video views, and individual stats, as well as amount of storage used and remaining.

Viddler's key differentiators compared to other video-sharing sites are as follows:

- Tags and comments for videos can be made in text or in video and are then inserted directly inside the video and bookmarked. This functionality makes user input video contextually specific, which is more useful to future viewers. Contextual tags also help to make internal search results more relevant, since Viddler searches within the content of a video, including the tags at specific points.

- Viddler gives a comparatively large file-size limit of 500 MB per video and no time limit.

- You can add branding, such as your logo, into the video itself.

Like other video-sharing sites, Viddler has a large and active community that you can network with by adding friends or joining groups related to a particular subject. Viddler also lets you share your video content with a variety of social media sites like Flickr, Twitter, and Digg so that you can leverage your own existing network to generate video views. To start, sign up for an account at www.viddler.com.

TIP 221 | Use Vimeo

Vimeo is a niche video-sharing site that emphasizes high-quality, original video. Because of this emphasis on the art of video production itself, the Vimeo community consists largely of video enthusiasts, including film-makers, commercial directors, and artists. These are the main differences between Vimeo and YouTube:

- Vimeo prides itself on high-quality video and was one of the first video-sharing sites to adopt high-definition-quality video uploads.

- The original video file can be downloaded once it's been uploaded.

- Videos can be password-protected.

- There are no ads on the video interface.

- User accounts are self-contained. In other words, if you're viewing a video on someone's account, you'll see only their own related videos in the sidebar, as opposed to videos that may have been uploaded by someone else but whose content is related. In this way you can increase the likelihood that someone will watch more of your videos rather than jump to someone else's user page from the related videos section.

The main problem as a business owner trying to use video as a market-ing channel is that Vimeo explicitly prohibits the use of the site for com-mercial use. As a marketer, even if you've created the video yourself, you'll be violating the terms of service if you upload a video that, even if it has value, ultimately is used to increase your brand awareness on the site.

So, while Vimeo is not an effective place to explicitly market your brand as you can do on sites like YouTube or Viddler, it can still be extremely useful in certain circumstances. For example, if your business is filmmaking or ad production, the site can be a good avenue via which to connect with other industry members. Also, if you're in the process of creating videos for your business, Vimeo can be a good way to get help and feedback from an audi-ence that is highly knowledgeable about the video-making process.

Use TubeMogul to submit videos

Uploading video to multiple video-sharing sites can be a time-consuming process. As a solution, TubeMogul (www.tubemogul.com) is a video submission platform that allows you to upload your video to up to twenty video-sharing websites at once, including YouTube, Viddler, Revver, and AOL Video. The only requirement to do this is to have accounts set up for each site to which you want to submit. TubeMogul offers three types of accounts:

- **Free:** a hundred videos a month; submission to eight video-sharing sites; unlimited storage; access to analytics; submissions to social networking sites

- **Business:** all "free" account functionality plus five hundred videos a month; submission to fifteen video-sharing sites; ability to upload files larger than 300 MB to sites that allow it; file download; global deletion; use of a URL uploader

- **Gold:** all "business" account functionality plus a thousand videos a month; submission to fifteen video-sharing sites; batch uploads; multiple users and campaigns

The major advantage of TubeMogul is that you can see statistics related to your videos' exposure on all video-sharing sites in one place. This lets you compare your videos' success among the sites so that you can see the relevant effectiveness of each in engaging your audience. Along with video views, comments, and ratings over time, you can access more advanced TubeMogul analytics such as tracking how long someone watched, what geographic region the person came from, where it was embedded, which blogs and sites are linking to it, and what the referring sites and keywords were that resulted in video views. You can also create custom groups of videos so that you can see cumulative statistics for videos of a certain type and subject matter and which sites they perform better on. Armed with this information, you can see the bigger picture of whom your video is reaching and what content engaged them the most on which platform. From here you can change your content accordingly so that your video content becomes more effective in converting casual viewers into customers.

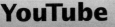

TIP 223 Understand YouTube

Founded in February 2005, YouTube is today the biggest video-sharing website online. According to Comscore, nearly 12 billion YouTube videos were viewed by users in the United States in February 2010,[1] and, according to YouTube itself, around twenty hours of video are uploaded every minute via browsers, e-mail, and mobile devices.[2] As a business wanting to market yourself using video, YouTube therefore represents huge potential exposure for your brand. This, together with the fact that the site is free, means that for many businesses YouTube is their primary channel for uploading and sharing video.

Another major advantage of YouTube is that because it is a Google property (Google bought it in 2006), its video content is integrated within regular Google search results. Therefore, videos uploaded to YouTube also receive exposure on Google search results to users searching keywords related to the video content. Especially if you have a new blog or website and are still building up search result visibility, YouTube can be an excellent supplemental tool for gaining search traffic until your site builds up its own credibility to improve its rankings.

When thinking about using YouTube to market your business, keep in mind two main key success factors:

1. The content should resonate with your target audience.

2. Your target audience should easily be able to find your content on YouTube.

Besides uploading your videos with the right supplemental information and in the appropriate category, the best way to connect with your audience is to be active within the YouTube community. Being active can mean making friends with other users, sharing your video with them, and building up subscriptions to other users whose video content relates to yours. By engaging with the right niche on YouTube, you can maximize the chance that the right target market will view your visit and fulfill the call to action you have in mind, such as visiting your website or buying your product or service. Overall, as long as you have the right strategy and the right type of content, YouTube can be a highly efficient, cost-effective way of generating targeted traffic and gaining brand exposure.

Create a channel

Once you've recorded your video, you'll need to create a YouTube account to upload it to the site. To do this, click the "Create account" link at the top right of the YouTube home page. When you enter your details for your new account, you'll be asked to select a user name, which will appear alongside any activity you do on the site, such as commenting on a video, and will hyperlink to your profile page. Therefore, to help build your brand exposure across the site, think of a user name that's related to your business; for example, if you sell hiking equipment and your company's name is "Seesun Hiking Equipment," you might create the user name *SeesunHikingEquipment*. Also, choose the type of channel you want (for more on this, see Tip 225).

Once your account is created, you can access your channel where you can see information such as your uploaded videos, your profile information, your subscribers, and your friends. To get to your channel, click "My Channel" in the dropdown menu under your user name at the top right corner of the home page. You can customize your channel in several ways to make it in line with your company branding in terms of colors, logos, and text. You can change several areas of your channel page by clicking the "Edit Channel" buttons that run across the top of your channel page:

- **Settings:** Here you can edit the channel title. Include your brand name in here if you can, as well as general keywords that relate to your business in the "Channel tags" section. Select the type of user you are (for more on this, see Tip 225) and check the box that says "Let others find my channel on YouTube if they have my e-mail address."

- **Themes and colors:** This is where you can change the colors to be consistent with your brand colors. If you have access to CSS skills, you can create your own theme using your own custom color palette by selecting the "show advanced options" link.

- **Modules:** Select the information elements you want displayed on your channel page such as your friends, subscribers, comments, and recent activity on your channel. These are all checked by default, so uncheck any that you don't want displayed.

- **Videos and playlists:** Select which video content you want to display; for example, only your own videos ("My Uploaded Videos") or other videos you like ("My Favorites").

TIP 225 Create a custom channel

By default, when you sign up for YouTube you're given a standard channel as a regular "YouTuber." However, if you're using the site to market your business, choosing a specialized channel can be useful because you can include extra information in your profile that relates to your industry. YouTube offers the following specialized channel types:

- **Musician:** A musician account lets you display custom elements unique to the music industry, such as music tour dates, information about your brand and label, and links on your profile page for customers to be able to buy CDs of your music. By selecting a specific music genre, for example, you make yourself more visible to people searching for a specific genre of music.

- **Director:** This type of channel displays extra "performer info" on your profile page that relates to your work as a director, including things like your influences and style of filmmaking. You can also include a customized logo in your profile.

- **Comedian:** This channel lets you display information unique to the comedy industry, such as stand-up tour dates, the style of comedy you do, and links for viewers to purchase CDs of your work. As with all specialized accounts, you can upload a custom logo to your profile.

- **Reporter:** In a reporter channel you can include information such as your preferred news sources, the areas of reporting you cover, and your writing influences.

- **Guru account:** This is intended for people who are experts in a particular field; it allows you to upload a custom logo and list your genre of work, such as "Financial" or "Home + Garden." If you're marketing your business on YouTube and aren't a director, musician, reporter, or comedian, this is the best type of channel to choose to display your industry and business information.

A major advantage of having a specialized channel is that users can search under a specific channel type, and if you're listed under these, you gain exposure to a more targeted audience that is looking specifically for your type of content. To change your channel type, click "Edit channel" on your account page and then "change channel type."

Think about search engines

Along with other media types like images and audio, Google's search results today pull in video content, sourced largely from YouTube. What this means is that if you take the time to optimize your video properly, it will be highly visible in search results, which will result in a good amount of extra traffic being driven to your videos. Besides making your video visible on Google's search results, optimizing your videos ensures that you're visible on internal YouTube search results. The search function on YouTube is the main way people find content on the site, so it's important to make your video page thematically relevant to the keywords people are entering in searches to find your content. Follow these steps to make sure your YouTube content is visible in Google's search results:

1. Research keywords. Using a resource like Google's keyword tool (for more on this, see Tip 227) can help you identify keywords your target market is using to find your content. The keywords you select should be general enough to attract a good amount of traffic while still being specific enough to attract targeted traffic.

2. Include them on your video page. Once you've identified one or two main keywords for your video, include them in your video title. For example, if your researched keywords are *New York City* and *real estate*, your title could be "Real Estate tips in New York City." Next, add these keywords into your description, but remember to keep it readable to a human visitor. Finally, add the keywords to your tags field (for more on tags, see Tip 227). Note that both your title and tags fields can be a maximum of 120 characters long, while your description can be a maximum of 5,000 characters.

3. Generate views. YouTube ranks videos not only by on-page relevance but also using factors like views, shares, ratings, comments, and the number of subscribers—in other words, the more popular a video is, the higher it will rank. For this reason, sharing your video and participating in the YouTube community is a key part of ranking both in internal search results and on Google's search results.

Tag your videos

Tags are a way of grouping videos on YouTube together within a similar theme or subject, which makes them easier to be found by users on the site looking for specific content. If you tag your video with a certain keyword phrase that someone then searches, it's likely that your video will show up in the search results for their query. Tags also affect how visible your video is in the "related videos" section of a page, which is another way of driving traffic to your own video content and channel. As a content provider, you can also subscribe to tags as a way of staying up to date with content in a particular subject, such as subscribing to tags related to golf if you're a golf coach.

Besides using tags that are relevant to your video content, you should try to use tags that are already popular within YouTube. By doing this, you increase the chances of more people seeing your videos, since more people are searching on those keyword phrases. There are two main ways to find popular tags:

1. From the main video page (www.youtube.com/videos), click on the category that relates to your business and browse through the most popular videos within it. On each video page, see what tags have been used so that you can apply these to your videos.

2. Look at the contents of the "trending topic" box at the top of the category page. It may be worth using moderately popular tags rather than the most popular ones, so that you won't be competing for views with as many other videos.

Once you've decided on your tags, enter them into the tag field underneath the title and description fields when you're uploading your video (for more about uploading videos, see Tip 228). You can enter as many tags as you like; the more you use, the more times your video will appear in search results. You can also add tags once you've uploaded your video. To do this, click the "Edit" button associated with a particular video. Once you've added your tags in the video information, click the "Save Changes" button.

TIP 228 | Upload your videos

To upload a video, click "My Videos" from the dropdown menu under your user name at the top right of the page. From here, click the "Start uploading a video now!" link and then the "Upload Video" button to locate the video on your computer. Although the video can be a maximum of 2 GB in size and up to ten minutes long, it's best to make it shorter (around two to three minutes) to keep your audience engaged.

Once you've selected the file you want to upload, click "Open" to begin uploading it. As it starts uploading, you'll be prompted to add a title, description, and tags associated with your video. The title should be a short summary encompassing what the video is about, while the description tag can contain a longer explanation. To encourage viewers to visit your site after they've watched your video, include your website URL in this description field and prompt your viewers to visit your site to find out more about the subject of the video. The tag fields are important since they affect your video's visibility on search results (for more about this, see Tip 226), so enter related keywords here, separated by comments. You'll also be able to select a category for your video, such as "sports" or "travel and recreation."

Each video that you upload contains its own individual URL, which you can share with others on your website, via e-mail, or on other social media channels you may have. Also, you'll be able to access embed code for each video so that you can display it in your own blog or website.

When you've uploaded all the video content you want to, you can organize them into playlists. By default, your "Favorites" are your default playlist, but you can create as many other playlists as you like. Playlists are a good way of grouping videos together in a series, such as a set of five "how to" videos. To create a playlist, choose "Playlists" from the dropdown menu under your user name at the top right of the page.

TIP 229 Create a call to action

Beyond just creating good content that appeals to your target audience, your video content should capitalize on people viewing it by creating a call to action that keeps them engaged with your brand. This call to action should encourage your viewers to perform a specific action that you define—whether it's to leave a comment, share the video with others, view more videos that you've created, or visit your website. There are several ways you can include a call to action when uploading your video:

- **In the description:** In your video description, provide text that encourages your visitors to take a certain action; for example, tell people where to find more information about a particular topic you're talking about in the video. When doing this, take care to keep this conversational and informative rather than a hard sell. If your desired action is for viewers to visit your website, sign up for a guru account (see Tip 225 for more on this), which will let you include your website URL in the description field. You can also think about sending viewers to a page on your website that provides information that's more specific to the information contained in the video. This may mean including the URL of a related subsection or category of your site. In this way, you create a more seamless browsing experience for YouTube visitors leaving the site and then visiting yours.

- **In the video itself:** Within the video, you can talk about how and where viewers can find more information, or you can ask them to leave a comment or to watch more related videos that are part of a series. You can also include the URL of your website in the credits at the beginning or end of the video.

- **Use annotations:** YouTube allows you to make annotations to your video once it's been uploaded. These are pieces of text that resemble speech bubbles that you can overlay on the video to provide more information to your viewers. To annotate a video, navigate to the "Manage my videos" section on your account and click the "Annotate video" button alongside the video to which you want to add annotations.

TIP 230   Leverage video responses

Besides commenting on a video in text format, you can upload video as a response to another video. Video responses let you give more in-depth and meaningful input on a particular topic, and they generally have greater visibility on a video watch page than a text response, since there are fewer of them and they appear immediately below the video. Posting a video response to a very popular video can be a good way of exposing your content to large numbers of people interested in the type of content you're offering, which will increase the amount of traffic to your own channel and watch pages and ultimately to your website (if the goal of your video is to send users to it). To find popular videos, search on keywords related to your industry or browse through related categories. If you have an existing video to use as a response, make sure it is closely related to the original video content or otherwise invest in the time to create a new response from scratch. Try to be among the first people to upload a video response so that your content gets more exposure over time and don't be offensive if you're posting a response of disagreement, as this could harm your brand's reputation to others watching the video. To upload a video response, click the "Post a video response" link under the video to which you want to respond. YouTube gives you two options: you can either record a new video or upload an existing video.

In addition to posting your own video responses, you can encourage viewers on your own watch pages or channel page to upload their own responses. This is an excellent way of encouraging interaction between your audience and your business that will also add value to other viewers who are watching. It's also a good method of idea generation and problem solving on a particular topic. Perhaps most important, all video responses contain a link to your original video below it in a sentence that says, "This is a video response to [video name]." This exposes your video to the audience of every viewer that posts a response, which in turn increases the viewings of your original video.

TIP 231 Share videos

Once you've created your video, you need to expose it to people both inside and outside of YouTube who may be interested in its contents. The more people who view your content, the more likely it is that they will share the video with others and return to your channel to watch more videos that you create. There are several ways you can do this:

- **E-mail:** E-mail your contacts about new video content from directly within the YouTube interface by clicking the "Share" link underneath the video on your video watch page. You can either e-mail your YouTube contacts or enter other contacts' e-mail addresses manually. Be careful not to do this too often, and be sure that you're letting people know about content they're likely to be interested in.

- **Post bulletins:** Send updates in the form of bulletins from your channel page to your subscribers about new videos you've uploaded. When you post a bulletin, it appears on both you and your subscribers' recent activity section of your home page.

- **Publicize on social media sites:** The "Share" link on the video watch page also lets you post a link to your video on other social media channels like Facebook, Twitter, MySpace, and Orkut. You can also enable Autoshare, which publishes your activity on YouTube (such as when you upload a video) to these other services.

- **Blog about it:** If you have a company blog, create a new post whenever you upload a new video on YouTube. You can embed the video in the blog post itself by copying and pasting the embed code provided on every video watch page.

- **Use other marketing channels:** For example, you could embed a video in your monthly newsletter or include the YouTube link in it for readers to access. You can also place links to your YouTube channel in online presentations or webcasts that you conduct, as a way to give your audience further resources on a particular topic.

Build subscribers

A good way of building up a regular, active user base for your content is to encourage users to subscribe to your channel. When they do this, they're notified of activity in your channel, such as new content being uploaded, or when you favorite or comment on a video elsewhere on the site. There are several ways you can build up a subscriber base:

■ Add a message encouraging users to subscribe within the body of your channel page and in the text of your profile page. You can also include your channel URL in the descriptions for each video you upload.

■ Let your contacts on other social media sites know about your YouTube channel. For example, add a link to your channel on your Facebook page with a note encouraging your fans to subscribe.

■ E-mail your channel URL to your existing contacts, such as business partners, vendors, or suppliers.

■ If you have a company newsletter, include a link to your channel page as an added resource within your newsletter.

■ Add people as friends within YouTube and then request that they subscribe to your channel. To add contacts, click the "Account" link dropdown from your name, and then click "Address Book" under the "Messages" tab.

■ Subscribe to other people's channels. Doing so makes them more likely to reciprocate by subscribing to your channel, but it's also a good way of keeping up to date with your industry and networking with other industry members. To find channels to subscribe to, click the "Channels" link at the top of the YouTube home page and then browse through categories related to your industry. When you find a channel you want to subscribe to, click the "Subscribe" button at the top of the page.

Before you invite people to your channel, make sure you have a good amount of video content uploaded and that you're active on the site, such as by commenting on and favoriting related videos. Having more content on it can convince YouTube users to subscribe to your channel page.

TIP 233 Participate in the community

Because YouTube is a video-sharing community, you'll be most successful in marketing your business on the site when you are a valuable, active
member. Besides allowing you to interact with others in your industry, being
active is the best way to spread awareness of your channel across the site.
The more awareness your channel has, the more people add you as friends
or visit your channel and subscribe to it. The larger your subscriber base
is, the more credibility you'll develop on the site and the more visible your
video content will be on the site as a whole. There are several ways you can
participate:

- **Comments:** Every time you leave a comment on a video, your user
name is hyperlinked to your channel page. Therefore, the more times you
leave a useful or insightful comment, the more chance you'll have that users
will click on your user name and view your channel content.

- **Post video responses:** Although they take more time to do than text
comments, they can be a more effective way of getting visibility to your
own content. To add a video response, click the "Add a video response"
link under the video to which you want to respond (for more on this, see
Tip 230).

- **Add friends:** On the home page of your YouTube account, you'll see
a box that says "Find your friends on YouTube." From here you can search
through contacts you already have in Gmail, Yahoo! Mail, and Facebook and
connect with those people who are already YouTube users. You can also
request to be friends with someone by clicking the "Add as a friend" link
on the person's channel page. Once you're friends with someone, you can
e-mail the person directly from within the YouTube interface. In the "Recent
Activity" section of your home page, you'll also be able to see your friends'
activity on the site, such as uploading a video or rating or favoriting other
videos.

- **Subscribe to channels:** This is a good way of being notified about
useful content you may be interested in from within your account. Subscribing to other channels also encourages channel owners to reciprocate and
subscribe to yours (for more on this, see Tip 232).

TIP 234 | Use Google AdWords

Besides using YouTube channels as a way to spread your video content to other users, you can advertise your product, service, or website to the site's large user base through YouTube's "self-managed" ad program. Self-managed ads are specifically aimed at small- to medium-business owners who want to create and manage their own ad campaigns, including the ad creative's and budget. Since Google owns YouTube, you can advertise on the site through Google AdWords, with your ads on the program being integrated into various areas of the site. As with regular Google AdWords ads shown on Google search results, the content of each self-managed ad is matched to the content of the page on which it's shown. AdWords also lets you display ads in two main places: alongside search results, alongside Web content, or on both. In the context of YouTube, this means that your ad will either display on internal search results pages or on video pages on the site where the content is related thematically to the contents of your ad. Using Google AdWords to display ads on the YouTube site is a good way of harnessing YouTube's large user base as a target audience for your product or service without your needing to take the time to create and upload video content to a channel page.

To start showing ads on YouTube, first sign up for an AdWords account at https://adwords.google.com. As with all Google AdWords ads, you can choose image, video, or plain text for your ad's format. To have your ads shown only within YouTube and not on Google search results or other Web properties, you'll need to specify this in your AdWords account by adding the domain youtube.com to your list of managed placements. To access this functionality, click the "Networks" tab at the ad group level and then click "show details" next to "Content: managed placements." As with all AdWords ads, how often your ads will be shown is based on an auction model: the more you're willing to pay, the more regularly your ad will be shown on the site.

TIP 235 Understand Promoted Videos

YouTube's Promoted Videos program can be a supplemental way of increasing views to your YouTube channel and video content on the site. Like using Google AdWords to advertise on YouTube, Promoted Videos are aimed at small business owners who are interested in advertising but want to manage their own campaigns and don't want to commit to a large budget. Promoted Videos work on the same relevance algorithm model as regular Google AdWords, where your videos appear above or beside internal YouTube search results for keywords that relate to your ad's content. They also appear alongside video content that is related in theme. This ensures that the audience viewing your video is more likely to be interested in its contents, as they're actively searching for similar content. Also like AdWords, Promoted Videos use an auction-based pricing model, where how much you're willing to spend relative to other advertisers determines how much exposure your Promoted Video will get. You set your maximum cost per click (CPC) for your keywords and determine a budget for your campaigns. For more on the CPC cost model in the context of using Facebook advertising, see Tip 104.

While both Google AdWords and Promoted Videos can help increase your brand's exposure on YouTube, the main difference between them is that Promoted Videos are intended to drive traffic internally to a YouTube channel or video watch page rather than to an external website. This means that your Promoted Video content needs to promote specific video content you already have on the site that you want to drive traffic to, rather than generally promoting your products or services. Within YouTube, a Promoted Video is clearly marked as such, so that viewers know it is an advertisement. As with regular videos, your Promoted Video will perform better if it features interesting, unique content.

The main steps involved in creating a Promoted Video are creating the promotion, selecting your budget and where you want your videos to show, and launching your campaign on the site (for more on how to do this, see Tip 236). To run a campaign, you need to sign up for an AdWords account at https://adwords.google.com, and you should already have a YouTube account. Once you have both, you'll need to link them together before you can create new video promotions.

TIP 236 Create Promoted Videos

Once you have an AdWords account and have linked your YouTube account to it, you're ready to start creating a Promoted Videos campaign. Rather than creating content that simply advertises your brand, product, or service, the aim of a Promoted Video is to drive traffic to more of your YouTube content or to your channel page. The call to action on a Promoted Video should therefore be an action like visiting a video watch page, leaving a comment on the video (whether in text or video format), or subscribing to your YouTube channel. To create a Promoted Video campaign:

1. Log on to your account at https://ads.youtube.com and click "Create a new promotion."

2. Choose the video that you want to be part of. Note that you have to already have uploaded your video to your YouTube account to use it in a Promoted Video. When choosing a video, you can select one you think is funny, useful, or interesting, or you may want to create a short-form "teaser" video that then links to the full-length version of it on a video watch page.

3. Write the text to accompany your video that accurately describes the video's content. For editorial guidelines, visit www.youtube.com/t/promoted_videos_editorial_policy.

4. Choose a thumbnail image that will be shown when your video is shown in search results but isn't playing. Try to select an image the sums up the main idea of your video.

5. Select the keywords for which you want the ad to appear. These should be closely related to the contents of your video to enable maximum relevance for YouTube users who will see the promotion.

6. Select your maximum cost per click (CPC). To have your video appear more often and in a more visible position on a content page or on search results, you'll need to have a higher cost per click (CPC) than other promoters. This means you're willing to pay more for someone to click on your video than someone else who is advertising on the same keyword.

7. Preview your promotion, and if you're happy with it, launch it.

SlideShare

TIP 237 Understand SlideShare

SlideShare (www.Slideshare.net) is a social networking website on which you can share documents and presentations with other SlideShare users and with anyone browsing the site. By uploading resources that can be viewed by others, you can build your business's reputation as a source of useful knowledge in a particular topic. Compared with other kinds of information like images, links, or blog posts, the documents you can upload to Slide-Share (such as PowerPoint or Word documents) are by nature more in-depth. This means you're able to provide a richer resource for your viewers, who may be potential partners or customers for your business.

SlideShare lets you share documents in a number of ways: you can e-mail the URL of the document to your network of contacts, you can embed it in your blog or website, or you can share the URL on social media sites like Facebook, LinkedIn, and Twitter from within the SlideShare interface. When you upload a presentation to SlideShare, it is automatically grouped with related content so that people viewing other related presentations or looking for content on a particular topic will be able to see your content too.

The more you interact with other SlideShare users, the more people will be exposed to the material you've uploaded to the site. You can be active on the site by doing things like commenting, tagging, bookmarking, and favoriting their slide shows or by joining groups on a specific topic where you can access presentations from other group members. If you find some users' material particularly useful, you can follow them to keep track of any new documents they upload. Finally, you can market your SlideShare presentation two ways: AdShare, which places targeted ads, and LeadShare, which allows users to enter their information. Overall, SlideShare's social networking and sharing functionality makes it a useful way of networking with others in your industry and of keeping up to date with industry-specific knowledge and research.

TIP 238 Create a SlideShare account

Creating your SlideShare account involves four main steps:

1. Sign up. Start by signing up for an account at www.slideshare.net. You'll be prompted to enter a user name and password, associate an existing e-mail address with your account, and select an account type. You'll select your account type based on the industry you're in, such as "Company," "Event Organizer," "University or School." Making this selection helps people find your content when they're searching or browsing on the site. Next, enter your geographic location, agree to the terms and conditions, and validate your e-mail address.

2. Find your friends. SlideShare prompts you to connect with people you already know who may already have profiles on the site. If your contacts aren't on the site, you can invite them to join. In either case, SlideShare lets you choose contacts to add by connecting directly with your existing Web-based e-mail accounts, such as Gmail, Yahoo! Mail, or Hotmail. When you connect with someone on SlideShare, you become the person's follower, which means you'll be able to see his or her activity on the site from your own profile.

3. Fill out the rest of your profile. Your profile information is visible to anyone on the site who accesses your material, so it's a good idea to fill it out as comprehensively as you can. Within your profile information, also include a link to your blog or website so that you can drive traffic to them from the SlideShare site and provide an avenue for people to find out more about you. Within your profile you can also add in tags related to your business. This helps people find your content when they search or browse on the site for a specific subject.

4. Start uploading. Once you've connected with friends and filled out your profile, you're ready to upload your first document or presentation. For more on how to do this, see Tip 240.

You can edit your profile details at any future point by clicking the "Edit profile" link in the left column of your profile page. In the edit section, you can also manage your contacts and your privacy settings on the site.

TIP 239 Create good content

The biggest factor in your success on SlideShare is the quality of the content you're uploading. Even if your presentations are exposed to large numbers of people, the real value to your brand in terms of their becoming regular readers or even customers is how useful they find your information to be. Best practices for creating good content include these:

- **Be useful:** Create a presentation where the primary aim is to provide useful, interesting, or unique information to your reader rather than one that is a thinly veiled way of pushing sales of your product or service.

- **Make it stand out:** Make your presentation different from competing resources on the same subject. You could take a unique angle on the information itself or in your physical presentation of the slides themselves.

- **Give practical advice:** Don't be too theoretical in your presentation. Rather, give practical advice such as how-to demonstrations that contain step-by-step processes or provide graphic illustrations of case studies.

- **Upload a lot of content:** The more content you have on SlideShare, the more credibility you'll develop on the site as a useful resource in your industry. To bulk up your content, upload past content that you created previously, such as presentations, white papers, or articles. Be sure that anything you upload is still relevant to your audience.

- **Make sure it's readable:** Presentations in the SlideShare interface are viewed at a 66 percent resolution, so make sure your text, graphics, and diagrams within the presentations are visible at this size.

- **Take out the animation:** SlideShare doesn't support dynamic elements in a presentation like Flash or transition animation. If you have these in your presentation, make a static version where you split out animated slides into several sequential slides that still make sense to the reader.

- **Include your contact details:** Someone may read your presentation without looking at your profile details, so include your contact details on the last slide.

TIP 240 | Upload presentations

The central activity you'll do on SlideShare is uploading presentations to your account. You can upload three types of content: presentations (Keynote or PowerPoint files), documents (Microsoft Word or OpenOffice), or spreadsheets (Excel, OpenOffice, or iWork). Note that files can be a maximum of 100 MB each in size. To upload a presentation, follow these steps:

1. Click the "Upload" button in the top navigation menu on the home page of your account.

2. Select the file you want to upload from your computer by clicking the "Browse and Select Files" button.

3. Enter a title, description, and tags for your presentation. The document's title will heavily influence whether it is clicked through from search results or category pages, so be sure to make this snappy and information packed and a good summary of what the presentation is about. Although only a title is mandatory, it's a good idea to fill out the description and tags as well, as they'll affect how easily you can be found by people who are looking for content related to yours—both on internal SlideShare search results and on search engines like Google.

4. Choose how visible you want your document to be from the "Privacy" dropdown box. You can share it with everyone or only with people you follow (i.e., your contacts), or you can make it private if you want it to be an internal document. If you make the document private, you'll be given a "secret" URL, which won't be visible on your profile but which you can e-mail to selected people, such as your colleagues or a prospective client.

5. Select a category for the presentation, such as "Finance" or "How to & DIY." This will ensure your presentation is visible to people browsing through these categories on the site.

6. Once you've finished, click the "Publish All" button. After the document has been uploaded, you'll be able to see it on your profile page under the "Documents" or "Presentations" section of the site, depending on whether it's a text document or presentation.

TIP 241 Use LeadShare

LeadShare is one of SlideShare's two business services that help you promote your account by encouraging people viewing your presentations to submit their details to you. This is done through a lead form that appears in several possible places: alongside your presentation, when they attempt to download it, within the presentation itself, or externally if you embed your presentation on your blog or website. The cost of LeadShare depends on the type of lead information you want to gather. For example, gathering a name, e-mail address, and company name costs $1 per lead, while a phone number or physical address cost $2 extra each (remember, though, that the less information you ask your audience to fill out, the more likely it is they'll fill out the form). To get started with LeadShare, you need to have uploaded at least one document or presentation to your SlideShare account. Then follow these steps:

1. When you're logged in, click the "Business" link in the top navigation menu.

2. Click the orange "Try LeadShare" button.

3. Fill in a title and opening message for your lead form. The more compelling your messaging, the more likely it is your visitors will fill in the form.

4. On the same page, select your targeted country for your lead form. For example, select "United States" from the dropdown list to only have your lead form shown to people in the United States.

5. Under "Advanced Options," you can select additional information you want your audience to provide (such as a phone number). You can also select where on your account you want the lead form to show.

6. Click "Continue to Step 2."

7. On the next page, select how much money you'd like to add to your account, fill out your PayPal or credit card details, and then click "Submit."

To view statistics for your campaign, such as the number of leads and the cost per lead, select the "Business" header link from the home page and then "View Your Campaigns" link under the LeadShare section. To create a new campaign at any time, click the "Create New Campaign" link on this page.

TIP 242 | Use AdShare

AdShare is SlideShare's advertising program that lets you promote your uploaded presentations or documents on the site. Used in conjunction with LeadShare (for more on this see Tip 241), AdShare is a good way to increase the targeted leads for your business as a result of your uploaded documents. An AdShare ad consists of a thumbnail image of the first slide of your presentation and the presentation's title. This ad is then placed near other related content on the SlideShare site—for example, alongside other presentations in the same category or on search results for keywords relating to your presentation's contents. AdShare is priced using a cost-per-click (CPC) payment model (currently set at $0.25), so you'll only pay when someone clicks on your ad. You can target your campaign to only promote certain presentations and only to SlideShare users in certain countries. To get started with AdShare, you need to already have presentations or documents uploaded to your account. Once you've done this, follow these steps:

1. When you're logged in, click the "Business" link in the top navigation menu.

2. Click the orange "Try AdShare" button.

3. Fill in your campaign name, select the documents or presentations you want to be promoted, and choose how much you want to spend.

4. Select your campaign targeting. For example, select "United States" from the dropdown list to only have your ads shown to people in the United States.

5. Also in this section, choose where in the site you'd like your ads to appear. They can either be shown alongside content in a specific category or any related content on the site (e.g., search results).

6. Click the "Create Campaign" button.

7. If you haven't already added funds to your account, you'll be able to do this using a credit card or PayPal account.

At any time, view statistics for your campaign including the number of clicks and your click-through rate by selecting the "Business" header link on the home page and then "View Your Campaigns" link under the AdShare section.

TIP 243   Join groups

Joining SlideShare groups is an excellent way of networking with other SlideShare users who are interested in topics about which you have expertise, while sharing your presentation within a group lets you expose content to a more targeted audience than just general site users. Groups can be an excellent way of gaining knowledge in a particular topic by learning from others who are sharing related information, and you can also use them as a forum from which to get feedback on aspects relating to your business, such as a new product or service you're developing that you outline in a presentation.

To find groups to join, use the SlideShare search tool to find users, groups, or presentations on a particular topic, such as "graphic design." On the search results page, click the "Groups/Events" tab and then click on group names in the results to see the group pages. To join a group, click the "+ Add to my groups" link at the right of the group page—this group will now appear in the "Groups" tab of your profile.

Along with joining existing groups, you can create your own group by clicking the "Create a group" link in the left column of your profile page. Be sure to search and see that no identical group already exists. Once you've done this, click the "Create a Group" link. You'll be asked to choose a group name, select a category into which it should be placed, upload an image, and select whether you want the group to be viewable to everyone (public) or private. You may want to create a private group only for your colleagues, whom you can then invite to view internal presentations that you upload. You can also choose how you allow people to join the group (for example, letting people join only with your approval), and you can decide on your posting settings (for example, letting only members post). If you do create a group, keep it active as a way to grow its membership but also as a way of publicizing it: group activities are published on members' news feeds, which keeps them returning and interacting in it.

TIP 244 | Promote your profile externally

The more you can promote your SlideShare presence externally, the more traffic you'll drive to your presentations, and the more readers you'll get. There are several ways you can do this:

- **Embed:** SlideShare lets you easily embed your presentations or documents into your website or blog so that your existing readers can access your presentations from within your website. If they want to see more, they can click through to your SlideShare profile from within the embedded file. To embed a presentation, copy the code in the "Embed" text box on the right side of the SlideShare presentation page and paste it into the code of the page where you want the presentation to appear.

- **Add to other social media sites:** From your SlideShare profile page, you'll see two links underneath your profile image: "Add SlideShare to your LinkedIn profile" and "Add SlideShare to your Facebook profile." When you sync with either or both of these sites, you can upload presentations directly from SlideShare into these two sites.

- **Publicize your URL:** Once you've uploaded a presentation, you can e-mail your contacts with the URL of your presentation, or you can share it on Twitter, Facebook, Delicious, and more by clicking the sharing icons beneath the presentation.

- **Add widgets:** SlideShare lets you embed widgets in other locations that pull through activity from your SlideShare account. For example, the "SlideShare Playlist" lets you customize a hyperlinked list of documents and presentations from your SlideShare account. To access this widget, select "Widgets" from the main menu of SlideShare once you're logged in. From here, select your preferences of which content you'd like to be pulled through. Based on these preferences, SlideShare will generate code that you can copy and then paste into the HTML of the page in which you want it to appear. Similar to playlists, "Presentation Packs" let you display a group of presentations in one widget, which can be useful if you want to display a set of presentations, such as those related to one single conference. Mini-badges are hyperlinked buttons you can include on your blog or website that link through to your SlideShare account. Finally, the sidebar widget contains a feed from your SlideShare account that you can embed on your blog.

Podcasting

TIP 245 | Understand podcasting

A podcast is a digital media file, typically in audio or video format, that is broadcast on the Internet (either in a podcast directory or on your blog or website) and that people can subscribe to. Like a radio show, podcasts are usually produced as a series that contains episodes created on a regular basis. Unlike a radio show, though, anyone without access to a radio studio can create a podcast using fairly basic technical equipment. The result is that the podcast genre has grown substantially in recent years, and today you can subscribe to podcasts on a large number of topics, from fashion and sports cars to guitar lessons or astronomy. There are two types of podcasts:

1. Audio podcasts. These contain sound only, which makes them relatively small in file size and so easier to download and play on any portable music player.

2. Video podcasts. These have both audio and video included, making them larger in file size and requiring a music player with video capabilities.

Whether you choose to create an audio or a video podcast, both can be an effective way to market your business by providing information, insights, and entertainment to your target audience in an audio format. The specific subject of the podcast you create can vary depending on your goal for it as well as your industry. You could create podcasts for sharing knowledge, entertaining, conducting interviews with experts, or simply to share opinions on a topic with others. Whatever you choose as your subject, you should have some authority in the area, and the podcast should provide some unique value to your audience (for more on researching topics, see Tip 246).

The basic process for creating and launching a podcast is to create the audio file and accompanying artwork, upload it to your site or podcast directory along with an RSS file so people can subscribe to it, and then market the podcast to your target demographic. Your audience then subscribes to your podcast and receives it automatically each time you publish a new episode. The rest of this podcasting section will describe this process.

TIP 246 Research topics

The first step in creating a podcast is to think of a topic to broadcast. Since you're using podcasting to market your business, think of a topic that's related to your industry, that would be useful or interesting for an audience, and that would preferably show your expertise and knowledge in that particular subject. For example, if you're a Web design firm, you could create a podcast series on how to design websites, while if you're a travel agency, you could provide a series of podcasts on a particular region or country. Or, if you own a chain of health clubs, you could record podcasts on health and fitness where you interview nutrition experts and provide workout tips. When thinking of a topic, it's important to know who your target listeners would be (for example, working parents or women under the age of thirty). Having a good understanding of this will help you create content that appeals to them, and it will also help you market more efficiently to those people.

Once you've decided on a topic, the next thing to think about is your podcast's structure and how you could break up the information from one episode to the next. A podcast series typically has one common overarching theme, while each particular episode can focus on a specific subtopic. A good way to get a feel for what makes for an engaging podcast and how it is best structured is to listen to other podcasts before you create your own. You can find these by browsing categories in podcast directories like Podcast Alley (www.podcastalley.com) or at Podcast.com (www.podcast.com) or by searching in Apple iTunes' podcast directory. Once you've decided on a topic, start writing out the podcasts so that there is a good structure to each episode.

A key factor in building subscribers to your series is to create regular podcasts, so think about whether you could commit to recording them regularly, such as once a week or once a month.

Creating a podcast can be a fairly simple process that requires only basic technical equipment. Still, if you'd prefer not to do the recording and editing yourself, a variety of websites will manage the entire process for you, from recording the podcast to publishing and hosting it on their site. Some examples include MyPodcast (www.mypodcast.com), GarageBand (www.garageband.com), ClickCaster (www.clickcaster.com), and BlogTalkRadio (www.blogtalkradio.com). Using these sites means you don't have as much flexibility as with creating your own podcast, but it saves you time and effort.

If you do want to create your own podcast, you'll need a computer with recording software and a microphone. Recording software varies in terms of complexity and cost, but free software such as Audacity (http://audacity.sourceforge.net) or GarageBand (free with most Macs) are good to start with. Technical pointers for recording the actual podcast vary according to the software you're using, and most programs give clear explanations and tutorials for how to get started. The common steps in recording an audio podcast are:

- **Recording:** Once you have your recording software and microphone up and running, you're ready to start recording your podcast.

- **Editing:** This is where you do things like lower the volume of certain tracks, remove silences, and take out background noise. Most podcasts begin and end with music, so part of the editing process also involves adding in music. Make sure that any audio you use is your own or that you have the rights to use it. Sites such as Royalty-Free Music (www.royaltyfreemusic.com) let you buy music to use without charging royalties. Recording software programs like GarageBand provide you with jingles and other sound effects that you can use within your podcast.

- **Markers:** These allow you to add things like chapter titles, chapter artwork, and URLs for each podcast chapter.

- **Artwork:** Having album art as part of your podcast is essential only if you want to submit your podcast to Apple iTunes. As with using music in your podcast, make sure you have the copyright to use images in your album art.

TIP 248   Create your podcast RSS feed

One of the unique features of a podcast is that it allows users to subscribe to it. This is done through the creation of an RSS feed that is based on the MP3 file of your podcast. The RSS feed for your podcast contains links to the podcast episodes as well as information about each episode such as the title and description, the language it's recorded in, and any copyright information. The feed URL is submitted to a podcast directory, and then when someone subscribes to your podcast, his or her feed aggregator (such as Google Reader or My Yahoo!) automatically downloads new podcasts as they become available. In the case of iTunes, readers will subscribe to a podcast, the episodes for which are then downloaded into their iTunes account as they become available. For more on RSS feeds, see Tip 11.

You can create an RSS feed for your podcast in a variety of ways. If you're using sites such as ClickCaster or MyPodcast to create, publish, and host your podcasts, or if you're using recording software like GarageBand, your RSS feed will be created automatically for you. To create an RSS feed yourself, you can use FeedBurner (for more on FeedBurner, see Tip 12), or you can use separate RSS creators like FeedForAll that may offer more features than the free software packages can offer. Alternatively, if you're hosting your podcast on your blog with Blogger or WordPress, you can use its RSS plug-ins to generate your podcast feed.

Once you've created your RSS feed, it's a good idea to validate it so you ensure that it doesn't contain any errors and that it conforms to common RSS standards. You can do this in a number of ways. One of the easiest is by entering in your RSS feed URL at a feed validator such as http://feedvalidator .org or at http://validator.w3.org. Once you've validated it, you're ready to submit it to directories where listeners can find it and subscribe.

TIP 249   Optimize for search engines

Making sure your podcast is indexed and visible on Google is a good way to target external traffic to your podcast and increase your subscriber numbers. Search engine traffic is of a high quality because visitors are actively looking for content like yours and so will be more likely to subscribe to your podcast once they click through from search engine results pages. There are several ways you can optimize your podcast to increase its search engine visibility:

■ **Add text to your podcast:** Add in keywords that you think people would be searching to find your podcast within the title and descriptions for each episode chapter. Also include your main targeted keyword phrase in the podcast's title.

■ **Optimize a landing page:** Creating landing pages for podcast episodes gives search engines context to the audio file to help them work out what the audio file is about. For each podcast episode, write a summary of the episode or transcribe the spoken words into a transcript. In both cases, include keyword phrases that relate to the podcast's content within the text. Doing this provides search engines with good text-based contextual information about the theme of the podcast episode. Be sure you don't overload keyword phrases in the text—keep the text natural so that it is still easy for a human to read. Once you've written the text, create a separate page on your site or blog that contains the text of the podcast and make the page title or blog post title the same as the podcast title. On the same landing page, include a link to the audio file, as well as to the feed URL for visitors to subscribe to future episodes.

■ **Optimize your RSS feed:** Besides external search engines like Google, podcast directories like iTunes contain internal search engines that visitors use to find new podcasts to subscribe to. To help your podcast achieve visibility on these internal search results, include text information within your feed, such as the author and title, chapter titles and information, and copyright information.

Upload your podcast

Once you've created your RSS feed and MP3 file, your next step is to upload it to the Web. There are several options for doing this. If you're using a site such as MyPodcast or ClickCaster, the site will host and publish your podcast for you automatically. If you have your own website or blog, you can upload it there, but remember that every time your podcast is downloaded it will use up bandwidth. If you do go this route, make sure you're aware of how much it will cost you if your podcast becomes very popular, resulting in a large number of downloads. When you upload your podcast to your site, you'll need to upload both the RSS file and the MP3 file for each episode into the same directory on your Web server. Then, each time you add a new episode, you'll need to make sure your RSS feed is updated to contain that new episode, and that the new MP3 file containing the new episode is uploaded into the same directory. If you don't want to host your own podcast but aren't using an all-in-one service on a site like MyPodcast, you can use a specialized podcast-hosting site like Liberated Syndication (www.libsyn .com) or Podbean (www.podbean.com).

As mentioned in Tip 249, if you have a blog, create a new blog post dedicated to each new podcast episode. Besides helping to ensure good search engine visibility through text-based content, a blog post will help to market your new podcast to your blog readers. Even if you don't have a blog, include a summary blurb in the resources section of your website for each new episode. In both cases, include the link to download the podcast file alongside the summary or blog post and use the podcast title as the anchor text within the link. If you're using an external company to host the file, such as those mentioned earlier, link to the URL of the external site where the podcast resides that your viewers can click on to access the episode.

TIP 251 | Submit to podcast directories

Once you've created your podcast and uploaded it to the Web, you can start to use ways to build your subscriber numbers. Besides marketing your podcast via external sources (for more on this, see Tip 252), one of the most effective ways to increase your podcast's visibility is to submit it to podcast directories such as these:

- **Apple iTunes:** This is one of the largest podcast directories; it contains thousands of listings of free podcasts on a broad range of topics. iTunes works by having you submit the URL of your podcast's RSS feed, but it won't host the actual MP3 file on the site. Therefore, to submit to iTunes you should first have your podcast uploaded, either on your own site or on an external podcast-hosting site (for more on this, see Tip 250). To submit your podcast to iTunes, log in to the iTunes store, navigate to the podcast page, and then click "Submit a Podcast" link in the right navigational menu. You'll need to provide your podcast's feed URL and other information about it, including the category into which it should be submitted. Note too that iTunes requires your podcast to have album art for it to be accepted into its directory. Once you've submitted your podcast, you'll get a confirmation e-mail to say that iTunes staff is reviewing your submission. Once it is approved, you'll receive another e-mail containing a link to the podcast within the directory. Once this happens, the iTunes server can take up to a day to index your podcast before it becomes visible on iTunes' internal search engine.

- **Other directories:** Not everyone may have access to iTunes, so to get the widest reach for your podcast, it's worth submitting to other directories as well. There are a large number of podcast directories in existence, including sites like Podcast Alley (www.podcastalley.com), Podcast Directory (www.podcastdirectory.com), and Podbean (www.podbean.com). Some sites require registration, while others let you submit your podcasts right away. Most directories contain specific categories to which you submit your podcast, which makes it easier for listeners to browse and find content related to a particular theme.

TIP 252 — Market your podcast

Besides submitting your podcast to directories (see Tip 251 for more on this), there are ways you can market your podcast to increase your subscriber base. Most of these involve leveraging existing audiences you have in other places to become subscribers to your podcasts as well:

1. Find your target market. Know where your ideal listeners are aggregated on the Web so that you can advertise your podcasts in that space. For example, if you create podcasts on Web design, participate in Web design forums or social networks and then provide your podcast as a useful resource in related discussions. As always with group participation on social media sites, be an active, value-added member of the group rather than simply pushing your own product.

2. Link to it. Everywhere that you have an existing online presence is a potential opportunity to link to your podcast. The first place to do this is to link to it from your blog or website, but you can also include links to new episodes from your Twitter feed and a link to your RSS feed from your Facebook page, LinkedIn profile, and other social bookmarking sites like Digg and Delicious.

3. Use your other marketing communications. Examples include linking to your podcast URL in your presentations or embedding links to the audio file within your press releases.

4. Provide widgets. These allow your users to embed your podcasts as audio in their site or on their Facebook page.

5. E-mail people. If you have a company newsletter, include links to new podcast episodes in each edition and provide a snippet of text information about each one. Because your newsletter audience is already familiar with your brand, there's a better chance they'll be interested in subscribing to your podcast content as well.

6. Advertise. Through self-service advertising programs like Google AdWords, you can advertise your podcast on search engine results pages or on pages where the content is related. Sign up for AdWords at http:// adwords.google.com.

7

Reviews and Opinions

AS A RESULT of social media's widespread usage and popularity, the influence of online communities on people's purchasing decisions is more pronounced than ever. Like never before, when people are in the research or "education" phase of the buying cycle, they have access to a wider audience of current, past, or prospective customers worldwide that they can consult before making their decision. From a business's perspective, it's therefore more important than it ever has been to monitor and improve your reputation online as a way of ensuring that prospective customers have a positive experience with your brand when they're in the research phase.

One of the primary sources of product research is the review website, whose overall goal is to help consumers make informed decisions about buying a product or service. There are two broad categories of review sites: those run by single individuals or groups of editors and those run by communities where members perform peer reviews. The strong adoption of social media in recent years along with technological ability has meant that peer reviews have become extremely influential. On peer-driven review websites like Yelp, Epinions, or Amazon, anyone can post his or her feelings about a product or service for all future buyers to see. As a business marketing yourself on these channels, it's essential for your brand reach to be featured on online review websites. But just being featured is not enough—the general opinion on that website about your business will determine your success. While your product or service should inherently be good enough so that you believe in it, there are several strategies for engaging with your customer on these forums. If you do it right, review websites can be an excellent tool for converting a prospective buyer into an actual customer.

In addition to the general review websites listed here, there are industry-specific review websites, such as tech review sites and travel websites. Having your product reviewed and spoken about on these niche review websites is a good way of exposing your brand to a more targeted audience that is specifically looking for your product.

Reviews and Opinions Overview

TIP 253 Respond to positive reviews

If your business is being spoken about on a review website, the most important thing to do is to engage with the conversation that's happening—whether it's positive or negative. This is especially important because the number of people reading your review is likely to be higher than you think for two main reasons:

1. Depending on the visibility of the review site's domain in search engines, people searching for your company name may see the review conversation in results and click through to the page, even if that was not their original intention.

2. Many review readers don't post but only read what's written, so the number of readers is usually higher than the number of posts in a review thread.

While it's important to handle negative reviews properly (for more on this, see Tip 254), you should also respond to good reviews as a way of showing the reviewer and future readers that you listen to your customers and acknowledge their feedback. When responding to a positive review, your intention should be to show appreciation for the good review rather than to solicit another sale or action from the reviewer, which could annoy the reviewer and undo the goodwill that has been created around your brand. Therefore, don't ask the person to buy your product and don't add the person to your mailing list. You also shouldn't offer them any kind of reward for the review, since this could be interpreted as a bribe either by the reviewer or by the people reading your response. Try to respond to a positive review as quickly as you can, which will improve your image as a proactive business. To stay up to date with new reviews so that you can respond quickly, make a habit of checking review sites regularly or subscribe to their content.

Although many review websites allow you to respond privately, it may be a better idea to respond publicly so that people reading the review can also see your response to the original poster.

Respond to negative reviews

Ignoring a negative review can make a bad situation worse, so you should always respond. When you do, keep the following best practices in mind:

- **Be polite:** Treat the reviewer with respect. Being rude is the fastest way to lose a current or potential customer and spread a negative perception about your brand and business.

- **Be humble:** If you genuinely are in the wrong, apologize and take responsibility for the situation.

- **Provide a solution quickly:** Respond as quickly as you can and always try to suggest a solution to the problem as soon as you can. It's very possible to turn a bad review around by being prompt, honest, and proactive. In doing this, you're giving yourself an opportunity to show real customer service—which may result in the reviewer's changing his or her opinion of your brand.

- **Don't become defensive:** Even if you think the reviewer is wrong or inaccurate, you will damage your brand's reputation even more by being defensive about the problem in a public arena. Even if you respond privately and are defensive, you risk angering your reviewer, who can then repost what you e-mailed. Rather, stay levelheaded by acknowledging the reviewer's feedback and calmly stating your point of view while staying objective. It's worth noting that readers are usually more likely to side with the reviewer than with the business that is involved.

- **Keep it simple:** Resist the urge to have a drawn-out public dialogue with the negative reviewer or with readers of that review. If someone says something negative about your brand, acknowledge it, but move on and talk about the solution as soon as you can.

- **Keep the review up:** Many businesses feel that the best strategy for dealing with a bad review is to get it taken down from the review websites. Most review sites won't do this and, even if they can, this is detrimental to your brand as you could come across as a company that doesn't promote open discussion or value its customers' opinion.

- **Learn from it:** If you were in the wrong, use review criticism constructively as a way to improve your business in the future.

Yelp

TIP 255 | Understand Yelp

Founded in 2004 as an "online urban city guide that helps people find cool places to eat, shop, drink, relax and play,"[1] Yelp (www.yelp.com) is an online review site that contains more than nine million local reviews.[2] Although originally started in San Francisco, Yelp has grown in size and now has a presence in all major cities, selected towns, and other locations in the United States, as well as in major cities within the UK, Canada, and Ireland.

Businesses with a physical presence can list their details on the Yelp site for their city—for example a restaurant, clothing store, movie theater, or dry cleaner in Los Angeles. Once the business's details have been added to the site, Yelp users can write reviews on the service and give a rating of between one and five stars. Due to its large user base and geographic reach, Yelp is a powerful channel of word of mouth within the community, which means that it can have a powerful effect on your brand's reputation. A positive review, for example, can result in a significant increase in customers. Yelp also attracts external traffic from search engines, and so listing your website as part of your Yelp business profile can be another channel by which to drive traffic to your site. On the other hand, negative reviews can have an equally strong impact on your business, and so it's important to have a strategy to deal with bad reviews too (for more on how to respond to negative reviews, see Tip 254).

Reviews on Yelp are based on a strong social networking platform. Via internal e-mail, members can connect with each other to share photos, compare reviews, blog posts, and more. This social networking aspect is fully integrated into reviews on the site: when you read a review, you can click on the reviewer's profile to read all the reviews he or she has created and to add the reviewer as a friend on a site. This helps other users place the reviews in context and judge the reviewer's opinions and perspectives against previous entries.

TIP 256 | Claim your profile

The first step in establishing your business's presence on Yelp is to claim your profile. Previously, business owners had to sign up as regular Yelp users to do this, but Yelp now allows you to create a specialized business owner's account. To sign up, go to https://biz.yelp.com and click the "Get A Business Owner Account" button at the right of the page. Since any Yelp user can add your business to Yelp without being part of the company, you should start by searching the directory to see whether your business is already listed. If your business isn't listed, click the "having trouble finding your business" link at the bottom of the dropdown box from the search field. On the next page you'll enter details about your business, including your business's name, physical address, Web address, and hours. Also select a category for your business, which will affect how visible you are in search results for users looking for a business in your industry, as well as how visible you are when they browse by category.

If your business is listed, you'll be asked to enter your details, including your name, e-mail address, and password. Next, you'll need to confirm that you're the business owner. Yelp verifies that you're the owner of the business through phone verification. When you add a new listing and add your associated phone number, the system will call that number and provide you with a code that you'll then enter into the site as confirmation. Once the verification process is complete, take the time to fill out your profile comprehensively beyond the basic details like your business hours and contact details. By adding things like a history of your business, photos of your location, and information about special offers you're currently running, you create a better hook for people viewing your page that encourages them to leave a review or visit your website.

Once you've claimed your business, you'll receive e-mail alerts when a new review is written about your business, and you'll be able to respond directly to reviewers via e-mail. As a business owner you'll also be able to see statistics on who has viewed your page.

TIP 257 | Solicit reviews

Once you've listed your business, the next step is to start getting reviews—preferably positive ones. Higher-profile and better-established businesses will naturally attract more Yelp reviews than small or new companies. If yours is one of the latter, there are two main ways that you can get others to write reviews of your business:

- **Ask your customers:** Even if you have happy customers, they may not think to write a review about their experience with your business on Yelp. Let them know you're on the site by linking to your Yelp profile from other online channels such as your blog, website, e-mail signature, and company newsletter. You can also publicize your Yelp profile in your offline materials, on your restaurant menu or in leaflets that outline your services and prices. If you have enough positive reviews, you are eligible to receive a "People love us on Yelp" sticker that you can display on your business's premises.

- **Ask your network:** You can also ask people with whom you have an existing relationship, such as your friends, suppliers, partners, or vendors, to leave reviews. Rather than e-mailing them all at once, e-mail different subsets of people around once a month and ask them to leave reviews. Although this process is more time-consuming, it's worth it to ensure that your profile has a more natural buildup of reviews added to it. When you ask someone you know to leave a review for your business on Yelp, ask the person to leave his or her honest opinion of your business rather than a "fake" review that's intended to blatantly drum up your sales. Besides looking made up to readers of your business profile, these kinds of reviews will be deleted if Yelp thinks they're not genuine. How the site decides whether a review is a fake depends on a variety of factors, such as how many other reviews the reviewer has written. For this reason it's preferable to ask people you know who are already active on Yelp to write reviews for you.

Use your account information

Once you've set up your business account and are starting to get reviews, there are several other ways you can use your profile to connect with the Yelp community:

- **Update with offers and announcements:** On the "offers and announcements" page in your Yelp business account, you can upload details about news, events, and special offers that your business is currently running. In addition to improving your brand image, keeping your profile current increases the chances that people will return to view it, as well as to share it with others they know. The other advantage of uploading offers and announcements is that these are indexed in Yelp search results, so that you get added exposure for people who are searching for related content. Note that you shouldn't use announcements to respond to reviews or to request more reviews.

- **View stats:** In the summary tab of your Yelp business owner account, you'll see statistics showing you how many people are viewing your Yelp page. This can be an effective way of measuring how successful your marketing efforts are in marketing your Yelp page. For example, you can track how many people view your page immediately after you post your Yelp profile on your Facebook page. You can also do this to track the effectiveness of announcements, discount promotions, or special offers that you display on your profile.

- **Install your badge:** Installing a Yelp badge on your website or blog encourages your existing readers, or customers buying products off your site, to visit your Yelp page and leave a review. To be able to install the badge, you first need to have a certain number of reviews written about your business. Once you do, click the "Get badges for your website" link on the summary tab of your business owner's account. From here you'll be given a snippet of custom code that can copy and paste into the code of the page where you want the badge to appear.

Get involved with the community

As with any other social networking site, you'll get the most use out of Yelp by being an active participant. Being involved in the site as a business owner makes both parties active in the review process, which makes for a more objective and balanced discussion around a particular business. Says Yelp, "The minute a business owner humanizes and puts a face on a business, it changes the conversation."[1] There are several ways you can be active in the Yelp community that help you become a value-added member of the site. Start by writing reviews of other businesses in your area. For example, you could review your favorite coffee shop even if you own a pet store. This is also beneficial for you as a business owner, since that business may return the favor and write a review for your company.

Yelp allows you as a business owner to recommend up to five businesses. While you can recommend businesses you know and like, it may be a strategic decision to recommend businesses that are in the same industry and location but aren't competitors so that they can refer their customers to you. For example, if you're a wedding planning service, you may want to recommend a wedding cake maker in your city, who can then recommend you back as a complementary service. In this scenario, each set of customers will benefit from the recommendations each business makes.

Take advantage of Yelp's social networking functionality by adding friends and building and maintaining your network of friends. Yelp helps you add people you're already connected with in e-mail programs like Gmail and Yahoo!, but you can also add reviewers as friends by clicking on the "Add as a friend" button on a user's profile page. It's also worthwhile to connect with other business owners on the site whose services complement yours (like the wedding planning/wedding cake example just mentioned). Once you're connected with them, you can form a mutually beneficial relationship by writing reviews and referring customers to each other.

TIP 260 Respond publicly and privately

When someone leaves a review on your Yelp profile, it's important to engage in the conversation and respond to the review (for responding to positive and negative reviews, see Tips 253 and 254). Yelp lets you respond both publicly, in the form of a comment underneath the review, or privately, where you can e-mail the reviewer once after he or she has written a review. Public responses are good for showing both the reviewer and any other person reading the review that you're a fan of open discussion, that you listen to your customers, and that you're prepared to find a solution in the case of a negative review. Public responses are also useful if you want to update information in the review or correct it, such as when someone mentions a menu item or drink that you no longer offer or when you can't resolve a problem through a private message on Yelp. To leave a public response, log in to your business account and then click the "Reviews" tab. From there you'll be able to add your comment, which will appear under that particular review on your business's profile page. As mentioned in Tip 254, always be polite, objective, and honest in your response rather than being defensive.

In addition to leaving a public response, Yelp lets you contact the reviewer privately via e-mail. As part of the site's efforts to combat spam, you will be able to send only one e-mail to the reviewer at a time until the reviewer writes back to you. In the same way, the reviewer is allowed to send only one e-mail back to you until you respond back, and so forth. If you respond privately, stick to the same rules that you do when you're responding publicly: be polite, don't try to solicit more from that customer, and don't be defensive. By following these rules, you increase the chance of the customer's responding to you in a continuing dialogue and of improving the customer's perception of your brand.

A good route to take may be to respond publicly and then follow up privately with the reviewer to reinforce that you've taken the feedback seriously. This may be even more important in the case of a negative review.

Epinions

TIP 261 Understand Epinions

Owned by Shopping.com, which was in turn acquired by eBay in 2005, Epinions is a consumer review site where users can review products or services in more than thirty categories such as books, music, electronics, and travel. Epinions calls itself a source of "unbiased advice," which means that if your product or service gets a favorable write-up on the site, others will see this recommendation as unbiased and are therefore more likely to trust it, which will in turn have more of an impact on whether someone else buys that product or service.

One of the key ways in which Epinions keeps its reviews credible is via its "Web of Trust," which is where users can indicate the reviewers they trust and those that they don't. Together with rating a review, your personal Web of Trust will determine in which order you see opinions on the site (for more about the Web of Trust, see Tip 264). The social networking aspect of Epinions also lets you connect with potential customers by adding them to your "Trust" list.

Besides writing reviews, users can rate reviews as being helpful or not and can leave comments on other people's reviews. Epinions provides a good way of monitoring your reputation online through its alert system, where you're e-mailed whenever a review is written about your product or service. Reviews on the site are supplemented with educational resources in the form of buying guides, how-to guides, and product definitions. Once you've decided on a product, the site also provides you with pricing comparisons and merchant availability for you to compare prices.

Epinions can also be used as a way to establish authority in your industry by writing related reviews yourself as a business owner. For example, if you're an electronics retailer, you could provide reviews on electronic equipment that would help to build your reputation as someone who's knowledgeable about electronics. If your reviews are particularly helpful, you can become a top reviewer, advisor, or category lead, which means more exposure for you on your site and more referral traffic to your website via your Epinions profile page.

Set up your profile

If you're writing reviews on Epinions as a way to establish yourself as a source of knowledge in your industry, the first step is to set up your user profile. As with most other reviews and social media sites, your profile page on Epinions contains personal information about you, including your biographical information and your contact details. This is an important part of building your credibility on your site, since your profile page will list your past reviews, how many people have visited your page, and how popular you are as an author within a particular subject category.

To create a profile, sign up by clicking the "Join Epinions" link at the top right of the home page at www.epinions.com. You'll be asked for a user name, a password, and an e-mail address to associate with your account. After you've confirmed your e-mail address, click the "Create your own profile" link to enter your personal information. In the "Account Options" column on the next page, select "Edit Public Profile" and enter your name, e-mail address, geographic location, biography, and a link back to your blog or website. Also include a contact e-mail address for people to get in touch with you directly if they prefer.

Your user profile shows your reviewer status—for example, general member, top reviewer, advisor, or category lead. Attaining a higher level of membership (above a general member) is a good way of increasing the number of people who will add you to their Web of Trust, which can lead to more visibility for your profile and more direct leads. Also, the more popular your review is and your status as a reviewer is, the more likely it is that your reviews will rank in search engines, which means more external traffic to your review and profile page from outside of the Epinions site. For more on these different member levels, see Tip 265.

Once you've created your profile, you can start writing reviews (see Tip 263) or adding people to your Web of Trust (for more on this, see Tip 264). As with any social networking site, the more active you are on the site, the more exposure you'll get for your profile page.

TIP 263 Write and rate reviews

Writing useful reviews builds your credibility as an Epinions user, which means that more users will add you to their Web of Trust (see Tip 264). Also, any review you write is linked back to your profile page via your user name, so the more reviews you write, the more exposure your profile page will get and the more traffic you'll drive to your website from your profile. To begin writing a review, click the "write a review" button on any product or topic page (if you want to write a review on a product that's not already listed on the site, you'll need to ask the category lead for that category to add it).

When you write a review, always aim to be objective and rational and don't review your own product. Rather, write about products that are related to your industry but don't compete directly with yours. For example, if you sell guided hiking tours, you could provide reviews on hiking accessories or gear under the "Sports & Outdoors" section. In this way you can give unbiased advice while improving your exposure within your industry on the site. Try also to stick to reviews in one category, which will help to increase your exposure to an audience that's more targeted to your business.

Below the review text, you can rate the product with from one to five stars. You can also rate other people's reviews as Very Helpful (VH), Helpful (H), Somewhat Helpful (SH), Not Helpful (NH), or Off Topic (OT). You can also choose to Show (S) or Don't Show (DS) Express Opinions, which are shortened versions of reviews. Rating other reviews helps to improve the number of opinions you're shown that you find useful.

As well as writing reviews, you can write opinions about more general topics where you provide advice to others, such as what kind of golf shoes to buy or how to choose a bartending guide. To write these opinions, click on topics for the buying guides in the "Advice" section of a specific category; for example, book-buying guides in the "Book" category.

TIP 264 Add people to your Web of Trust

Epinions' "Web of Trust" system helps to tailor your experience with the site so that you're shown more reviews that you find useful, since you trust the opinions of the people who write them. Alongside any review you read, or in someone's profile page, you can click the "Trust" link, which adds that reviewer to your Trust list. In the same way, if you find a review unhelpful or offensive in any way, you can click the "Block" link for that reviewer. If you change your mind, you can return to the reviewer's profile and click the link that says, "Remove [user] from your Block/Trust list." The more users you trust or block, and the more you rate reviews (from a sliding scale of "Very Helpful" to "Off Topic"), the better the site is able to learn what kinds of reviews you prefer. Once you've been doing this for a while, you should see more reviews from people you trust and fewer from people you've blocked. The list of people in your Web of Trust is visible in your profile, and you can choose whether to make this visible to others or not. Unlike your Trust list, your Block list always remains private.

The Web of Trust concept works similarly to the people you trust in real life—you may trust them because you've known them for a while and you know their past reputation, or you know people who recommend them, or they have interests similar to yours. When deciding whether to trust someone on Epinions, the logic is the same: spend some time reading the user's profile and some of his or her past reviews and see who else is in the person's Web of Trust. See whether this user has preferences similar to yours or has written a lot of reviews in your industry.

Just as building up a Web of Trust enhances your own user experience, becoming a member that other people trust can also be a valuable way of improving your brand's reputation on the site. The more people who add you to the network, the more your profile will be viewed and the more people will get to know you as an authority in a particular area. In addition, if you receive enough trust from other Epinions users, you can become a top reviewer or a category lead (for more about this, see Tip 265).

Become an elevated member

Besides being a general member, you can become a top reviewer, advisor, or category lead if your reviews and ratings are frequent and useful enough. Being an upper-level member means your reviews are given more exposure on the site, and you'll develop a more solid reputation as a reputable source of knowledge in your particular area. Your member status is also shown alongside your profile name in reviews that you write and on your profile page, which further helps to build your credibility. The three kinds of elevated memberships on Epinions are:

- **Top reviewer:** If your reviews are of a consistently high quality and enough people add you to their Web of Trust, you can be chosen to be a top reviewer in a particular category. As a top reviewer, your reviews are given increased visibility to other members, which means you'll be seen as a highly credible member on the site. You'll also be more likely to earn more Income Share, which is a bonus that Epinions distributes to writers who contribute the most useful reviews. The amount of Income Share you can earn is determined by how often your reviews are used by Epinions users to make buying decisions—whether it's a positive decision to buy a product or a negative one not to. Top reviewers are evaluated around once a month, so you'll need to continue writing a minimum number of quality reviews in a particular category each month to keep your top reviewer status.

- **Advisor:** Epinions advisors are members who help other users find the best content on the site by rating the reviews they read. As an advisor, your ratings are weighted more heavily than other members in that category, and you have a greater influence over the reviews that new members can see. Epinions advisors are chosen by the community every eight weeks on a peer comparison basis and are selected based on the frequency and quality of their ratings and review comments. It is possible to be a top reviewer as well as an advisor if both your ratings of other reviews and your own written reviews are of a consistently high quality.

- **Category lead:** This is the most powerful type of member that oversees a particular category on the site. As a category lead, your reviews are weighted more than anyone else's and are therefore the most visible on the site within your particular category. Category leads can choose advisors and top reviewers, and they can add new products to the site for others to review.

TIP 266 Monitor your brand

Epinions is a good channel through which to stay aware of what's being said about your product and your brand, as well as of what people are saying about your direct competitors and their products. An efficient way to stay up to date with this information is to subscribe to reviews for a particular product—whether it's yours or your competitor's. The most important thing for you as a business to do on a review website is to engage in the conversation that's happening around your brand. Subscribing to reviews means you can follow up quickly with the reviewer, which is particularly useful if your product receives a negative review as you can contain the damage to your brand's reputation by attempting to rectify the situation as quickly as possible. If, on the other hand, you receive a positive review, subscribing to alerts means you can quickly contact the member concerned and thank him or her for it. Be sure that in the case of a positive review you don't ask the reviewer for anything more, such as pushing another one of your products or asking the person to write more reviews. As with all review sites, you should take the time to listen to what's being said about your product and use the criticism constructively to improve your product offering in the future.

When you subscribe to a review on Epinions, you'll be alerted whenever a new review is added, which means you won't have to keep checking that review page for updates. To subscribe to a review, click the "Subscribe to new reviews" link alongside the product description on the review page you're interested in. You can do this for as many products as you like. To view all the alerts you are receiving, click the "E-mail Alerts" link under the "Settings" section of the left navigation menu on your profile page.

Besides subscribing to reviews for your own products, you can use Epinions as a way to stay aware of your competitors and what's being said about them. To do this, subscribe to a competitor's review page in the same way that you would do for your own products.

RateItAll

TIP 267 Understand RateItAll

RateItAll is a consumer review website that pitches itself as the "fun and social way to find and share reviews about everything." Unlike other review sites, RateItAll doesn't limit itself to a particular category of product or service, so users can rate things like games, art, travel, music, movies, drinks, and sports teams in addition to traditional services like restaurants, bars and clubs, and products. In addition to writing reviews on the site or e-mailing them in, users can create and submit lists and can isolate opinions via filters on particular demographic groups. Because of this wide range of reviews and review formats, the site allows people to give not only opinions about a product or service but also their opinions on other angles of the product, its general genre, and the product as compared to other products. As a business owner, RateItAll can provide a good way of finding out the general consumer perception of your brand, particularly in terms of how they see it in your industry as related to your competitors.

RateItAll places a strong emphasis on social networking, which allows you to find other users on the site with similar interests and tastes. If you like the opinions a particular reviewer has, you can add them to your Trusted Network, which means you see more of his or her reviews. The site makes it easy for you as a business owner to connect with potential customers or other people or businesses in your industry. You can also promote your site, product, or service on the site and have other people rate it.

RateItAll has an "open door" policy with its content, which means any Web publisher can use RateItAll content on its site. The site gives revenue-sharing opportunities to business owners through a partnership with Google AdSense, where you can earn money by allowing ads to run alongside your content. Finally, RateItAll uses RSS so that you can subscribe to topics or reviewers you're interested in because they relate to your brand or your industry.

TIP 268   Fill out your profile

To create a RateItAll profile, sign up for a profile at www.rateitall.com by clicking the "Register" link at the top right of the page. Enter a user name, password, and e-mail to associate with your account and then click the green "Sign me up" button. On the next page, the site will connect with existing contacts you have on sites like Gmail, Yahoo! Mail, or LinkedIn that are also RateItAll users. Next, add an image to your profile and click the "Finish!" button. Once this is done, you can enter other profile details such as your geographic location, personal details, and a biography.

The information that is shown on your page consists of activity on the site from you and your contacts. Your home page feed is divided into three sections:

- **"Me"** shows your own recent activity on the site, such as reviews you've written, ratings or comments you've made, or lists you've created.

- **"Everyone"** shows activity from everyone on the site.

- **"MyFeed"** is a personalized information stream showing news about keywords, categories, and friends you're interested in. To change these settings, click the gear icon at the right of the feed section to bring up a window divided into four tabs: on the "Keywords" tab, select keywords related to topics you're interested in, such as *cell phones*, *New York*, or *U.S. Open*. In the "Community" tab, choose which people's activities you want to see—for example, only friends or friends of friends. Similarly, you can choose keywords that you don't want to see information on by adding them to your block list. The "Saved Topics" tab lets you see content that you've subscribed to via the "Fave" buttons on pages around the site, while the "Story Types" tab lets you choose the type of information you'll see within "MyFeed," such as reviews and ratings but not quizzes.

In all three tabs, you can click the down arrow icon under the "right now" heading on the left to view only certain types of information published, such as only reviews. This is a temporary filter that can be changed at any time.

TIP 269   Get your business listed

RateItAll's "Promote" section lets you add your business, product, or service to the site's database so that people can review it. Encouraging reviews of your brand, product, or service is an effective way of increasing brand exposure, monitoring your brand's reputation, and engaging in conversation with prospective customers. To add your business to the RateItAll database, go to www.rateitall.com/promote and click the "Get started now!" button. You'll be asked to enter the name of your business or product to see whether there are other instances of your product that are already listed on the site under various categories. If there are, click on the brand or product you want to promote. To mark yourself as the product or service owner, click the yellow "claim this page for free" tab alongside the info tab at the top of the page. Once you've confirmed you're the owner via digital signature and the claim has been approved, you'll be able to update the page's information yourself and control what other viewers can see on the page.

If your business or product isn't already listed, click the "Continue" button at the right of the results page. You'll be asked to select the type of listing you want:

- **Local business or service:** Examples include bars, restaurants, mechanics, or laundromats. For this type of listing, you'll need to enter a physical address.

- **Website or blog:** This is applicable if your business operates online—for this listing, you'll need only your website or blog URL.

- **Other:** Use this option to promote anything that doesn't fit into the preceding categories, such as travel attractions and destinations, nonfiction books, authors, architecture, magazines, or fashion trends.

Once your business is added, you can subscribe to any updates on it by clicking the RSS icon at the top of the reviews column. From here you can start getting others to write reviews on your site (for more on how to do this, see Tip 270). Since RateItAll is fair and objective, you can't control how others review your product, but you can have an effective strategy for responding to positive or negative reviews (for more on this, see Tips 253 and 254).

TIP 270 Encourage others to leave reviews

Once you have your business, product, or service listed on RateItAll, you can start encouraging people to leave reviews. The best way to do this is to market your review page to your existing network. There are several ways you can do this:

- **Share the page:** When you're on the review page, use the "Share this page" section in the right column to e-mail it or add it to your Facebook account or Twitter feed or click "grab embed code" to place the widget within your own blog or website (for more on this, see Tip 273) so that people can add a review without leaving your site.

- **Blog about it:** Include a link to the RateItAll page from your blog or create a new blog post about a new product or service you're selling with a link to your RateItAll review page contained within the post.

- **Let people know they can e-mail:** RateItAll lets users write reviews without visiting the site by sending them as e-mails to reviews@rateitall .com. The e-mail should contain the product in the subject line, the star rating as the first line of the e-mail, and then the review below it, and pictures can be attached as an optional extra. Also, every item on RateItAll has a unique e-mail address that is linked to your page's URL in the format reviews+[unique id]@rateitall.com. You can find this e-mail address by clicking the "e-mail your review?" link at the top of the review page. Use this feature by including the e-mail address alongside products on your websites to encourage more user reviews. Once the e-mail has been sent, RateItAll automatically adds it to the related page on the site.

- **Connect with others:** By using RateItAll's social networking functionality, you can connect with other users on the site who will see your activity on the site in their "MyFeed" section. Therefore, the more active you are, the more exposure your profile and business listing will get among your contacts.

TIP 271 Connect with other users

RateItAll has social networking functionality that lets you connect with other users on the site as a way of building relationships with potential customers and increasing your brand exposure. Broadly speaking, you can either connect with people on the site that you already know or add people as connections that you don't know personally but whose reviews you find interesting or useful or who write reviews on products related to your business offering.

As a business owner who writes reviews on the site, you can encourage people to follow you as a way of establishing your credibility as a source of knowledge within a particular category. Once you're connected with another RateItAll user, you can contact him or her directly from within the site.

There are several ways you can add connections to your RateItAll account:

1. Search for people you know: Click the yellow "Invite friends" button in the right column of your home page when you're logged in. RateItAll will connect with existing Web-based e-mail accounts you have such as Gmail, Yahoo! Mail, or LinkedIn.

2. Add useful RateItAll users: You can add someone as a connection by navigating to his or her profile page and clicking "follow me" under the profile information in the right column of the profile page. Once you're following someone, activities that he or she does on the site, such as favoriting a product or writing a review, will be published to the "MyFeed" section of your account's home page (as long as you've enabled friends' activities to show through there). You can also subscribe to that user via RSS or receive an e-mail whenever he or she posts a new review.

3. Encourage people to follow you: Adding a link to your RateItAll profile on external sites like your blog, Facebook, or MySpace page can be a good way of encouraging more people to follow your reviews and activity on the site.

4. Take quizzes: Quizzes are a way for the RateItAll site to see whom you're most compatible with in a particular area, which lets you connect with people in your industry or with those who have the same interests as you. To start, click the "Quizzes" menu item in the top navigation menu.

TIP 272 — Create and share lists

RateItAll lets you create lists about anything you are interested in. For example, if you're a landscape gardener, you can start a list containing your favorite plants or plants that work well in small gardens. If you're a bicycle shop, you can start a list of your favorite bike routes in a particular city. The real power of lists comes not from creating them but from getting other RateItAll users' input on the list you've made by rating or reviewing it. Doing this is a way of encouraging a discussion around a particular topic that relates to your brand, product, or industry.

To create a list on RateItAll, follow these guidelines:

1. Log in to your RateItAll account and click the yellow "Create a list" button.

2. Think of a name for your list, such as "top 10 bike routes in San Francisco."

3. Click the green "continue" button.

4. Select a category for it, such as "Movies," "Sporting Goods," or "Destinations" under the "Travel" sections.

5. Describe your list, add a photo, and add keyword tags. Tags are an important way of ensuring that your list is visible to people searching for related content.

6. Click the green "Continue" button.

7. Begin adding items, filling in the description and a link if necessary and/or a photo.

8. Once you've added your list, you can click the "Edit List" or "Edit Items" tab to change your list's details.

9. Once your list has been published, people can suggest things to add to it, which you'll then see in your message center. You can either approve or reject the suggestion.

Once you've created your list, you can promote it by sharing it so that others can review and/or rate it. To share a list on sites like Facebook or Twitter, click the "Share this page" section on the right-hand side of the list page. You can also e-mail your list to RateItAll contacts or to other people you know who aren't on the site by pulling in contacts from Web-based e-mail accounts like Gmail or Yahoo! Mail. The useful part of this sharing functionality is that anyone can share the list—not just the creator—and can do it without needing to be logged in to the site.

TIP 273 Add the consumer review widget

The RateItAll consumer widget lets publishers of blogs or websites integrate RateItAll's ratings functionality into their own site about their own products or service. By including the widget in your site, you can encourage customers to interact with your brand and give their point of view about your offering—all while not requiring them to leave your site to do so. RateItAll's review widget can be placed anywhere you'd like customer feedback about something you're selling or talking about, such as on a blog post, a product page, or even the home page of your website.

The widget lets users do two things: either they can enter their own reviews and ratings of your product or service, or they can read ratings and reviews that others have written about the same thing. They can also search on keywords in existing reviews or click through to the related review page on RateItAll. To submit a review, users need to register as RateItAll users. If they're not already registered, they can do this from within the widget by adding a user name, e-mail address, and password and then entering the review. The widget also interfaces with Facebook so that users can connect with this review functionality from within their Facebook account.

To install the RateItAll widget on your site, first navigate to your review page on RateItAll. At the right of the page, in the "share this page" section, click the "grab embed code" link. This will take you to a page where you can customize the widget to your own preferences: choose among three sizes, eight different colors, or add custom branding such as your logo and a link to the review page on the RateItAll site. Once you've finished selecting your options, copy the code and paste it into the code on your blog or website where you want it to appear.

Yahoo! Answers

TIP 274 Understand Yahoo! Answers

Yahoo! Answers is a free, community-driven opinion site on which anyone can ask or answer a question on a variety of topics. Unlike a chat room, Yahoo!'s activity centers on a question and answer format rather than a free-form discussion. For a business looking to market itself, Yahoo! Answers is a useful site to engage on when the business centers on knowledge sharing, such as if you're a consultant. That being said, if you're a retailer selling a product, you can still find opportunities to provide knowledge about the specifics of a particular product type as an answer to a question being asked.

Although you need to be registered to ask or answer on Yahoo! Answers, anyone can view pages on the site, which also have excellent visibility on search engine results pages. To encourage a quality information exchange, Yahoo! Answers awards users points for answering questions, which allow you to escalate through "levels" that have accompanying privileges, such as being able to ask more questions on a given day. True to its social media nature, Yahoo! Answers lets the community decide which answer is best based on a voting system.

The primary advantage of being active on Yahoo! Answers is that you can build your reputation as a knowledge expert on a topic related to your line of business. As your credibility and visibility build, you can generate more traffic to your profile page, which contains a link to your website and therefore means more traffic to your site. Because of its niche nature, Yahoo! Answers may not result in large volumes of traffic to your site, but rather is better as a source of highly targeted traffic from people actively seeking out the product or service you're offering. Another advantage to your business on Yahoo! Answers is if your website is listed as a resource that supplements a particular answer. In these cases someone else is endorsing the information on your site, which will result in good brand exposure and another source of qualified traffic to your site.

TIP 275   Set up your profile

Your Yahoo! Answers profile page contains information about you, including a summary of your activity on the site, such as recent questions and answers, how many points you've earned, and who your contacts and fans are. Create your profile by logging in to http://answers.yahoo.com with your Yahoo! account (if you don't already have one, you'll be prompted to create one). Once you've logged in, click the "Edit My Preferences" dropdown link under the "My Activity" tab on the home page. Choose a nickname and profile picture that will appear alongside any of the questions or answers you submit to the site, and select your privacy preferences below that. In the "About Me" section, enter details about why you are qualified to answer questions in your particular category and include a link to your website to back up your credentials. Once you've confirmed your selections, click the blue "Preview" button and then "OK" to confirm.

As with any other social media site, the more you network with other users, the more benefit you'll gain. Once you add people as contacts, you'll see their questions and answers by clicking on the "My Network Activity" link under the "My Activity" tab. As opposed to contacts, fans are Yahoo! users who have added you to their own network of contacts so that they can follow your activity on the site. Having a lot of fans is an excellent way of building your credibility on the site and exposing your knowledge to as many people as possible.

There are two main ways to add Yahoo! Answers contacts:

- **Add them from their profile:** When you are browsing someone's profile page, click the "Add to my contacts" link. Or, if you're on a question page and you want to add either the questioner or the responder to your contacts, roll over the person's profile picture and click the "Add to my contacts" link from the pop-up window that appears.

- **Add your existing contacts:** On the "My Activity" tab, click the blue link on the page that says, "Invite your friends to join your network on Yahoo! Answers."

TIP 276   Ask and answer questions

Once you've set up your Yahoo! profile, you're ready to start answering questions. Questions that are asked and answered on the site are organized into categories and subcategories that cover a broad range of subjects such as politics, sports, travel, dining out, business, beauty, and pets. To find categories, click the "Browse Categories" tab from the home page; clicking any category link on this page will take you to the category page containing links to its subcategories. Below the subcategory items on the page are questions within that category that are organized in three tabs:

■ **"Open":** Each question is open for a period of four days, during which other members can answer it. If no one answers it, it expires and is deleted. The question creator has the option of extending this answer period by an extra four days before it expires.

■ **"In Voting":** Once the question has been online for at least four hours and there are one or more responses, the person who asked the question can choose the best answer. If the question asker doesn't select a best answer within the four-hour period and there are two or more responses, the questioner can put the question up to the community to vote. The best answer is also put to a vote if the person who asks the question takes no action and the "open" period of the question expires. When this happens, the question will appear in the "In Voting" tab. The voting period is two days.

■ **"Resolved":** Once the best answer has been chosen, the question is considered answered and can't be answered anymore, although you can still leave comments and rate the best answer. If this is the case, you'll see the answer in the "Resolved" tab.

To answer a question, start by browsing to the category or subcategory related to your business—for example, "Books and Authors" under "Arts & Humanities" if you're a bookstore owner. When you find a relevant question, click on it, and on the question page, click the blue "Answer Question" button. On the page that follows, type in your answer, provide relevant sources, and then click the "Preview" button. If you're happy with your answer, click the "Submit" button.

TIP 277 | Give quality answers

When answering questions on Yahoo! Answers, use the following guidelines to get the most value out of the answering process and exposure for your brand:

- **Try to answer first:** The first answer under a question is typically above the fold of the screen, which means it gets more exposure than those that fall below it. Many visitors don't realize that there is more than one answer under the first one, particularly if the question and answer take up most of the space above the fold.

- **Give a quality answer:** Take the time to research your answer and then explain it clearly and simply. Doing this gives you a better chance of having the question rated as the best answer, which means it will be shown first above all other answers. You also earn extra points for having your answer selected as the best response (for more on the points system, see Tip 279).

- **Include links to your site only if they're useful:** When you answer a question, you'll be given the option to include URLs of sources for your information. Include resources other than your own here, unless you have a page of resources on your site that are highly relevant to the question being asked. It's important to note that soliciting or advertising on the site goes against the Yahoo! Answers' community guidelines, and your answers will be flagged and removed if you do so. If you do provide your own link, always ask yourself whether the link you provide genuinely provides useful answers or simply advertises your product. For guidance, stick to including your link to your website or your own content once in every ten answers and provide the most specific link you can rather than your home page.

- **Sign your name:** To add credibility to your answer, leave your full name when you answer and make sure you have the option checked to link to your profile page. This allows people who liked your answer to click through and view your profile page, from where they can visit your website listed in the "About Me" section, or they can e-mail you or IM you directly.

TIP 278 · Answer relevant questions

To get the most use out of Yahoo! Answers as a way of improving your brand's reputation, concentrate your activity on the site within a category related to your business or industry. There are several ways to keep up to date with questions being asked in a particular category:

- **Search:** The search box is featured in the header of every page on the site, so start by searching on keywords related to your industry, such as *motorcycles* or *Yamaha* if you sell motorcycles. In the results, browse through open questions that you can answer.

- **Browse:** Yahoo! Answers lists categories and subcategories that you can browse through to find questions to answer, such as "Cars & Transportation" > "Motorcycles" or "Maintenance & Repairs."

- **Subscribe:** Unless your area of expertise is extremely specific, it can be time consuming to keep up with questions to answer in every category that's applicable to your industry. As a solution, you can subscribe via RSS for any category or subcategory on the site. So, as a motorcycle dealer, navigate to the "Motorcycles" subcategory in "Cars & Transportation" and scroll down to the right column, where you'll see an RSS icon and a link that says *RSS*. You can also create an RSS feed based on a particular keyword search. To do this, enter your keyword search and then click the "RSS" link in the left column on the results page.

- **Use search engines:** As well as searching for questions within Yahoo! Answers itself, you can enter your keywords into Yahoo!'s regular search engine and then click the "Answers" tab in the results page to see questions and answers that are featured from the Answers site. Questions featured in regular search results will get more traffic than other questions, so answering these is a good strategy if you have time to answer only a couple of questions a day or week.

TIP 279 **Earn points**

Yahoo! incentivizes its users to provide genuine, quality answers through a points reward system: the more questions you answer, the more points you earn, while the more questions you ask, the more points are taken away. This is because you're seen as using up resources when you ask a question and contributing to the site when you answer them. You can also earn points for other activities on the site; for example, if your answer is selected as the best answer, you'll earn ten points, while if someone gives you a "thumbs up" on an answer you wrote, you'll earn one point.

As you earn more points, you'll be promoted to higher user levels on the site: to move from level 1 to level 2 you need at least 250 points; to move to level 3 you need 1,000 points; to move to level 4 you need 2,500 points; and so on. Each level has accompanying privileges that allow you to rate answers, comment on more answers, and ask more questions. For example, as a level 1 user, you can ask five questions and answer twenty per day, but you can't rate any answers and you get only a total of twenty votes for an answer per day. In contrast, a level 3 user can ask fifteen questions and answer sixty. The site's level structure means that the more you participate on the site, the more visibility you'll gain with other users.

Your Yahoo! Answers profile page shows you a tally of the points you've accumulated. This means that the more points you earn, the more credibility you'll be shown to have to people viewing your profile page (as well as on the pop-up window if you roll over the avatar on the answer page). Note that Yahoo! Answers frowns heavily on what it calls "point-gaming," which is where you deliberately try to increase your points on the site without adding any value through questions that are "advice-seeking" or answers that are "knowledge-worthy."

If by providing consistently good responses that are often chosen as the best answers you become known as being especially knowledgeable in a particular category, you have a chance of being selected as a "top contributor." When you're awarded this status, you'll have a "top contributor" badge that will show in your profile and as part of your avatar when you participate on your site.

TIP 280   Be active to be visible

Even if you don't have the time to answer large volumes of questions on Yahoo! Answers, it's better to spend shorter amounts of time on the site more regularly rather than to spend a longer time on it more sporadically. Besides establishing yourself as a genuine, value-added member, regular activity on the site encourages a more steady flow of traffic to your site from your profile page. Yahoo! Answers also encourages regular activity by rewarding you with points each time you log on (for more on the points system, see Tip 279). Two other main ways to be active on the site are:

1. Add a badge: Embedding the Yahoo! Answers badge on your blog or website provides your site visitors with an extra information resource in the form of questions and answers from the Yahoo! Answers site. You can customize the badge as much as you like so that it relates to your industry and to the subject on the page it's embedded on—for example, you can include only questions in a particular category or questions related to a particular keyword or only questions that you've answered. Change these options, as well as the badge's look and feel, by going to http://builder.answers.yahoo .com. Once you've selected your preferences, copy the code that is generated and paste it into the code of the page on which you want the badge to appear.

2. Build up your contacts: Your activity on the site, such as answering a question or rating an answer, is published to the news feeds of your Yahoo! Answers contacts, which means the more contacts you have, the more people will see your answers, ratings, and comments on the site.

As with all social media efforts, you should track the effect your activity on the site has on your site traffic. Based on these numbers, you may be able to identify the shortest amount of time that you can spend on the site to give you the maximum return. In other words, there may not be much of a difference in terms of your site traffic between your answering ten questions and answering twenty-five. However, since you earn points and move up levels the more questions you answer, it's harder to track improvement in the perception of your brand to other Yahoo! Answers users that could result.

TIP 281 Don't spam

Because Yahoo! Answers is a knowledge resource, it has a strict antispam policy that prohibits businesses from using the site as a way to solicit customers. At the same time, Yahoo! Answers realizes that businesses with specific knowledge may be well positioned to answer questions in their area of expertise, and they may have further resources on the topic that the user would find helpful. Because of this, it's acceptable to answer questions while being associated with your business. However, keep these guidelines in mind:

- **Provide information, not pushes for your product:** Always give proper information in an answer rather than using your answer as a thinly veiled way to push your product. For example, if you are a tax software company, answering a question about the difference in tax rates in certain states would be acceptable, while answering a question about the best tax software to use would not.

- **Keep your answers relevant:** Keep your answers relevant to the question being asked and don't stray off topic.

- **Don't provide your contact details or Web address in your answers:** If people want to find out more about you, they can click through to your profile page for your contact details listed there.

- **Don't ask and then answer your own question:** This is a common spamming technique; answer only genuine questions that others have asked.

- **Be careful when linking to your own content as a source:** A common form of spam is to use your own URL as a source in every answer, even if it's not genuinely appropriate or relevant to the question being asked. Always use sources that are genuinely useful to the answer and never use affiliate sites or sites that have no proper content as source links. Supply a link to a page on your own website only if it specifically relates to the question and is a proper knowledge resource (such as a white paper or research article).

By providing quality answers, people will perceive your brand as being a valuable resource and will be more inclined to click through to your profile page and contact you directly if they want more information. Also, the more useful your answers are, the more chance you have that they'll be selected as the "best answer," which gives you increased visibility on the site.

TIP 282　Understand eHow

Founded in March 1999 and now owned by Demand Media, eHow is one of the oldest how-to resources on the Internet. The site provides simple, actionable advice in the form of step-by-step instructional articles, videos, and quick guides where several articles on the same subject are combined into one general resource. eHow articles cover a broad range of topics such as education (e.g., "How to gear up for college"), investing (e.g., "How to determine portfolio values"), and cooking (e.g., "How to make gourmet hamburgers"). Users can also publish an "I Did This," which is a story and photo slideshow that documents their personalized experience of completing a particular how-to.

Besides the large amount of content featured on the site, eHow's social networking functionality lets you connect with other people in your industry and potential customers by adding friends, joining groups, favoriting articles, and participating in forums. More recently, eHow launched a mobile version of the site for the iPhone and an application for the Android phone. This mobile functionality means users can access the site's information to solve practical problems (such as tying a bowtie or hanging a painting) while on the go.

eHow draws its content from Demand Studios, a content creation network where anyone can apply to be a writer. Writing articles for Demand Studios that are then featured on eHow can be an excellent way for you to establish credibility as an expert in your industry and position yourself as a useful resource for potential customers. Your article's becoming popular on the site can mean a significant increase in traffic to your site (according to statistics from the beginning of 2010, eHow receives almost 60 million unique visitors a month[1]). The site's million-plus articles also have good visibility on search engines, which means that a popular article on eHow tends to generate large amounts of search engine traffic as well. Depending on the article's content, you're paid either a flat fee or a share of revenue. For revenue share, you'll earn a portion of the money that Demand Studios makes from your article—this is determined by a variety of factors including how many people view your article and which category your article is in. While this compensation is a good incentive to write for the site, in a social media context it's best to think of eHow primarily as a way to build your brand's reputation online by being an expert in your topic.

TIP 283 | Apply with Demand Studios

To write articles on eHow you first need to submit an online application with Demand Studios at https://www.demandstudios.com/application .html?role=Writer. In addition to filling in your details, you'll need to attach a writing sample or a URL of one of your published works and your resume. Because of this screening process, you should have writing experience or a basic ability to write in order to apply. If you don't, you could enlist the help of someone within your organization (such as an in-house copywriter or press release writer) who is better suited to the task. Either way, whoever writes articles for eHow in your business should have specific expertise in the topic they will write about as it relates to your industry.

After submitting your application, Demand Studios will review it within seven days. Once you've been approved, you'll be supplied with login details in order to access your Demand Studios writer account at www .demandstudios.com. Before writing your first article, it's a good idea to visit the Writer Resource Center once you're logged in, and read the Writer Welcome Packet. Once you've done that, write your biography and upload a photograph of yourself into your Demand Studios account. Your biography will be appended to each eHow article you write, so it's important to make this biography informative enough so that readers can find out more about you and why you're qualified to write about your particular topic.

Once you've written your biography and read the introductory material, you can start to browse under existing topics that eHow needs content for under the "Find Assignments" section of your account. You can search on keywords or filter by categories such as "publisher" (in this case you'd filter for all eHow content). Work that is available for assignment is displayed in this tab with the title, rate, and subject category it fits into. You can also suggest your own topic that is then submitted for review by Demand Studios editors. Once you've written your article (for more on how to do this, see Tip 285), you'll submit it through your account for checking by a copy editor, who will either approve it or will send it back for changes to be made. Note that if changes have been requested, you'll get the opportunity to do only one set of rewrites. For this reason, take the time to write the best article you can, and check and recheck it again before you resubmit in order to catch any spelling or grammatical errors. Once your article has been approved, you'll see it under the "Published Work" tab of your account, which means it will be published on the eHow site.

TIP 284 | Join eHow

As well as applying to write for eHow via Demand Studios (for more on how to do this, see Tip 283), you should also join eHow in order to access the site's social networking functionality and engage with the eHow community. To join the site, go to www.ehow.com and click the "Join" link at the top of the home page or go to https://forms.ehow.com/register.aspx. You'll be prompted to associate an e-mail address and enter a user name and password in the pop-up window. After you've entered them, click the "Register Now" button.

Once you're logged in, you'll see several different tabs in the middle of the page that displays different information such as your articles, friends, videos, and subscriptions. Click the "MyProfile" tab to access your profile. Clicking on this tab will take you straight to the "Me" tab of your profile, which displays information such as your recent activity, a list of your friends, the groups you belong to, and articles you've marked as favorites. To fill out your eHow profile information, click the "Edit Profile" link in the left navigation menu when you're on this "Me" tab. You'll be able to enter personal information about yourself here including your first name, last name, company website, geographic location, and more about yourself.

Also in the "MyProfile" section, the "Friends" tab shows everyone you're connected with on the site. To add someone as a friend, click on the author's name in an article to reach his or her profile page and then click on the "Add as a Friend" link underneath his or her profile picture. Once the person receives your request and approves it, you can communicate directly on the site. You can also subscribe to someone so that you can keep track of his or her activity on the site, such as when the person publishes a new article. To subscribe to someone, click the "Subscribe" link underneath his or her profile picture.

A good way of showcasing your knowledge on a particular topic is to feature articles in your profile. You can choose up to five articles by clicking the "Articles" tab within the "MyProfile" section and then selecting the articles you want featured.

TIP 285 Decide on an article topic

Whether you select an existing topic for which eHow needs content or suggest your own topic to write on, your article should be useful and high in quality to achieve good visibility amid all the other competing content. Keep these best practices in mind for writing good article content:

- **Write what you know:** Stick to your area of expertise. Besides demonstrating your knowledge in your industry, your article will be better if you do this, as you'll be able to provide unique insights as a result of your firsthand experience. For more on sticking to your niche in the context of blogging, see Tip 16.

- **Be original:** Check to see whether the article you're intending to write has already been written. If it has, think of an original angle or another topic that is still related to it.

- **Write what's popular:** Conduct your own keyword research using free keyword tools such as Google's keyword tool, which will help you pinpoint search trends of information people are looking for in your industry.

- **Write simply and well:** Using a simple writing style that explains steps clearly and precisely will help your article to be better received. Also, make sure it is grammatically correct—if you need to, designate someone in your company who has an eye for correct grammar to write your articles. You can also have a friend read it over after you've read it or, at the very least, use eHow's built-in spell check tool when you upload your article.

- **Don't write on a topic that will become dated:** If an article is about a finite event or topic, you'll stop generating page views from searches after that event ends. Therefore, write articles on "evergreen" topics that won't expire; for example, write an article such as "How to play soccer" rather than "How to Get Tickets to the 2010 Soccer World Cup."

- **Give advice that can be acted on:** Your article should provide action steps rather than general theoretical opinion. Says eHow in its FAQs, "Vague instructions that do not provide detailed step-by-step instructions and leave the reader to make intellectual jumps from step to step will be removed."

TIP 286 Drive search traffic to your articles

Since eHow is an established and credible URL, articles on the site tend to be indexed quickly and extensively in search engines like Google, Bing, and Yahoo! Especially if you're still building the credibility of your own domain for your blog or website, having an article on eHow can be a great supplemental way of exposing your brand on search engines and driving traffic to your site. While many of the best practices of search engine optimization are explained in the blogging section (see Tips 27–32), there are specific things you can do in the eHow context to ensure that your article has good visibility on search results pages. Before you start, research two to three keyword phrases for which you want your article to be visible (for examples of how to do this, see Tip 28).

- **Optimize specific areas of your article:** Include your keyword phase in your page title, subheadings (if it makes sense to the reader), and in the body copy. For example, if your main targeted keyword phrase for an article is *vegetarian lasagna*, your article title could be "How to make vegetarian lasagna."

- **Use synonyms:** Including synonyms in your article is a good way of reinforcing your overall theme to search engines. You'll also help the article be visible to people searching on different words that have the same meaning, such as *soccer* and *football*.

- **Link to your articles:** Apart from on-page copy, a major factor in how a search engine ranks content is by looking at the quality, quantity, and thematic relevance of links pointing to that article from external sources. The first way to ensure a lot of links is to include all related articles you have in your "Related articles" section when you're entering your article in the site (for more on how to do this, see Tip 287). Then link to it from external sources including your blog, website, and other social media sites (to find out how to market your blog elsewhere, see Tip 291). Also include your keyword phrase in the external link text, which is another way of helping search engines determine the thematic relevance of the destination article.

- **Don't sacrifice quality:** Although you should include targeted keywords in your article, don't sacrifice your article's quality for the sake of ranking high in search engines. Write your article for human readers first and search engines second.

TIP 287   Upload your article

When you write an article for eHow, you'll need to upload it via your Demand Studios account (for more about applying with Demand Studios, see Tip 283). When writing an eHow article, follow these best practices:

- **Add a title:** Your title should explain exactly what the article is about in a clear, concise way while still making sense in the "How to . . ." sentence format.

- **Add an image:** This is the general image that sums up the main topic of your article, so keep it closely related to your content. Beware of copyright issues and give credit if necessary.

- **Introduction:** This should be a very brief, informative summary of what people can expect to learn in your article and can include background information that doesn't fit in the practical steps section.

- **Steps:** Keep your steps as simple as possible, by writing one step per idea. The minimum number of steps is three, so write more steps rather than too few.

- **Images:** Upload images that relate to each of the steps.

- **Tips and warnings:** Add any other information that won't fit in the steps but that will help your users understand the process better.

- **Spell check:** Keep your article professional by ensuring that it's free of grammar and spelling mistakes.

- **Categorize:** Choose an existing category for your article, such as "Business" > "Marketing & PR" > "Direct marketing." This is important for your article to be found by people conducting internal and external searches for your article content.

- **Add keywords:** These are important to ensure your article gets visibility on the site and in search engines.

- **Related articles:** You can add other eHow articles that help drive traffic between them and your article.

- **Resources:** Be careful about linking to your own site. If you do, make sure the page you link to is specific and is relevant to the article.

- **Submit:** Once you're ready, submit your article. If it's approved, you don't have to do anything more. If rewrites are needed, you'll be sent the changes to make.

TIP 288 Don't spam

Even if you have good intentions as an author, there are several things you should bear in mind to prevent your article from being rejected by Demand Studios. Even if your article is accepted by Demand Studios and it appears spammy (this is highly unlikely), other community members will pick up on this, which can damage your brand perception on the site. The main pointers to avoid a spammy article are:

- **Be useful:** Always provide useful content first, with referral traffic being your secondary goal. The purpose of your article should be to share knowledge, rather than to overtly push your product. So, for example, if you sell bicycle equipment, your article could be about how to fix a bicycle puncture or how to maintain your bike. Anything that pushes your selling the bike itself, such as "How to find a bike at Acme bike dealer," would be considered solicitation and should be avoided.

- **Stay on topic:** Don't wander off the topic. To ensure that you stay on topic, write about a simple topic or break down a complex topic into subarticles.

- **Don't offend:** Avoid articles that are controversial, that give advice on something illegal, or that could be offensive to others.

- **Don't repeat content:** Search for the article to see if it's been written first.

- **Be objective:** Although there may be different ways to do something (e.g., how to hang a picture), which means your article will contain a certain degree of bias, stay away from subjective or opinion pieces.

- **Don't plagiarize:** Always cite your sources, even if you're paraphrasing someone else.

- **Keep your resources relevant:** Whenever you cite resources, make sure they're genuinely useful to the reader. If you do link to your own site, link not to a product page of your site but to an article you've written or a blog post that provides more insight into what you're explaining.

Participate in the community

Engaging with the eHow community is the best way of getting your article exposed to as many people as possible on the site. eHow gives you several different ways to network with other users:

- **Add friends:** Adding friends is the first way to build up relationships with others on the site. Once you've added people as friends, you can rate and comment on their articles, which will encourage them to do the same for yours. For more on how to add friends, see Tip 284.

- **Comment on articles:** Each time you comment on an eHow article, your name appears alongside the comment with a link to your profile, which makes it a good way of driving traffic to your profile page. Providing insightful comments is also a good way of showing off your in-depth knowledge about a particular subject.

- **Rate articles:** To rate an article, mouse over the empty stars that have a gray outline at the beginning of the article alongside the title and the author's name. Click on the number of stars you want to give the article to assign it that particular star rating.

- **Join groups:** Groups are a great way to interact with eHow members who are specifically interested in the knowledge you have to offer. For more on groups, see Tip 290.

- **Participate in the group forum:** eHow contains a general forum for general questions related to the site, as well as a place to find out about promotions and competitions currently happening on the site. To access the forums section, click the "Community" tab and then "Forum." As opposed to eHow groups, forums are related to activity within eHow rather than knowledge about a particular subject.

- **Add "I did this" stories:** Alongside each eHow article you can click the "I Did This" button and recount your personal experience with following the article instructions. You can add photos along with your text, which is another good way of spreading the word about your brand. Unlike regular articles, there is no set format for an "I Did This" article, which gives you more flexibility.

TIP 290 Join groups

eHow groups are dedicated to specific subject areas, so joining a group related to your industry is a good way of exposing your articles to a more targeted audience. To find groups related to your area of expertise, click the "Community" tab on the eHow home page and then click the "Groups" link. In the text box, search on keywords related to the group you're looking for, such as "recipes" if you're a catering company. eHow then returns all related groups in search results below, with each result showing the number of members and a summary of what the group is about. Click on a group you're interested in, such as the "Foods Galore" group, to see the group page. On the group page you'll see a feed of recent activity by group members, and below that, links to recent discussions between group members. Groups also contain blogs where members can create new posts containing links to articles they've written on the site. As with a regular blog, you can add images and related tags and the link to your article, and other members can comment on the blog post.

To join a group, click the green "Join this group" button on the top right of the group page. As a group member, you'll be able to participate in discussions, upload media such as photos and videos, write new blog posts, add events, and interact directly with other members. The "Members" section of the group shows you all eHow users that are group members; for each member, you can click through to his or her profile and add the person as a friend. In the "Discussion" section, you can ask and answer questions from group members, which further highlights your expertise. The "Take this group with you" link on the group home page provides you with code that you can embed on your blog or website to pull group activity through to your site. You can also subscribe to a group page via your RSS reader.

Market your article externally

Once you've written your article, interacting with the eHow community (see Tip 289 for more on this) is a good place to start to drive internal traffic to it. Along with doing internal marketing, though, you should market your articles externally. By exposing your article to your existing networks, you get the most leverage out of the time spent writing your article by getting more page views from people who aren't just other eHow users. You can market an eHow article externally in several ways:

- **E-mail it to people:** E-mail a link to your eHow article to friends, colleagues, business partners, and those you do business with and encourage them to pass the article on to their own network.

- **Publicize it on your site:** Write a blog post about your article if you have a company blog and post a link to it in the resources section of your website.

- **Use your other social networks:** Link to your article from social media sites like Facebook, LinkedIn, or Twitter. Doing this means you not only drive audiences from other sites to your eHow article, but you also improve your content offering on those sites by providing more useful resources.

- **Include it in your newsletter:** If you have a company newsletter, include a resource section in each edition where you link to new eHow articles you've written.

- **Bookmark it:** Add your article to Digg, Delicious, StumbleUpon, or other social bookmarking sites you use. Be careful not to submit too much of your own content to these sites—for more on these sites, see Chapter 5 on social bookmarking.

- **Include a badge:** eHow provides you with badges that contain links to your own eHow articles. By embedding this widget in your site, you provide your blog or website audience with further general resources in your industry, as well as drive traffic to your articles on the site. To access the eHow badge, log on to your eHow profile, click the "My Profile" tab, and then click the "Get Started" button at the bottom of the left column under the "Custom widget" section.

8

Wikis

DERIVED FROM the Hawaiian word meaning "fast,"[1] a wiki is defined as a website that anyone can edit. Like a blog, wiki content is uploaded through a content management tool and published on a central Web server so that it is accessible via a particular URL. Unlike a blog, though, wiki content is designed to be edited by a group of people as opposed to one main author. It is this fact that fosters group collaboration and idea sharing and is what makes it such a powerful tool. Through the "group edit" environment, wikis encourage social interaction, which makes them one of the oldest social media tools around and one that long predates the current social networking trend. As long as wiki interactions and processes are managed correctly, they can be a fertile atmosphere for generating new ideas, solutions, and strategies.

Wikis fall into two broad categories: public and private. Public wikis, the best-known example of which is Wikipedia, allow anyone to add, edit, or remove their content. In addition to general wikis like Wikipedia that cover a wide range of subjects, there are many niche public wikis dedicated to specific subjects, such as travel or technology. As opposed to public wikis, private wikis are accessible only by a specific group of people who are required to log in to the site to access information and/or edit the contents.

Wikis can be used both internally within a business and externally in more of a social networking context. Used internally within a business, wikis allow for easy information sharing between a company and its employees. They can also streamline communication for things like brainstorming, planning, managing projects, sharing projects between employees, and generating ideas. More recently, as business use of social media to connect with their customers has grown, businesses are also using wikis as a channel to engage in conversations with their customers. Compared to

305

traditional communication mechanisms like FAQs or "contact us" forms, wikis can be more meaningful for both parties. For example, a company wiki could allow a customer to get involved in the conceptual stage of new product development. Since customer input is more constructive at an earlier stage, the end product or service is better, which benefits both customers and businesses.

Wikis Overview

TIP 292 | Contribute to niche wikis

Contributing to general wikis like Wikipedia (for more about Wikipedia, see Tips 297–301) means you can contribute content that will be exposed to a large audience. However, if you want to reach a more specific audience, it's worth contributing to subject-specific public wikis. Doing this lets you provide useful content to a more targeted audience that is specifically interested in topics related to your area of expertise. When contributing to any niche wiki, make sure you provide useful information rather than using the site as a way to sell your product. You can also use niche wikis as a way to find new information in your industry or to source new ideas for products and services within your business. Wikis can also be good for networking purposes—most wikis have communal areas or forums where you can connect with other users by discussing topics related to the wiki.

Niche wikis exist in a broad range of subject areas such as travel, finance, and technology. Some examples of subject-specific wikis include:

- **Wikitravel:** This worldwide travel resource (www.wikitravel.org) contains guides and articles on destinations around the world.

- **Wikia:** The Wikia domain (www.wikia.com) contains more than seventy-five thousand subject-specific wikis with communities attached to each. Some examples of topics include finance, recipes, psychology, family ancestry, and song lyrics.

- **Dealipedia:** This wiki (www.dealipedia.com) focuses specifically on business deals such as IPOs, mergers, acquisitions, and venture capital investments. Anyone can add or edit a deal on the site, and you can subscribe to RSS feeds of deals within specific categories such as technology, mining, or health care.

- **WikiMapia:** A collaborative mapping wiki (www.wikimapia.org) where the overall aim is to provide a comprehensive and up-to-date map of the world in multiple languages. The site lets anyone add, edit, or delete locations on the map, as well as add or edit information on any location contained within it.

TIP 293   Use wikis internally

Using wikis within a business provides a platform for employees to share information and collaborate on team projects. Some ideas of how wikis can be used to streamline processes within your organization include:

- **Storing information:** You can share and store information that affects all your employees—operation procedures, legal and HR documents, knowledge documents, and the like.

- **Collaborative document creation:** You can create shared documents for which you want group participation and input from many different employees. For example, if you're creating a proposal for a customer and want multiple people's input on a document, you can post the document to a wiki page that everyone can edit.

- **Project work flow:** This can include any processes or tasks that involve multiple groups of people, such as flow diagrams, brainstorming, task delegation, data capture from projects, or virtual meeting and conference call support. The ability of wikis to track changes from multiple sources means that project managers can easily see the history of a project's development and who contributed at each stage of its completion.

- **Marketing:** Wikis can be an effective way of selling projects to your internal stakeholders. For example, if you have a research and development team working on a product, you can get other teams, such as salespeople and marketing personnel, to give feedback on the product via a wiki that everyone can see. In this example, the research team would have better ideas for the product, and the sales team would understand it better when it comes to selling it.

The first step in using a wiki internally is to select the wiki software to use (for more about choosing wiki software, see Tip 294). Once it's installed, you'll need to educate your employees about using it. Fortunately, most wiki software is easy enough that anyone can use it without needing any special technical skills. You will, however, need to train your employees about the shift in business processes that comes with wiki usage—for example, instead of sending a group e-mail, you'd now be able to post that information to a wiki page.

Choose wiki software

A wide range of wiki software is available, each one with different costs and capabilities. When choosing which one is right for your business, you need to consider several factors. First, think about cost. As with a blog, you can choose free or paid wiki software, and you can host it on your own servers or have someone else host it for you, in which case you'll pay for the hosting space. Paid wiki software typically has more extensive functionality and applications than free software, so it's better suited to larger businesses with complex business processes, a significant number of employees, and a bigger budget. If you're a small or medium business owner, free software that allows simple collaboration on a Web platform should be more than sufficient. Some examples of popular wiki tools follow, all of which offer basic wiki functions such as varying member levels and version control:

- **Wikispaces:** Of the three levels of accounts available here (www.wiki spaces.com), the free version gives 2 GB of storage and allows unlimited users. For a monthly fee you get 5 GB of storage plus extra features like your own domain name and custom themes.

- **Socialtext:** Depending on the package you choose, this offers from 1 GB up to unlimited storage. Socialtext (www.socialtext.com) also offers other products, including blogs, spreadsheets, and integrated social networking and microblogging capabilities that help employees interact with each other.

- **Google sites:** These sites (http://sites.google.com) allow unlimited users, and you need only a Google account to sign up. The free account provides 100 MB of storage, while the Google Apps Premier Edition provides 10 GB of storage.

- **PBWorks:** While this tool isn't free (the Business Edition costs $20 per user per month after an initial thirty-day free trial period), PBWorks (www .pbworks.com) gives you unlimited user numbers, storage, and uploads, and you can also get functionality specific to four industry categories: professional services, law firms and attorneys, design and marketing firms, and general corporates.

For an extensive comparison, WikiMatrix (www.wikimatrix.org) provides a good side-by-side comparison of all major wiki tools.

TIP 295 Use wikis to communicate with customers

Besides improving information sharing and collaboration within a business, wikis can be used to communicate externally with customers. Wikis are democratic by nature and allow barriers between customer and business to be broken down so that both parties can communicate openly and freely with each other. The result is a better collaborative environment, which can have a positive impact on problem solving, idea generation, and general customer service. For example, a wiki can be a more effective place for a customer to get specific answers to a question about your product or service rather than reading general FAQs, which may not give the answers they're looking for.

The other main strength of a wiki compared to other communication platforms like blogs or forums is that information on a wiki is typically organized by subject rather than by date. This means that customers can browse through a logical subject hierarchy for the information they need, rather than needing to search through archives that are organized chronologically. Also, compared to blogs, wikis don't have one main author so that they provide a less intimidating medium for customers to communicate. Using wikis to interface with your customers also has other advantages:

- They can be virtual focus groups if you involve your customers early on in the brainstorm process when you're developing a new product or service. By allowing them to give feedback via a wiki early on in a product's developmental life cycle, you know that whatever you develop will have your customers' needs in mind and is therefore more likely to be received well.

- Customers can become empowered by help from other customers within the wiki environment.

- Wikis encourage a community to be built around a particular topic. Then, by being involved in a discussion along with your customers, you can connect directly with them in a way that wouldn't be possible with traditional "push" forms of marketing.

Remember that wikis allow customers themselves to change the document, edit, and make additions, as opposed to just leaving comments below an unchanged original document. Therefore, you'd want to restrict customers' editing rights for certain types of documents such as pricing agreements or legal documents.

TIP 296 Implement wiki processes

If you're using a wiki to communicate with your customers, it's a good idea to have certain processes in place to make sure that it runs smoothly and effectively:

- **Designate a wiki champion:** If you're a small business, you yourself could track what's being added to your wiki by your customers and employees. If you're a larger organization, you could designate a "wiki champion," a person within your business who is responsible for assimilating information on the wiki and keeping it up to date. If your wiki is large enough, you could assign several champions responsible for different wiki categories. Responsibilities of the champion could include keeping track of edits, removing spam, and pulling information from blogs and other corporate channels to archive on it. The easiest way to do this is to subscribe to changes on the wiki so that you or your champions are automatically alerted when any information changes.

- **Educate your users:** Although most wiki software comes with built-in help, make sure documentation on using the correct syntax and saving and publishing pages is easily accessible to them. You could publish a "Are you new here?" wiki page in a prominent place on the site that includes a style guide as well as notices of where feedback is currently needed on the site and where new information has recently been added.

- **Use the information you gain:** While a wiki is an excellent way of communicating with customers, it's powerful only if you act on the insights, criticism, or other feedback that your customers add to it. To make sure you do this, take the time each week or each month to meet with your champion and run through new additions and discussions on the wiki. Then formulate steps you'll take to act on this information. For example, based on new feedback, you may change the way you're running a service in your business, or you may use a suggestion from a customer in your development of a new product.

Wikipedia

TIP 297   Understand Wikipedia

Combining the words *encyclopedia* and *wiki*, Wikipedia is a free, community-based online encyclopedia that is written in wiki format. Cofounded in 2001 by Larry Sanger and Jimmy Wales, Wikipedia is today the sixth-most-popular site on Alexa (www.alexa.com)[1] and is the largest general wiki online. Managed by the not-for-profit Wikimedia Foundation, Wikipedia is written in multiple languages and has a significant depth of content: as of January 2010, there were more than three million articles on the English Wikipedia site alone.[2]

True to its wiki nature, Wikipedia is community-based, meaning that anyone can add or edit its contents. To manage this constant flow of edits, the site has a large team of volunteer editors and administrators who track changes and make sure that any content added to the site sticks to Wikipedia's content guidelines. These guidelines are important to maintain a level of content quality and to prevent spam articles from being added in the place of genuinely useful information.

Although it's a comprehensive repository for shared knowledge, Wikipedia content is not written solely by experts, so it's important to follow up on the site's information with external sources (usually listed at the end of an article). Other disadvantages of the site are that content can be biased, can omit information, and can often lack citations of external sources. Nevertheless, the site's collaborative nature means articles are intended to be continually improved over time by different people until the article is, according to the site, "well-written, balanced, neutral, and encyclopedic, containing comprehensive, notable, verifiable knowledge."[3]

Because Wikipedia is essentially a social media site containing an active community, you can use it to gain exposure within your industry in several different ways. For example, by connecting with other Wikipedia members, you can build relationships with industry members, and by writing useful content related to your industry, you can develop your credibility as a knowledge resource on a particular topic. Also, due to the sheer volume of traffic the site receives, if your site is listed as a resource, Wikipedia can be an excellent source of site traffic.

TIP 298 Know what to use it for

- **It won't improve your rankings:** Wikipedia's size and the number of inbound links pointing to it mean it has a huge amount of credibility (and therefore excellent rankings) on search engines. In the past, many website owners used this fact to gain inbound links to their site from Wikipedia, which would in turn improve their own sites' rankings. However, to combat misuse of the site for this purpose, and to ensure that only relevant resource links were added, Wikipedia implemented the "no-follow" attribute in 2007 on its outbound links. So, although having a link to your site from Wikipedia will mean more traffic to your site, it won't improve your site's search engine rankings.

- **You can't self-promote:** Wikipedia prohibits any kind of self-promotion, advertising, or solicitation, so you shouldn't write an article simply to advertise your business, products, or services. In addition, even if you do write useful content, you shouldn't write it for the sole purpose of including a link back to your site. Says Wikipedia, "You should avoid linking to a website that you own, maintain or represent, even if the guidelines otherwise imply that it should be linked."[1] You should provide only resource links to an article that are genuinely useful to the article itself and that provide more resources for the reader. A better strategy is to write or conduct useful research in your industry and then market it to others. As you become known as an expert in a particular area, others are more likely to use your content as a resource.

- **Use it as a knowledge-sharing tool:** Instead of promoting your business, think of Wikipedia as a way to build out and provide information to the community that is related to your business and in which you have expertise. For example, you could add or edit information to a wiki about travel in Spain if you conducted tours to a specific region in the country or if you studied the history of the area. By adding genuinely useful content in this way, you build up a credible reputation as an expert in that particular topic. If people do want to find more about you, they can contact you via your user page.

TIP 299 | Create a Wikipedia account

To edit an existing page, you don't need to be a Wikipedia member. However, if you want to start a new page, upload images, rename pages, or access watch lists to track changes on a particular page, you'll need to create an account. Another benefit of creating an account is that as a registered user you can connect directly with other Wikipedia users via e-mail. And each time you edit a page while you're logged in, you'll get full credit for that edit on the "History" tab accompanying every page. People viewing this page can then click on your name to view your user page and contact you directly if they want to find out more. Therefore, be sure to fill out your user page carefully and comprehensively since it can help to promote you as a useful resource in your industry. Although you can include links to your website and can list your e-mail address on your user page, your page should be primarily a way to provide more information about you as an author and not a place to talk about your business. To get the most benefit out of it, you should edit content that's related to your industry to "sculpt" the audience that will be viewing your profile to those who are interested in your topic of expertise.

To create a Wikipedia account, follow these steps:

1. Click the "Log in/create account" link at the top of any Wikipedia page.

2. Click the "Create one" link in the sentence that says, "Don't have an account?"

3. Choose a user name and password to associate with your account. To enhance the networking capabilities of the site, enter an e-mail address as well, so that you can allow other members to e-mail you directly via your user page.

4. Click the "create account" button after verifying the text.

5. Once you've been signed up, navigate to your user page from your home page and add your details. Note that as for all other content on Wikipedia, you should keep the tone on your user page neutral and as unbiased as you can.

TIP 300 **Start adding and editing content**

There are two main ways you can contribute to Wikipedia content:

1. Start a new page. To begin writing an article, start by searching for the topic and then clicking "Go." If there is no existing page, Wikipedia will let you create a new page via a red link to the article name. Click on this article name to begin writing. When writing an article, keep it objective and neutral and consider whether its content is appropriate to an encyclopedia. In other words, you shouldn't write content that is subjective, such as personal essays or opinion pieces. Also make sure your article is well referenced and is backed up by credible sources: in the "External Links" section, include resources for further reading, and in the "Reference List," include sources you used to write the article. When you're finished, click the "Show preview" button and then "Save page" to add the page to Wikipedia's index. For more help on this, see http://en.wikipedia.org/wiki/Help:Starting_a_new_page.

Besides starting a new article, you can edit existing articles or create "sub-pages" that concentrate on specific elements within that particular subject.

2. Edit an existing page. There is a good chance that an article you want to write has already been added to the site. In this case, you can still add value by editing and providing useful extra resources to the existing content. Editing the page is a simple process, and you don't have to be a registered member to do so. To start editing a page, navigate to the page you want to edit and then click the "Edit this page" tab at the top of the page. If you want help on using the special wiki markup, you can click the "Editing help" button near the "save" button at the bottom of the page. Whenever you edit a page, add a reference to back up your information. When you're finished, click "Show preview" or "Show changes" to see what is different between this version and the previous one. If you're happy, click the "Save page" button. For more information on editing a page, see http://en.wikipedia.org/wiki/Wikipedia:How_to_edit_a_page.

TIP 301   Track what's being said

Since Wikipedia is such an influential site, large volumes of people are likely to see any content that is written about your brand or your business on it. It's important, therefore, to keep track of what's written about you so that you can correct any mistakes and factual inaccuracies and undo any acts of vandalism to the page. As always, when editing a page on Wikipedia, especially content written about your own business, keep the information neutral and unbiased and always back up content that you add as part of the edit with credible sources.

In addition to tracking what is said about you, you can use Wikipedia as a way to find out more about your competitors and about progress and events in your industry. The site can be a good starting point in getting a feel for how your business and your competitors are positioned and how you fit into the context of your industry as a whole. Content on the site related to your industry can help you think of new research papers or articles to write, or which product surveys to conduct, or even identify gaps in the market for new products or services that you could offer that your competitors don't.

There are a few ways you can keep track of new information added to pages on which your brand or business is mentioned. You can simply search for your business or brand name on Wikipedia and then bookmark those URLs in your browser for future reference. If you're a Wikipedia member and are logged in, you can view a watch list of pages you specify to see which edits were made to the page. To add a page to your watch list, click the "watch" tab at the top of the page you want to be tracked. While a watch list is useful, it doesn't actively alert you when a change has been made, so remember to check the page regularly to see what, if anything, has been changed.

Notes

Introduction
1. Australian Bureau of Statistics Tourism Satellite Account, 2007–08, www.abs.gov.au.
2. http://blog.facebook.com/blog.php?post=287542162130.
3. http://blog.twitter.com/2010/02/measuring-tweets.html.

Tip 115
1. www.orkut.com/Main#MembersAll.aspx.

Tip 128
1. http://blog.ning.com/2009/12/happy-new-year-to-our-1-9-million -ning-networks.html.

Tip 134
1. Comscore, "*comScore Media Metrix ranks Top 50 US Web Properties for September 2009*," www.comscore.com/content/download/3435/62071/ file/comScore%20Media%20Metrix%20Ranks%20Top%2050%20U.S.%20 Web%20Properties%20for%20September%202009.pdf.

Tip 207
1. http://wiki.creativecommons.org/Frequently_Asked_Questions.

Tip 218
1. comScore Media Metrix, December 2009.

Tip 223
1. http://www.comscore.com/Press_Events/Press_Releases/2010/4/ comScore_Releases_February_2010_U.S._Online_Video_Rankings.
2. www.youtube.com/t/fact_sheet.

Tip 255

1. www.yelp.com/faq#what_is_yelp.
2. www.yelp.com/press.

Tip 259

1. www.igreenbaum.com/2008/04/dealing-with-comments-yelps-best
-practices.

Tip 282

1. http://www.demandmedia.com/2010/01/05/press-releases/new
-ehowcom-android-application-takes-how-to-articles-videos-and
-community-mobile.

Chapter 8

1. www.mauimapp.com/moolelo/hwnwdshw.htm.

Tip 297

1. www.alexa.com/topsites.
2. http://en.wikipedia.org/wiki/Wikipedia:Size_of_Wikipedia.
3. http://en.wikipedia.org/wiki/Wikipedia:About.

Tip 298

1. http://en.wikipedia.org/wiki/Wikipedia:External_links.

Index

About the Author

Catherine Parker is a South African social media and search engine optimization consultant and Web copywriter. Through her work as a search engine marketing specialist at three digital agencies—Quirk eMarketing in Cape Town, Greenlight Marketing in London, and iProspect in San Francisco—Catherine created strategic search marketing campaigns for a variety of international clients in industries such as health care, retail, financial services, and travel. It was while working in San Francisco that she was exposed to using social media as a way to further drive targeted traffic to websites and as a way to increase brand exposure and manage clients' brand reputations online. More recently, Catherine worked at CBS Interactive (formerly CNET) in San Francisco, a premier online content network for information and entertainment that relies heavily on social media to connect and engage with its online audience. Catherine now works as an independent consultant, helping small to medium businesses grow their brand through social media, search engine optimization, and action-oriented Web copy. The idea for this book came from a belief that any business owner can use social media to attract and retain customers—no matter how big or small the company is and no matter how basic the owner's technical knowledge.